1
2
3
4
5
6
7
8
9
10
11
12
13
14
15
16
17
18
19
20
21
22
23
24
25
26
27

1

2

3

4

5

6

7

8

9

10

FROM
OVERWHELM
TO FLOW

FROM
OVERWHELM
TO FLOW

SAILING THE SEAS OF SELF WITH
COURAGE, MEANING, AND RESILIENCE

DESSY T. LEVINSON

CRATE
NEW YORK
2025

Published in the United States by CRATE MIND Inc.
CRATE.COM

Library of Congress Control Number: 2024923564
Names: Levinson T., Dessy, author
Title: From Overwhelm to Flow: Sailing the Seas of Self with Courage, Meaning, and Resilience
Description: First Edition. | New York
Identifiers: ISBN: 979-8-9918121-9-1 (hardcover)
ISBN: 979-8-9918121-8-4 (ebook)
ISBN: 979-8-9918121-7-7 (open market)
Subjects: Business & Economics / Leadership | Self-Help / Personal Transformation | Behavioral Sciences / Cognitive Psychology

 CRATE

To my mother and father, who gave me their everything
and to Lawrence, Cassandra, and William,
who became my all.

CONTENTS

She said: write truth as if it were a poem.
Grab light half-glimpsed—
snuck in,
peripheral,
pre-whispered.
Tiptoeing on the outskirts of awareness,
unlock your will with courage and less pride.
Divine some hope as act of the imagination,
then stand still

and in the darkness, see the tunnel eye.

INTRODUCTION

Here's the story: this book is a love letter—to you, to myself, and to the universe. There's a lot of pain in the world, and while I'm not about to engage in hair-splitting as to whether this moment right now is worse than any other time in human history, on this we can likely agree: we're currently on the dark timeline and the walls are closing in. I've been sweating over this book for several years. Not just over the words that fill it, but what those words should be about, what they mean, who might want to read them, rinse and repeat ad nauseam. And what I discovered after all the sweating is that the experience of writing is rather emblematic of the experience of existing. We want to have the courage of our convictions, we want even to *have* convictions, and we want to matter in a way that will make us feel like we belong on this pebble of a planet in the boondocks of the known universe.

Because the truth is that we often feel alone, tiny, and lost. And my job as a weird, out-of-place immigrant kid and an even weirder, slightly less out-of-place adult has been to say the soft things out loud. Not just voice them, but understand them, explain them, and make them less scary—partly as a service to others, but mostly as a way of keeping myself within squinting distance of sanity.

This book started as a summary of the things I wanted to tell my coaching clients so I didn't have to constantly repeat myself. Then, it evolved into what I wished my teen children knew before becoming adults and what I hoped my parents could learn before becoming dead. Now I have made my peace with the fact that this is just the book I've been writing for myself, as well as for anyone else who thinks that humaning[1] is hard and wishes there was a way we could do it with more clarity, agency, and trust that things might actually be all right.

For most of my life, that last part—trust—completely eluded me. My dad always said, "Trust, but verify," which (as much as I love him) entirely misses the point of trust. So, I set out to make sense of my experience of becoming an adult while simultaneously looking for an edge, an out, a secret that would give me the decoder ring for navigating my thoughts and emotions while keeping them from swallowing me whole.

I think I found it.

I understand how this assertion might sound grandiose, and I promise it's nothing as pithy or as cryptic as '42'. Instead, it is a deep dive into examining how our experience as a conscious organism able to narrate its own existence has fostered and served us, how it has hindered us, and what the evolutionary catches are that——when understood——could turn into potential advantages.

That may still sound a bit vague, so before we begin, allow me to set the table by sharing five premises that shape how I coach and, more importantly, how I parent, love, create, and pick myself off the proverbial floor when the going gets tough.

First: **humaning is hard.** This is because we gather incomplete and often conflicting information, compelling us to make choices

---

[1]   *I know that isn't an actual verb, but it should be.*

while convincing us there is a *right* answer. This difficulty increases further because we are complex systems formed by increasingly complexifying relationships. We are programmed by *nature* to diminish threats while amplifying rewards. We are taught by *nurture* to imitate and then influence. Yet, amidst all this programming, an emergent narrative arises—a sense of self, striving for greater continuity and cohesion.

Our organism is at the mercy of two opposing forces: the urge to venture out and the desire not to die. Many of the choices we make are effectively steered by the biological urge toward *surprise minimization*, which brings us fear and anxiety but also safety; and *active inference*[2], the optimization that can only come through exploration, which grants us curiosity and joy but also risk and disappointment. This tension bubbles up to consciousness, registering as internal conflict and eventual suffering. Stability and Plasticity, Exploitation and Exploration, Constriction and Expansion, Phobos[3] and Agape[4], Truth and Beauty—we have many names for the seemingly opposing forces, yet we are perpetually torn in choosing between them.

"Purity of heart is to will one thing," said Kierkegaard, but unfortunately for us, such clarity of choice often appears superhuman (or relegated to enlightened creatures who aren't us). We struggle with conflicting desires: the need to rest and the hunger for success, the hope for attachment and the titillation of independence, the siren call of a double-chocolate-chip muffin and the commitment

---

[2]   *Active inference and surprise minimization are key concepts in predictive processing theory: a framework for understanding how the brain works. Active inference refers to the brain's process of actively engaging with the environment to gather information and test its predictions. Surprise minimization is the brain's tendency to minimize the difference between its predictions and actual sensory input. We'll explore these ideas in much greater detail in the coming chapters, so hang tight!*

[3]   *In Greek mythology, Phobos is the personification of fear and panic. The term is derived from the ancient Greek word φόβος (phóbos), meaning "fear" or "terror." In this book, I occasionally use Phobos to represent the constricting, aversive emotional energy that drives us away from perceived threats or discomfort.*

[4]   *Derived from ancient Greek ἀγάπη (agápē), Agape represents a form of love that is unconditional, selfless, and all-encompassing. In philosophical and psychological contexts, Agape is often associated with a sense of universal love, compassion, and connection. I use Agape to represent the expansive, connective emotional energy that draws us toward growth and deeper engagement with life and others.*

to sensible nutrition. These desires appear in tension, but they serve a hidden function: to deduce or confirm who we believe we are. Through each of our actions, we strive to maintain a coherent identity and reconcile it with the choices we're making.

Second: **Everyone's the hero of their story.** No one wakes up, brushes their teeth and unironically thinks, *I'm going to be the bad guy today.* Contrary to what popcorn movies have taught us, the choice between good and evil is not actually a choice. Even when we know we're acting in direct opposition to the status quo, we believe it is because we alone see something that's fundamentally wrong with the world and can fix it. Even if we feel like the victim or villain, we are still the main character; still secretly in the right. This path leads to both the French Revolution and to fascism, and it is one we must tread carefully. Thankfully, most of our choices are not nearly as cataclysmic. They involve choosing between two jobs, two mates, or two activities. Indeed, the choices between two incongruent positively-charged things or two unpalatable negatively-charged ones are the primary ways choice (and its accompanying conflict) presents itself.

For the most part, when individuals behave hurtfully to themselves or others, they either feel justified based on their perception of reality or act out what was done to them (which remains mostly unconscious). The latter is so common I bet it has happened to each of us—likely this week. As Parker Palmer writes, "Violence is what we do when we don't know what to do with our suffering." *Not* looking away from our suffering requires us to become conscious of it, and this not only hurts, it also introduces a posse of feelings like regret, fear, vulnerability, guilt, even shame. In response, we hide and pass around our pain like a hot potato, repeating patterns that were handed down through generations.

And that, conveniently, brings me to my *third* premise: **in order not to become unwittingly harmful, we must become uncompromisingly brave.** To avoid panicked, unconscious reactivity, we must choose disciplined, conscious self-examination. When we feel triggered by our discomfort, we can learn not to contract away from it but to expand toward it with courage and curiosity. Doing so feels counterintuitive. Let's be frank: there's a reason we've evolved to maintain homeostasis; steering away from the unknown is how we've survived long enough to reproduce[5]. But what keeps us safe on the macro level does not always help us on the micro level of building a meaningful life. We must recognize that even maladaptive behavior is a form of adaptation and learn to feel compassion toward our organism and the organisms of others, all of which are doing their best to survive. Unless we become willing to look into the shadowy corners of our psyche, we are unlikely to have a chance to rewrite our script.

So, how do we become brave? Well, that is my *fourth* premise. **We must become willing to examine the internal stories that scare us most.**

If making a decision is all about selecting the story we would like to define our sense of who we are, then our difficulty with choice stems from our insistence on a fixed narrative of that self. A story that resonates viscerally is a story that can become true. Powerful narratives are, in fact, mental models. We feel overwhelmed when our mental models are unclear—when our stories don't add up. These models aim to explain (or predict), warn, and inspire. They are always driven by emotion, and that emotional energy comes in two forms: an expansive feeling—what the ancient Greeks called *Agape* (a mixture of connectedness, awe, yearning, and love) and a constricting one—*Phobos* (the aversion, resistance, and scarcity mindsets that all live under the umbrella of anxiety and fear). The energy of *agape* can lead us out of the labyrinth of our suffering, helping us find our way back to our core and each other. *Phobos* will trick and unmoor us, whispering in our ear, encouraging us to

---

[5]   *This is also likely the reason for our entertainment-industrial complex, fast food, and social media.*

remain small and alone. Every myth teaches us that we must choose repeatedly between these two ways of being. It is better that we do it consciously rather than not.

Fifth: **"The opposite of a fact is falsehood, but the opposite of one profound truth may very well be another profound truth."** This is a quote from the quantum physicist Niels Bohr, also echoed in the writings of many wisdom traditions. In many ways, grokking that fifth and final premise is what this entire book is all about. Most important things are not in a binary yes/no state of veracity. Rather, they are in tension with their opposing states, like a taut string stretched between two points. Emptiness is a prerequisite for form to appear. Darkness is the necessary space that light travels through—where it can create contrast and become seen.

Is it dark or light at dusk? The answer is yes.

Is it dark or light at night? It is mostly dark.

Is it dark or light in a vacuum space where no light enters? It is momentarily dark but there's the continuous potentiality for light to appear.

Literalists may object here that such hazy continua allow for equivocation, that they reek of subjectivity and come dangerously close to the views that posit everything is true or that nothing is. I understand these objections. After all, if a train is headed for you, you don't need to oscillate about the distance of the train's approach; you need to get the hell off the tracks. That is precisely the fact-or-falsehood situation Bohr spoke of. For the purposes of our experience, the laws of thermodynamics are facts. The apple will fall off the table—when rolled. The train will hit you—if you remain on the tracks. But making a choice about one's future, deciding on whom to love, defining what makes a life well-lived or a society moral—those are questions of great multifaceted truth that we must not view through the same aperture as a rolling apple.

When it finally shifted within me, this frame change—allowing me to see things as a "yes-and" proposition—shattered my egoic fixedness with the power of a supernova. It brought the realization that in containing the multitudes of reality, we can begin to engage with our own complexity, aligning seeming contradictions and thereby creating positive (constructive rather than destructive) feedback loops. When our internal narratives expand to tolerate and even contain their opposites, we not only become happier and more at ease, but we also become kinder to ourselves and to the world at large. All we give up in return is fixedness—including fixedness in our story of self.

Why should you believe me? If you are wondering about my qualifications, I have many—but also, none will be sufficient. I often say that the best founders (and especially founding teams) feel like the Avengers—you have no idea what each of them is doing there, but it seems inevitable that these are exactly the right individuals to be fighting this battle. Notably, each of the Avengers has paid dearly for their powers. Bruce Banner isn't The Hulk because he was a nuclear physicist (though the knowledge comes in handy); he is the Hulk because, below all that scientific rationality, there was a Mariana Trench of emotion—particularly anger—which the exposure to gamma rays allowed him to unleash. Similarly, I am writing this book not because of the vast reservoir of psychology, philosophy, and cognitive science I've studied obsessively over thirty years. Nor is it based on my experience building ad campaigns in consumer advertising or working with high-performing individuals as a venture investor and coach. The years spent as a creative director, investor, and executive coach certainly helped me build pattern recognition, but I oriented toward theory, psychology, and creativity, and chose those jobs because I was haunted by my own gremlins. My own dualities caused so much inner turmoil that I intuitively knew that I either had to figure out a way to live with the extremes of reason and emotion I'd been given, or they would swallow me whole.

So, while books like this one are often framed as expert books based on doctorates and accolades, and while (to be honest) I've considered jumping through the regular hoops so I can fit that mold, I'm hopeful that what makes my work compelling is that I don't easily fit *any* mold. I've done everything in life by figuring things out from the ground up and finding a way to work with the system, around the system, and sometimes to teach *my* human system that there are better ways.

In undergraduate and graduate school, I became immersed in critical theory, psychology, philosophy, and even classical Greek literature, continuously obsessed with deducing how humans human. I then spent two decades across three successful careers—advertising, venture, and entrepreneurship—doing just that. It took me a while to realize that the more pertinent answers were hidden not in academic books but in my lived experience as an only child moving across multiple continents, provinces, and schools, and then as a young professional trying to make it in the most competitive city in the world.

I had the luck of growing up in an immigrant home where books were our most valued (and sometimes only) possession and where I was the product of two adults on seemingly opposite sides of the path threaded between reason and emotion. My dad is a physicist who taught me tireless scientific rigor and the responsibility to constantly question my hypotheses. My mom is a powerhouse of emotion from whom I learned that giving of yourself till you collapse is *one* way to outrun your fears. I like to think that uniting such ice and lava created obsidian[6], but truth be told, the jury's still out. Being bequeathed high volumes of thought and emotion enabled me to have three distinct[7] careers in New York City, a place that surely demands all the thought and tears one is willing to offer it. I used the psychology I studied to become a creative director selling people beautiful stories, then leveraged critical theory for another eight years as a startup

---

[6]   *Not sure if this works outside of Minecraft. Also, some days the obsidian feels like ash, and I've learned to contain that too.*

[7]   *In reality, I've seen that nothing in our work is separate either from our life or from the previous or future roles we hold. If we are lucky and intentional, the steps flow into each other to become a journey.*

investor, helping founders build their strategic narratives; and now I'm an executive coach and founder, helping humans intentionally examine and craft their most meaningful stories. At each stage, I've become more convinced that the stories we tell ourselves steer not just the companies we build but the lives we live. With each new level, I thought I'd gotten to the bottom of how narrative works. But it wasn't until I became a parent and watched two characters craft themselves seemingly out of thin air that I perceived something altogether obvious: we don't begin the same stories we finish. Story-building is how we make decisions about who to become.

So, how do we hold all of this? I have struggled with that question for most of my life. In accordance with the dualities handed to me by my parents, I've refused to choose between reason and emotion. As a teen, I was the rebel and the A+ student. I marveled at the wonders of physics and stayed up reading poetry. I wanted to be an artist *and* a scientist. Despite my father's well-intentioned urgings to just breathe through my feelings and let them go, I continued to deepen their intensity, using emotion as fuel for creativity while struggling to remain tethered to reason. My willingness to walk that razor's edge gave me superpowers like drive, empathy, and inspiration. It also became my kryptonite—flooding my brain till it felt like a jammed-up steam valve ready to explode, keeping me awake till sunrise, frantic with thought; then later, after the terrorist attacks of 9/11, overwhelming me with panic attacks that made each breath feel like a dance with mortality.

This tension of opposites is not unique. In fact, I've seen it fuel many of the founders I coach, and I suspect it is over-represented among creative individuals, including entrepreneurs. We tend to run from vast amounts of inner tension, which fuels our drive by motivating us to externalize turmoil, compensate, and solve seemingly outward problems by combining ruthless strategy with bursts of creativity. It all delivers high impact at a very high price. But unless we can intentionally align what we perceive as dualities, we end up pitting parts of ourselves against each other, fanning internal tensions that sooner or later explode into conflict.

Still, a wonderful and deeply inconvenient thing about our psyche is that—if we pay attention—it won't let us get away with lying to ourselves. I left first advertising and then finance because my nervous system convinced me (perhaps erroneously) that I needed to choose between profit and meaning. Since then, I have begun to examine what each of these terms means rather than taking the external answers as gospel. In order to balance the pragmatic with the inspirational, I needed to follow my obsession with reconciling thoughts and feelings full-time. At first, I approached the problem through what I thought was the best angle—technology—and set out to build an app that would quantify the qualia[8], enumerate momentary states (i.e., feelings), and track their effect on long-term traits (meaning personality or character). I hypothesized that if we could decode how our system functions, we would know which parts to fix. In hindsight, addressing the human condition by building algorithms is probably the most hubristic, reason-as-ego path I could have taken. My initial hypothesis worked, but more importantly, it opened the door to something far deeper and more fluid—something that requires embracing rather than fixing.

Then, the pandemic hit. Our personal, organizational, and societal cracks rose to the surface and started to widen. Founders whom I had occasionally coached began calling and messaging in a panic. Not only were their startups struggling, but their families and bodies were all in various states of collapse. My days became split between app-building and full-time coaching. Suddenly, algorithms weren't enough to address our stressors. At times of real threat, reason can be a helpful container, but what sustains us are our feeling-based narratives of trust, hope, and curiosity. I saw quickly that no app alone could help individuals find restful sleep

---

[8]   *Qualia here refers to subjective, conscious experience, as we become cognizant of it.*

or persevere through the stress of looming uncertainty. What *did* help were the warm Zoom conversations and even warmer silences when tears spilled over. I realized that healing lay in lending out my nervous system—together with all I had learned first-hand about holding highly-charged emotion in a container of reason. I also realized that the most powerful stories that change minds and shift behavior are woven not of algorithms or words but of emotion. Finally, I could no longer deny it (or perhaps I had nowhere left to run): I was not a thinking creature who felt things. I was an organism overwhelmed by feeling-based signals who occasionally thought that she was in control.

The premise of this book, then, is that our emotions and their accompanying narratives are the primary components of what we call a *self*. Without them, we become stripped of our ability to make choices. If we become cut off from emotion, we can continue to string together logical thoughts, but others perceive us as flat, lacking personality, and devoid of depth. Still, however much we may know this intellectually, we often remain scared of what our emotions might unleash. The somatic pings of our nervous system (what psychoanalysts called *the unconscious* and Greeks named *psyche*) feel unpredictable and irrational. They seem to have their own agendas, sometimes directly contradicting the one we consider ours. And yet, ignoring the wisdom of our psyche is how we've gotten to our current state as individuals and as a society: we are disconnected from our bodies and each other, overwhelmed, and in denial.

How can we learn to listen to the different layers of information inside us? And how do we differentiate which internal messages can help us and which are left over from our past, no longer serving the present? I did indeed build "an app for that," where you can press a button and be given some pointers on what to do next[9]. In the

---

[9] *Check the appendix for a complimentary three-month subscription to the CRATE app.*

process of building and testing, however, I uncovered that we are far too complex for a one-size-fits-all solution.

So, more importantly, I bring you a framework. I developed and tested it over the past five years, during more than a thousand hours of coaching and thousands more hours of research, study, and deep conversation with some of the best neuroscientists, psychologists, and somatic practitioners I could find. The framework combines five domains: Clarity, Regulation, Agency, Trust, and Energy (CRATE). Each unfolds into three aspects rooted in 4E cognitive science[10]—Embedded Prediction (your *Story*), Embodied Action (your *Stance*), and Extended Cognition (your sense of *Self*). CRATE is designed to help us contain our most powerful emotions and transform our overwhelm into a state of continuous flow. Two of its dimensions––Clarity and Agency––are the rational components that you, I, and every organization I've coached for require in order to function optimally. The other three (Regulation, Trust, and Energy) are our fuel; they are the relational components, which (I was surprised to discover) are even more crucial to our well-being and long-term survival.

The CRATE framework and this book aim to help us integrate the rational and emotional parts of our conscious experience so we don't have to hide from either. The thought-based interpretations of our emotions—what we refer to as our internal narratives—can be crafted into powerful tools that counteract fear, grow resilience, and create meaning. Continuing to react or passively ignore our emotions leads to knee-jerk, stress-driven behavior that leaves us feeling like we have little volition, control, or purpose. Learning to notice and metabolize emotion, on the other hand, unlocks exactly what it says on the tin: *Clarity* to know where you stand, *Regulation* to withstand whatever happens, *Agency* to act, *Trust* in your relationship with yourself and others, and *Energy* to get up and keep going for the first, or the fifty-first, time.

---

[10]   *4E Cognition is a growing field of cognitive philosophy that combines research on the embedded, embodied, enactive, and extended conceptions of mind.*

So, wherever you are right now and wherever you are headed on your journey, this is the point when you get handed a map and a crate full of tools. You then set off to discover who you may become once you are no longer fighting yourself. Using this framework has transformed my life and the lives of many of my clients; it is also the backbone of an app that has evolved into so much more than a set of cold algorithms.

But first, here is a quick overview to guide you through this book:

In **Part I**, we will leverage the latest discoveries in neuroscience to demonstrate how we are not one concrete self but a constellation of granular, relational, and emergent impulses driving us toward homeostasis. When we refer to our *self*, we mean a gathering of narratives expressed through behavior intended to keep us safe, then reflected by those around us. We will delve into the conscious and unconscious states that, when relationally reinforced, form the long-term traits we describe as our personality.

In **Part II**, we will bring it to our home and office. We will meet several of my clients and see how the CRATE framework helps steer us toward states of flow. Through client examples, we will examine the following prompts:

- **Clarity:** What narratives are driving or stymying you? What do you hold to be true, and how might that be preventing you from seeing new possibilities?
- **Regulation:** What emotional states are activated at a given moment? How can you adjust their volume by shifting their intensity and valence toward what helps you most?
- **Agency:** What is available to be done? What is the clearest path between something you genuinely want and the actions you can take to achieve it?
- **Trust:** Do you believe you can succeed? How has fear served and protected you until now? How is your relationship with

your self and others hindering or enabling you, and how can you grow embodied confidence?

- **Energy:** How will you get up, and how can you keep going beyond your current limitations? What are the physical, social, and creative engagements that connect you to greater sources of energy and meaning?

Part III is the *So what?* section: both a rallying cry and an honest conversation about how lasting change happens at the edges of our comfort zone. We will examine the interconnectedness of the Courage to Care, The Meaning to Act, and The Resilience to Create, and why I believe that orienting toward these three is how we enter and remain in continuous flow. Lastly, we will touch on the importance of moving beyond the individual self: how doing so allows us to form better families, lead better teams, and create a more resilient future not just for ourselves but for all organisms we encounter.

———

If you are wondering about the latest research on consciousness and our sense of self[11], this book attempts to gather some of the most convincing discoveries in neuroscience and psychology to answer a few simple yet infinite questions: What's going on in our heads? How do we exist in the present moment, at once conscious of our possibility and accepting of our limitations? What should we actually *do*? And, more importantly, how do we make the discomfort of reality feel worthwhile by processing, combining, and generating new output of care, action, and creativity? Is struggling with all this our burden or our salvation, and might they be the same thing?

Before we dive into the how, on the off (yet pretty plausible) chance that you become distracted from this book by the very things

---

[11]   *And who isn't?*

we are trying to address––the insistent emotions tugging on the sleeve of your attention––here is the TL;DR[12]:

Most of the time, you are not the master of your thoughts or behavior. You are not observing the real world, deducing next steps, and then intentionally executing them. For the most part, you only come online milliseconds[13] after the rest of your organism[14] has computed threat and opportunity and begun the survival-appropriate response of fleeing or pouncing. All of your actions (assuming you have not had the great misfortune of suffering brain damage) are spurred by drives, emotions, and feeling-based thought narratives, which is to say they are all motivated by *energy in motion* pointing you toward something or away from something else.

Now, why does this matter?

In early-stage investing, there's often oscillation between assuming that every idea is full of potential and knowing that more than 70% of startups fail within their first decade. Ideally, that primes the investor to give every idea the benefit of the doubt— project the opportunity they are exploring into the ever-narrower percentage of successful companies, while also assessing how likely that future is to occur. The best investors become deeply comfortable with uncertainty—they know that they can't actually know the future and that they're placing a bet based on reading a particular configuration of tea leaves, which might well change tomorrow. Most, however, are less comfortable with the unknown. This results in countless attempts at de-risking: believing that if you are great enough at picking the right founders, calculating unit economics, or comprehending market dynamics, you can beat the odds and ensure that a given startup lives long and prospers.

---

[12]   *TL;DR: Too Long; Didn't Read.*

[13]   *300-600 milliseconds to be exact. Mele, A. R. (2009). Effective Intentions: The Power of Conscious Will. Oxford University Press.*

[14]   *Comprised of your nervous system, limbic brain, and a vast set of evolved drives.*

While this example may seem niche, each of us does a version of this in our day-to-day lives. We read the tea leaves, make a choice, and then convince ourselves that if we only work hard enough, look good enough, be nice (or aggressive) enough, we will control the outcome and ensure some version of success and happiness.

Unfortunately for us, Bohr was right and the most effective direction points toward combining the truth of uncertainty with the projection of our hopes. Whether you are investing in an idea, building a business, or creating something even more ambitious, such as art or another human, there is a very important balance between engaging with the outcomes you can effect while accepting the ones that are beyond your comprehension or control. Making you comfortable with this duality is the objective of the CRATE framework.

By the time you are done reading, you will understand how our emotional system has evolved within organisms in general, how it functions within your organism in particular, and what you can do to re-frame your relationship with it. I invite you to face uncertainty while courageously tethering to care and acting on meaning. I am betting that this is the path from overwhelm to flow and the very essence of resilience.

I too need help tethering, breaking frame, and shifting the stories in my head—this is lifelong work. I've been able to build multiple businesses, earn financial stability, co-create a family, and maintain a loving relationship that continues to deepen after two decades. (This, by all accounts, is a not-insignificant portion of a flourishing life.) Yet I continue seeking ever bigger answers and feeling the restlessness in my chest, even as I deepen my sense of grounding and trust.

I don't think I've got it all figured out or that I have somehow arrived at a nirvana-like state where painful moments can never again unsettle me. They do. Just two weeks ago, another war erupted in the world, and a week ago, there was yet another school shooting[15]. This week, my teen daughter cried in my arms with stress, and my stomach sank as I felt small and powerless to ease her anguish. While these examples of tumult are not all of the same magnitude, each of them sneaks into my sleep, sits heavy on my heart, and requires deep conversations and even deeper contemplation.

The difference from ten years ago, or even five, is that I don't feel unmoored. I feel spacious. I watch myself go through a seven-session day and stand up from my desk, stirred but not shaken. I hold my daughter while she stresses, hold space for a founder while he cries, hold the news gingerly while I read about loss after loss, and I find myself able to hold... all of it. Able to make my heart larger, my mind more spacious, my nervous system ever more grounded––able to surf the waves of emotion and contain all their multitudes. My word these days is *tenderness*. I use it as a synonym for courage.

How did I get here? Well, to quote Robert Frost, "The only way out is through." After traveling through an ocean's worth of internal turmoil, I've reached the edges of my world and peered past the place where all of my maps ended. What waited for me has been magnificent. And now that I finally have my sea legs under me, I'm writing about it so that your journey might prove to be slightly easier. I hope to give you a way to explore your own map and then move far beyond it.

Now, welcome aboard. Here be monsters.

---

[15]   *The worst part is, it doesn't matter when you read this; the timing is still likely to be true.*

PART I

LEARN WHO YOU ARE

1

FIRE AND ALGEBRA

How the World Became Story

"The mind is its own place, and in itself can make a heaven of hell, a hell of heaven."
— John Milton

I'm fourteen years old and standing on top of the world. I've come as a tourist, yet I'm certain I've always been here and will always return. Below me are hundreds of windows, some blinking into evening wakefulness, others opaque. Each whispers a story. I picture a short-order cook returning from work, a waitress pulling up stockings, a musician waking up, an opera singer staring at the bathroom mirror, a writer looking back at me. I see hope and alienation, love and heartbreak. To my teenage mind, there's an entire universe distilled into this twenty-block radius. It feels more real than the wind on my face, the sting in my eyes, or the chill on my cheeks. It's the deepest breath I've ever taken, and I never want to exhale. That afternoon at dusk, as I stand on the platform of the Empire State Building, I promise myself that I'll return to these windows. I will live among them, uncover their stories, and then, finally, I will feel less alone.

I'm forty years old and looking out at the gathering storm clouds above me. I've returned as an expert, yet my palms are sweaty, and my heart thunders insistently in my chest. Gray carpet bounces off a gray sky, draining color from the buildings outside. There are rows of chairs, some of them occupied by humans, others by laptops, jackets, and stray notepads. This time, I'm in a large conference room on the fifty-second floor of that same building, and everything feels smaller and older. I'm struck by how much farther all the other windows appear. A crowd of founders and investors mingle, waiting for my breakfast presentation to start. Coffee cups and business cards exchange hands. I see hope and desire, ambition and trepidation. I swallow hard and ignore the pit in my stomach. As I begin to speak, I feel distinctly adrift and alone.

————

We forget to remember the things we've unlearned. I think of the *me* who stood atop the Empire State Building at fourteen, then at forty, and then more recently again for my daughter's twelfth birthday, and also four years before she was born, the day after my husband and I were married. A string of pilgrimages—each time I queued up for the elevator ride, each view had a slightly different sky, the sky had a different season, the season had a different *me*.

They say time is elastic, but it's also a spiral looping in on itself, circling to retrace the same patterns, conscious and unconscious, closing in toward a center, a core, a becoming and unbecoming of self.

New York City put a spell on me. For years, its thread pulled me through a labyrinth of school and work. With every step, I mapped out my way back to it. And when, at twenty-two, I found myself looking at the airport runway, about to depart my regularly-scheduled Canadian life and start a new one amidst big buildings and even bigger dreams, a suspicion crept in at the edge of my mind. Up there, on the observation deck, I had uncovered a secret. It would bring me everything I'd asked for, and ask for everything I had.

Like all powerful stories, the magic of New York lies in its emotional resonance. Emotions are not mere footnotes in our narrative—they are the authors of our stories. Neuroscience reveals that every decision we make is influenced, if not dictated, by our emotional states—a dance of neurochemicals like serotonin and dopamine, painting the outlines of our fear and desire.

Both the wide-eyed, dreamy teenager and the jaded professional are facets of who I've been. But I am no more those women than the ship of Theseus is its fourth or four-thousandth plank. The first memory makes my heart swell and my sense of the world expand; the second feels wistful and slightly constricted—as if a fist is closing in on my heart. I love them both because, more than just describing the scenes they recall, they remind me how our inner worlds are constructed—the dream of falling in love with a place and the reality of living in it. Each is true for a different part of me, and each speaks to a core that has remained unchanged: the desire to connect and to be understood.

To unravel this longing, we can travel back even further to a six-year-old immigrant kid, tucked under covers in a mid-size town near Toronto, Canada, reading *Twenty Thousand Leagues Under the Sea* way past her bedtime. That book's narrator is a scientist imprisoned aboard a submarine that traverses the deep seas for reasons as mysterious as its captain. The curious, answer-seeking voice of Professor Aronnax is one of the most salient memories I have of that year, surpassed only by the powerful presence of Captain Nemo. As an only child in a strange land, those men became my friends and echoes of my inner voice. Their world, full of adventure and reluctant companionship, was more comforting than my actual reality. Being with them felt safe, and over time they became inhabitants of a vibrant inner world populated by disparate fictional heroes, all of whom guided both my inner and outer choices.

Those dreams of daring, together with the movies I grew up watching—from *Working Girl* to *Crocodile Dundee*, from *Moonstruck* to *Annie Hall*—all set me up to fall under New York's spell. At fourteen, the city's promise as the effervescent center of the universe felt like the answer to a question I didn't know I had. The story resonated because, at one level, it has always been true. New York brims with possibility: excitement and opportunity lurk around every corner. It's also a story I *wanted* to be true: a real place where humans connect by peering into neighborhood windows as if looking into each other's souls. To this lonely teen, being anonymous yet seen was the promise of a lifetime. What sealed the deal was having just watched *Frankie and Johnny*, the film version of a Terrence McNally off-Broadway play where a waitress and a short-order cook find one another through the urgent proximity that only a cramped city can bring. It was a story of love thrumming through asphalt veins, and I was done for.

I tell this anecdote to illustrate how stories move us. Sometimes literally, across countries and continents, and often through time. They are the narrative that binds the "I" at this moment to the "I" of last year and the one at fourteen. We think that we have a story, but the story has us. We think we are visiting a place until we find ourselves having become it. The common thread through all of it—

our emotion—is what births and sustains identities and places (and they are not two different things, anyway).

This sense of identity through time is underpinned by our brain's ability to weave narratives and store them as memories. But our memories are not static; they are dynamic entities, constantly being rewritten each time we recall them. We integrate new experiences and perspectives into our existing stories, subtly altering the fabric of our remembered past and, consequently, of our sense of self.

This book is about why the stories we tell ourselves shape our reality and, more concretely, about the source of their power: the invisible energy in motion that courses through our mind and body, animating every turn, every move, every decision. This force, often relegated to the realm of the intangible, is in fact deeply rooted in our biology. It is the embodiment of our brain's *predictive processing*—constantly anticipating, adjusting, and reacting to the world around us. Emotion is not some otherworldly, woo component. It's also not something we opt to experience only when convenient and disregard when not—though we certainly try.

Predictive processing—a cornerstone of contemporary neuroscience—postulates that our brains are always making predictions about future experiences based on our past. Sending out emotional signals and using them to direct us toward or away from a stimulus, these predictions shape our entire perception of the world. They are the language our nervous system uses to communicate with us, transmitted through somatic (sense-based), kinetic (movement-based), and conscious (thought-based) channels.

As we navigate life, our emotional responses are not just reactions; they are anticipations of what our brains predict to be significant based on our past experiences. This entwinement of emotion with predictive processing illuminates why we feel compelled by specific narratives and how they become integral to our identity.

Whether we call them *emotion*, *feeling*, or *psyche*, these are the underlying currents of consciousness, guiding our decisions and shaping our personal narratives. My journey from Frankie and

Johnny's windows of teenage longing to the carpeted boardrooms of grown-up life wasn't a path guided by chance; it was a dance of prediction and emotion, each choice steered by invisible hands that I have only recently learned how to hold.

THE INSIDE STORY

There's likely a voice in your head. It might not be telling you to drive out the English as it did for Joan of Arc, but it's probably wondering if you forgot to lock the door, why Jack hasn't responded to your email, and what your colleagues said about you at the team dinner you missed. If you're lucky, the voice does more than stress. It tells you how relieved you are to have finished last week's project. It salivates at the sushi yo u'll order tonight. And it wonders about the sound of your future grandchildren's laughter.

We narrate our lives because that's the only way we know how to process reality. From an early age, we practice this innate ability to encode and decode high-impact information. "Look, plane!" is one of the first dramatic stories a toddler tells her mother. The sky was clear, and then something unexpected happened. That seemingly basic change––and the emotional accompaniment of joy or fear, surprise or trepidation––are at the core of every dramatic story we tell, whether it is to ourselves or others. As we grow, these stories become more complex: *I thought he liked me, but he only wanted my toys. I thought I'd never get the job, but I clicked with one of the partners.* Stories don't have to be epics that feature us as the Mother of Dragons, though if you squint, we're not far from those narratives either. And more often than not, we cast ourselves not exactly as the hero but as the quirky underdog, victim, or villain, all alone against the world.

Stories are not just a matter of entertainment or even of education. By enabling us to perceive the world and ourselves from an ever-expanding perspective, internal narratives become crucial to our survival and give us a processing space for our emotions. *Emotions* are the reactor core that powers every narrative, both within and without.

If I tell you that I visited New York, that's not a story; it's a statement. If, instead, I tell you that I visited New York and that from the first moment I emerged out of Penn Station, I had an uncanny feeling; that something in me changed as I walked spellbound along its sidewalks, convinced that I knew what was around each corner; that it felt not like a visit but a homecoming and over time all of it became reality... now we have a story: one that explains causality, introduces potential, and conveys emotion––enough to unfold an entire chapter, or even a life.

The Argentinian poet and author Jorge Luis Borges once wrote, "Art is fire plus algebra." This is particularly true for stories and how we make sense of the world. We need the fire of our nervous system with its energy in motion compelling our sensory pings of emotion and igniting our need to compose a story. And we need the algebra of the mind—calculating what just happened and what's about to happen, then deducing and embedding the story's message. When it comes to communicating with others, these functions are clear and can produce incredible art. But what happens when we are communicating with ourselves and when much of the process happens unconsciously?

With those internal explorations, we take the disparate moments, the happenstance, the fortune and misfortune, and weave a thread of cause and effect that we hope can lead us to the center of our labyrinth. Many of us tend to think that life is a linear, set journey and that we choose a path from A to B (ideally, from struggle and inexperience to success and serenity). We think that the conflicts we face are external, and the bad guys are easy to spot; that time is continuous, predictable, and slowly streaming out like grains of sand; that there's a reason why things happen and that if we only work hard enough, we can resolve our struggles and reach a meaningful, happy end. That's the story (and the movie) I spent the first thirty years of my life believing. Unfortunately for all of us, it's not how reality seems to work.

To start, we may be good at building stories, but we're even better at telling ourselves tall tales. After safety, feeding, and mating, sense-making is the activity that uses the most significant portion of our mental abilities. Yet we almost never tell ourselves facts; instead, we shape the narrative inside our heads to script a movie that features us as its star. We think we have a clear sense of what we want and how we act, but we filter perception, match patterns, and engage in all sorts of cognitive somersaults—all unwittingly and before breakfast.

If you're like me, you might be thinking your sense of reality is much better than the average person's. Unfortunately again, exceptionalism is one of the most pervasive and foundational tall tales we concoct! We each think, *yours might be a distorted sense of the world, but mine is certainly true.* Whether that makes us the most magnanimous leader or the most despicable person on earth, the important part is we believe our estimate to be current and verifiable, and over time, it becomes exactly that, as we play the roles we have set for ourselves.

Stories seem magical because they have the power to change our reality. Still, I'm a scientist's daughter who learned to question everything at around the same time I learned how to walk. I subscribe to Arthur C. Clarke's view that magic is just a sufficiently-advanced technology—that if we look in the right places, we can deconstruct how and why something works and then intentionally shift its course.

About a decade ago, I began experimenting with a hypothesis: what if we narrate the world as we walk through it and thereby actually affect it *and* ourselves in the process? What if we could deconstruct that action and thereby change our very experience of the world[1]?

---

[1]   *I realize that I stumbled accidentally onto something similar to what enlightenment traditions have taught over centuries. I tread carefully as I wonder whether each of our different cultures and modalities are not pointing at a similar truth about the nature of the I-Thou relationship between the experiencer and her environment.*

To test this, we need to understand how stories work, and to do *that*, we need to delve into their very core: emotional motivation.

THE FIRE OF EMOTION

We are eager, *and* we are trepidatious. Even on a calm, unremarkable day, our default stance tends to oscillate, alternately orienting toward approach or avoidance, toward interest or fear. I'd like you to picture a Cartesian plane (that X-Y graph that looks like a cross, separating space into four quadrants). The X axis is your path: on the left side is the avoidance-worthy, negative stuff like snakes and dark alleys and PowerPoint presentations; on the right side are all the approach-worthy, positive things: your loved ones, great music, and a delectable meal. Now, for the Y axis, if you look up to the very top, that's where the highest energy shoots up—when you want to race in panic or jump for joy. Its opposite—at the very bottom—is your lowest, barely-registrable energy level; that's when we want to curl up for a good nap (on the bottom right) or when we feel so depleted as to be burnt out (on the bottom left).

Now, take a deep breath and check in with your body[2]. Where on this graph are you right now? If you've been feeling stressed about your latest project and the associated thoughts feel anxious and frantic to you, you're probably somewhere in the upper left (high energy, negative valence); if, on the other hand, you are curled up on the couch enjoying the time you've allotted to reading this book, you are likely somewhere in the bottom right, probably towards the middle neutral-to-low energy, positive valence).

What we just did was plot your *affect*, which is the scientific term for emotion. The dual function of the word should not be lost on us here: your affect *affects* you by hueing your world in different shades of positive or negative valence (attraction or aversion). The mental charting above is how your emotions communicate with you. Is there

---

[2]   *If you have no idea what I mean by this, don't despair! We will cover Regulation in great detail in Chapter 6.*

something you really need to avoid, like that big project or dark alley? Your hypothalamus–a small but crucial part of the brain located just below the thalamus—is triggered, activating your sympathetic nervous system. The sympathetic nervous system is one of the two modes in which your body's communication system operates, also known as the fight-or-flight response.

This activation stimulates your adrenal glands to release adrenaline (epinephrine) into your bloodstream, rapidly preparing your body to respond to the perceived stressor. Your heart rate will elevate, your muscles will tense, and your breath may become more rapid or your palms sweaty. Your sense of this will be to experience high energy and negative (aversive) valence, thereby orienting *away* from the thing that prompted this response. You might act by running, fighting, or (if the energy state is not as high) simply avoiding. If the trigger was internal (meaning that you had a thought), you might undergo all of this inwardly while never shifting from your seat. The main part you are likely to notice in your conscious mind will be some mental narrative that is frustrated, anxious, stressed, bitter, guilty, jealous, angry...all the way down to despondent.

Let's play out the inverse, positive scenario. Is there something good happening, such as reading this book that's possibly delivering some insight? Great! Your response will be more nuanced, depending on whether the positive thing involves food, a loved one, or a pleasant experience. Either way, multiple areas of your brain–such as the ventral tegmental area (VTA), *nucleus accumbens*, and parts of the prefrontal cortex–will all become activated and take notice. The VTA releases dopamine, a neurotransmitter associated with seeking and finding reward. If this is a relaxed, positive experience (such as reading), your *parasympathetic* nervous system will take over, and you will feel warm and contented. Your heart rate will slow down, your breath will deepen, and you might even start to feel a little bit sleepy[3]. It's interesting to note that your mental narratives are less

---

[3]   *This, incidentally, is why many of us fall asleep while reading.*

likely to be as active or elaborate here as when you are negatively valenced (or upset). If you are excited (which is a high-energy state still keeping your *sympathetic* nervous system activated), you might notice thoughts of anticipation, joy, ebullience, or curiosity. If you are relaxing and feeling that *aahh* of a long exhale, you will likely notice fewer thoughts, and you will just breathe slower, settle down, and feel ready to chill.

Now, how does our brain *know* that the project is to be avoided or the book approached? Your immediate response might be to say that you decided this, but wait—you haven't started working on that presentation yet, and you're just at the beginning of this book. How do you know what's good for you and what isn't? Better yet, if you are walking down a path and something starts to shift in the grass, do you have time to look closer and decide whether it's a chipmunk or a rattlesnake?

If we had to check each detail and deduce on a case-by-case basis whether something was to be approached or avoided, that would take a lot of effort. What's more, if there was something pointy in that dark alley or something poisonous in that grass, a wrong decision might be our last. So, our organism has evolved not to ask us. Our limbic brain (the hypothalamus and VTA)[4] doesn't wait to receive clearance from the prefrontal cortex, where the higher-form cognitive functions reside. When it comes to how we react when a change in our environment appears, we're lucky if we get notified *at all*. Research[5] has shown there's a 300-600 millisecond lag between response activation and conscious awareness—we react physically before we 'feel' a positive or negative response. We act and *then* we story.

---

[4]   *Technically, the VTA is located in the midbrain, but it is a key component of the mesolimbic pathway, which is involved in the processing of reward, motivation, and pleasure. It is a major source of dopamine neurons, which project to various parts of the brain, including limbic regions like the nucleus accumbens.*

[5]   *Libet, B., Gleason, C. A., Wright, E. W., & Pearl, D. K. (1983). Time of conscious intention to act in relation to onset of cerebral activity (readiness-potential): The unconscious initiation of a freely voluntary act. Brain, 106(3), 623-642.*

Emotions are the basis of the narratives we construct, and those stories become emotional triggers themselves. Our nervous system reacts to a story with another set of emotions, which turn into another set of narratives or further reinforce the original. Rinse and repeat, over and over. This is how we get caught in rumination loops where one stray comment can ruin our whole afternoon, causing us to dredge up the hundred and eight other memories of when someone treated us unfairly or when we said the wrong thing. A small tip here is to remember that if your mind is spinning in a stream of narration, your nervous system is likely in sympathetic mode. As you'll remember, that is the fight-or-flight response and so your brain will be looking for things that might harm you and prioritizing extremes in the stories it tells you. In Part 2 of this book, we'll learn to notice and examine these mental loops and how to reliably step outside of them. But first, we need to understand the evolutionary dynamics that ensnare us in such predicaments to begin with.

Looking out from that conference room inside the Empire State Building, a new part of my story began to form. Two opposing conclusions settled inside me: the almost-tearful relief of *I made it*, together with a furrow-browed confusion: *...but I don't think this is it*. Intuitively, I reached for a tool I've since learned to be the Swiss Army Knife in our toolset: curiosity. Why wasn't my story lining up? Wasn't this—success, esteem, a sense of coming full circle—the whole dream I'd been chasing? Where did the voices in my head come from? Who, exactly, led me here?

THE ALGEBRA OF PREDICTION

As far as we're aware, the human brain is the most complex organ in existence—at least, that's what the human-brained scientists have told us. But, presuming this fabled bundle of neurons is at least pretty good (having invented things like quantum physics, rock music, medicine, and the air fryer), it may be interesting to know that it essentially operates as a prediction machine. Using the senses, the brain continually parses its environment, identifying what is most salient to its organism at any one point, and then optimizing to gain the greatest advantage while expending the least effort. Its ability to process and interpret vast amounts of sensory information allows us to interact with our environment in meaningful ways, adapt to new challenges, and make decisions based on information gathered from both past experiences and current situations.

To do this quickly and efficiently, the brain uses *Bayesian inference*—a form of probabilistic reasoning—to make predictions about future events. Over the past decade, research has solidified this theory[6], showing how the brain calculates probabilistic predictions to better understand and navigate the world it inhabits.

Bayesian probability is a mathematical approach for representing uncertain knowledge. It states that probability must be updated when new evidence is encountered; it also expresses how strongly prior knowledge should be considered when interpreting new data. In recent years, neuroscientists such as Karl Friston, Andy Clark, and Anil Seth have expanded upon this same principle to illustrate how it applies within the brain itself: neurons in higher-level cortical areas appear to update their inputs using Bayesian probability. Specifically, these neurons can combine confusing or unclear sensory input with expectations based on prior experience and then react most efficiently.

This suggests that the brain develops predictive models about upcoming events and updates those models as more data becomes available. The model assumes that any given situation can be represented by a set of probabilities, which are then updated based on new information or evidence. Karl Friston, the most revered and cited neuroscientist in the field, has extensively explored this concept, known as *predictive processing*, which has become one of the most widely-accepted hypotheses of how living organisms

---

6   *Friston, Karl. "The Free-Energy Principle: A Unified Brain Theory?" Nature Reviews Neuroscience 11, 127–138 (2010)*

infer information so as to survive and thrive in their environment. According to predictive processing, when faced with conflicting data points, living organisms revise their beliefs so that they match the strongest evidence. They *actively infer* the causes of sensory inputs and then update their model to minimize the surprise of prediction errors. Hence, we are not just passively predicting sensory information but actively engaging with the environment to confirm or update these predictions. At its most basic state, our living brains are non-conscious prediction machines that scan the environment and attempt to approximate our next state with as little error as possible. They do this via the dual processes of active inference[7]–linked to adaptability and plasticity–and surprise minimization–linked to efficiency and stability.

To illustrate all this fun terminology—and where predictive processing runs into complications of consciousness—let's consider three brains: mine (an overly introspective human), that of Irvine (a sweet but not very intelligent cat), and that of Lex (a slug in our garden, who technically has a set of ganglia—distributed neurons—rather than a brain). Irvine, Lex, and I are all thirsty. Each of our bodies will have registered a decrease in its homeostatic state and predicted that order would be restored if we were to become *not* thirsty. How each of us addresses this will differ based on how conscious we are of our state and what affordances our environment provides us.

Lex, who is (as far as we can discern) entirely unconscious, will continue crawling around the garden and may attempt to orient toward some droplets if they[8] are in close enough proximity to water to sense it. Since slugs can recall experience, Lex may actively infer a state of greater thriving near the sprinkler where they previously

---

[7]   *Active inference is a fundamental principle in neuroscience that describes how organisms actively sample their environment to reduce uncertainty and optimize their predictions. For a detailed overview, see: Friston, K., Daunizeau, J., Kilner, J., & Kiebel, S. J. (2010). Action and behavior: A free-energy formulation. Biological Cybernetics, 102(3), 227-260.*

[8]   *Slugs have both male and female reproductive organs*

encountered a small puddle, and so head in that direction. If they were to arrive at that spot and find that the ground is dry, Lex would then update their predictions to no longer anticipate water in that spot. All of this will happen non-consciously, and whether or not Lex finds water (and survives) is, to a great extent, dependent on circumstances.

Irvine, my cat sleeping next to me, will awaken with a vague sense of unease[9] and head downstairs to his water fountain. He will not introspect about why he is going there, nor will he reflect on having had water once he's done drinking it. However, he *does* know where his water is and will meow if the door is closed, or even come back upstairs to get my attention if something has gone awry and the water isn't there. While I would not deem Irvine's actions to be particularly conscious, they are not entirely *un*-conscious either; he exhibits volition (wanting water), object persistence (knowing where the water is, even when it's out of sight), and an understanding of cause and effect (knowing I can open the door or make water appear). While he's unlikely to declare a big conspiracy (or blame his sister Amelia) if the water is missing, Irvine has what we might term *core consciousness*, as an organism wanting water and having the agency to get it.

Now, what about my human experience of thirst? Here, we have a layer cake of conscious and unconscious dynamics at work. The very fact that I started writing about thirst and that it was the example most readily available to me makes it likely that I was experiencing some degree of it. As I began this section and deepened the example, I realized that I am indeed thirsty and that my body is anticipating (read: eager) to be in a state where my thirst would be quenched. While I, too, have object persistence and know to go downstairs and pour myself water from the fridge, I have an added layer that Irvine and Lex lack: my ability to make my drives conscious and then *choose* how to respond to them. These choices tie to more than just

---

[9]   (*positive approach, mid-level energy; probably plotted somewhere slightly above the X-axis line in the top right quadrant*)

memories of the water's location; they are linked to my memories of how I've behaved in the past with regard to thirst or even general deprivation; they are linked to my autobiographical sense of self.

Therefore, I can *choose*[10] to defer getting water until I am finished with this example. The slight discomfort of delayed gratification is lessened by the desire to make my point about the power of consciousness and our intentional actions. It is furthered by holding a narrative of being the kind of person who is able to withstand discomfort. My sense of self as a disciplined writer and teacher is, in this case, stronger than my sense as an organism needing water. Or so I thought. About a paragraph ago, I found myself lifting the almost-empty teacup on my desk and drinking the few drops left—— in a wholly unconscious act that did not fit my intended narrative.

The interesting part here is that I have some choice over both my actions and the conclusions drawn from them—though the exact extent of free remains up for debate. I could conclude that the best-laid plans of theorists and writers are no match for the powers of biology. I could frown that the facts didn't follow my envisioned narrative and conveniently ignore the teacup incident, pretending that it didn't happen. Or, I could do what I'm actually doing, which is to weave in the unpredictability of reality so as to highlight the larger point I will be making about the importance of internal fluidity in the face of change.

THE SPECTER OF CHANGE

The Greeks refer to a dramatic change in narrative as *peripeteia*, commonly translated as a reversal or surprise. It's at the heart of every classical tragedy, and not so coincidentally, it is also at the

---

[10]   *Robert Sapolsky would argue that I am not choosing anything but am instead responding to a complex interplay of genetic, environmental, and neurobiological factors. For a detailed exploration of this perspective, I refer you to his books, "Behave" and "Determined."*

heart of how our brain endeavors to predict the future. Simply put, shifts in opportunity are the pivot point where the story turns.

Change is why we expend all this effort–why we create conscious narratives based on semi-conscious emotions based on unconscious predictions, why we need to have predictions and then regularly update them.

Change is both titillating and dangerous. It's also constant, inevitable, and directly tied to our survival. We evolved simple (core) consciousness as a way to quickly parse and react to changes in our environment. We evolved complex (autobiographical) consciousness as a way to avoid or exploit it. Story, then, is the term we use to describe the *conscious* means by which the autobiographical self combines narratives of prediction and happenstance to navigate the labyrinths of change and the uncertainty that they induce. We do this to address questions as abstract as the human condition or as practical as deciding when to interrupt our work to get some water.

So what is so scary about change, you ask, chin tilted defiantly upward? "The universe is made of distance and dust," wrote the poet Anna Leahy, expressing a sentiment at once beautiful and terrifying. The more we understand the cosmos and our place in it, the more aware we become of the haphazard nature of existence and our potential removal from it.

Human beings share with all other living beings a basic predisposition toward surviving, thriving, and potentially multiplying. Darwin summarized it in the second chapter of his *On the Origin of Species*––"living things like to stay alive." This prosperous aliveness is what Antonio Damasio, a kind and warmly engaging Portuguese-American neuroscientist, terms *homeostasis*: a state that we strive toward with every axon of our nervous system. The problem is that entropy and change threaten homeostasis. Change is, at best, disruptive and, at worst, terminal.

To survive, we've evolved to spend a large amount of our cognitive resources parsing, understanding, and reacting to change. If it feels threatening—as most unusual, sudden, or unfamiliar change does—our instinct is to flee, mentally or physically. On a more abstract level, this seems to be why new ideas falter when attempting to cross the chasm to mass adoption. It's not that we don't want anything new or better; it's that novelty has often been dangerous, and so our instincts work against our desire for innovation.

Remember those non-dual dichotomies—such as love and fear—that I mentioned in the introduction? Stability's sister, Plasticity, appears to be its opposite until we look a little closer. Stability (which we can link to surprise minimization) is how we maintain the status quo. If all we wanted were not to encounter any change, we would stay in the back of our proverbial cave (or our comfortable modern home), and we would be safe. We would also eventually starve to death. If we wanted to search for food or a mate, we would have to overcome our hesitation and venture out into the unknown, bravely encountering change after change and inferring what is relevant and most beneficial to our thriving. That continuous adaptability is what Plasticity (linked to active inference) is all about. To our organism's needs, they are both opposing and not. We do have to choose between them at every turn, and yet, we must continuously alternate our stance so we can respond optimally, whether it be by retreating *or* approaching.

While change is indeed scary, it also heralds advancement and thereby aids survival. Those humans who dared to venture out of the cave (or village) were far more likely to hunt a bigger game or find the newest berry patch. The adventurers who dared to sail across the vast oceans struck gold (sometimes literally). Those of us who are differently-minded in the present stand a significantly better chance of becoming prosperous entrepreneurs, engineers, and creatives. Even in modern days, when the world appears to come into our stability-friendly homes through a digital screen, venturing out exposes us to chance and allows us to serendipitously encounter ideas and people that can expand our horizons.

Change, then, is the proverbial double-edged sword. It can bring danger or our greatest desire; in either case, it is charged with drama, suspense, and a sense of momentum. Change is also never passive. If we don't want disaster to come swinging for us, there's a window of opportunity when we can make a choice and volitionally direct the ensuing shift. If the point of our nervous system is to coordinate not dying, our brain (and its narratives) has the more surgical task of making choices that optimize our experience and enable us to not only avoid pain but also to achieve pleasure. To extrapolate from Darwin, *survive* happens through instinct, while *survive optimally* gets there through consciousness and narrative prediction.

And that's where things get more complicated. Because as you will see, it's not just choosing that trips us up, but also figuring out what to choose and clearly defining for ourselves what an optimal existence actually is.

We, humans, evolved a continuum of traits from stability to plasticity. We needed to stay safe at the back of the cave so as to avoid getting eaten, and we needed to venture out of the cave in search of berries and meat. Conversely, we needed to be open and outgoing enough to meet new mates so as to diversify our gene pool, and we needed to be cautious or adversarial to save our skin and defend what's ours. This tradeoff between expanding outward, seeking, and being open to growth versus constricting inward, protecting, and remaining alive is the opponent processing that enables growth in organisms from simple amoebas onward all the way to you reading this book.

It's a dance of expansion and constriction—*Agape* and *Phobos*, *Yin* and *Yang*—that appears to be the core dynamic of life. It works beautifully, but it comes with one not-so-simple catch for us humans: we seem to be aware of almost every turn. As we become conscious of the tense dualities we must navigate, the ensuing internal conflict regularly overwhelms us.

WHEN THE WAVES RISE

Overwhelm (which we will cover in great detail in Chapter 3) has many faces, and there are multiple ways to dissect it. Internal overwhelm is the point when our sensory tension becomes difficult to contain. It causes our stress to spill outward, in the form of anger and sadness, or to spill inward, deepening into behavioral sublimation, anxiety, and somatic disturbances such as poor sleep, addiction, digestive distress, and perhaps even inflammation and autoimmune illness. External overwhelm is often sensory—the migraine that hits after a tense meeting, the back that gives out, the blurred vision after hours spent staring at the screen. These internal and external variants go hand in hand, and one begets the other. Still, the reality in all cases is that we become overwhelmed when our predictive models fail repeatedly or when we are merely convinced that they will. Therefore, learning when to heed our unconscious predictions or when to interrupt them, bring them to the surface in the form of narratives and examine or even alter them, is what this book (and framework) are all about.

Change presents a fork in the road, not just in terms of having to make the choice whether to approach or avoid a given stimulus, but also in having to decide whether we even have the resources to make that choice. If we feel tired, effort (whether it be the physical, cognitive, or the emotional effort of tuning into a difficult emotion and working through it) feels like a Herculean task. Our unconscious inferences about the world become inaccurate: we get clumsy, make mistakes, or stop trusting the acuity of our senses. That costs us more effort, which becomes experienced as frustration or conflict—with ourselves because we are disappointed in our actions, or with others because they are nearby and easier to blame.

When we're depleted or exhausted, the decision-making capacity required to navigate change feels overwhelming, creating internal friction. This is because we've inferred that we lack the energy or resources to effectively manage the choices that change demands.

Such a sense of depletion doesn't just leave us feeling overwhelmed; it also traps us in a state of internal strife as we're torn between the need to adapt and our perceived incapacity to do so. Change leads to choice, choice leads to conflict. It's the vicious cycle of rumination and stress, leading not just to overwhelm but to eventual burnout.

On the other hand, when we are well—physically, mentally, and emotionally—we possess a sense of agency, and the same stimulus of change can lead us to greater clarity. Being in a homeostatic state equips us with the resilience to face change head-on. In such moments, we don't just react to change; we actively engage with it, transform it, and create something new. We assess our constraints, lean in with curiosity, and choose our course of action based on the convergence of all we have discerned. This type of choice, born out of a sense of agency and internal trust, brings about further clarity and energy. It turns what we might otherwise experience as chaos into a structured path forward, aligning with our innate drive as living organisms to not just survive but thrive in the face of new circumstances and then become generative. Here, change leads to curiosity, which then leads to convergence, or what is commonly seen as creativity.

We'll delve deep into Clarity in Chapter 5, but for now, here is the most useful takeaway: Pain (especially emotional pain) is how we experience our resistance to change. Yet, change offers the possibility of relinquishing pain or building an altogether different relationship with it. How do we reliably navigate our way to the second—more complex, yet also more promising—option? Why does it seem so difficult to do, and why do we often overshoot our attempts, arriving instead at a tangle of exertion and control? To answer those questions, we must take a closer look at who exactly is telling your story.

2

AN ALCHEMY OF BECOMING

Crafting the Story of Self

"We don't see the world as it is, we see it as we are."
— Anaïs Nin

The bedroom is vast and dim. Brown drapes are drawn across massive windows and around me the air feels cool. I can make out furniture outlines and see that my parents' bed is empty, covered with a checkered wool blanket. A large mahogany chest serves as its headboard, looming at the edge of my vision. I'm staring at it all from behind the wooden periphery of my crib, trying to put a foot between the rounded bars, experiencing momentary fear when my ankle seems stuck, then figuring a way to turn and pull it out.

Were I a good enough artist, I could draw you the entire dimly-lit scene from the vantage point of a toddler inside her crib. It would be highly detailed, down to the pattern on the swaddling cloth my mom folded in two and used instead of a pillow. The cloth has line drawings of little red birds and the cracked eggshells from which they hatched. There's also a white plastic music toy in the shape of a bell that hangs on the wall above my bed. Though you couldn't make it out in that light, it has a picture of an elephant's head and a cord you can pull to make it sing. Try as I might, I can't recall the melody.

According to my parents, I slept in that crib till I was about two and a half, so that's the oldest I would have been while forming parts of this memory. The likelihood that an adult retains such a clear image from when they were a few years old is––while not zero––infinitesimally small. This is because the hippocampus, the part of the brain critical for forming explicit, detailed memories, is still maturing in those early years. I've verified that the swaddling blanket and the bell did, in fact, exist and that there are no photos or remnants of either to have shown me their details later in life. Nonetheless, I suspect that this memory––one I've held as a tether to my earliest autobiographical self––is more or less a confabulation. While certain aspects, like the emotions associated with the memory, may be accurate, the specific details are likely reconstructed and embellished over time, influenced by my brain's desire for a coherent narrative. The images of the cloth, crib, and even the bell probably have some veracity, yet my sense of an "I" who likes to experiment, ponders deeply, figures out how to take risks, and then gets herself out of sticky situations is a little too on the nose not to raise a rational eyebrow. Still, I am so fond of that memory—have anchored my earliest childhood to it so strongly—that I simultaneously believe and disbelieve it. At the very least, I choose not to dismiss but to hold on to it as an example of the brain's capacity for storing and creatively modifying our past in the ongoing dance between memory and imagination.

Aside from procuring a time machine, I have no conceivable access to my childhood bedroom. Yet I can use the above scene as a jigsaw puzzle, surmising that the objects I've mentioned were salient enough to my young mind to have etched themselves deeply in my recollections, and that the moment of getting my foot stuck may have triggered a strong emotional response making it more likely to become embedded in memory. My fondness for that scene and the many times I have recalled it in my adult years–usually as a point of pride about how far back my memory extends–have ensured that it not only remains accessible but is strengthened every time it is taken out of storage and polished. Still, my memory is neither as clear nor as coherent as I would like to believe. My parents can recount plenty of embarrassing incidents from my youth that I have conveniently blotted out (read: repressed). More tellingly, the experienced reality of a two- or even a five-year-old child does not feel, from the inside, the same as being in an adult's head. I likely had *some* sense of self when those memory snapshots occurred, but that sense was less separate or continuous than the self who is telling this story. The objects I have been using as "proof," while possibly accurate, were captured as freeze-frames, then strung together and embellished much later into the continuous narrative that I can now run like a film in my mind's eye.

So, who was I at two months or two years, and how does that person connect to the *me* at forty-two and the *me* who will one day (hopefully) be eighty-two? While you may not be nearly as fascinated by your earliest memories, or you may have access only to relatively recent recollections, I am hopeful this chapter can quickly illustrate the ways our autobiographical memory—and the ways it parses what is most salient to remember—become the key beats to the story we tell about our Selves.

WE ARE RELATIONAL

To better consider our early memories, we might turn to Jean Piaget, a Swiss pioneer of child psychology who, during the 1920s, became deeply intrigued with how human development evolves from the earliest stages of life all the way into adulthood. A personal incident spurred Piaget's curiosity: when he was fifteen, his childhood nanny wrote to his parents to beg forgiveness for having falsely claimed that she fought off a kidnapper. Piaget was shocked—not by his nanny's deceit, but by the fact that up until that moment he had grown up with a detailed memory of having watched the incident as a young toddler from his stroller. Learning that his recollection of the distant past was not just inaccurate but completely false, Piaget developed an ardent interest in how memories are formed. Soon he had three perfect subjects—his own children—whom he closely observed from infancy onward, noting how their ability to understand the world transformed as they grew. Piaget discovered that children progress through distinct stages of cognitive development, each characterized by a qualitatively different mode of thinking.

He posited that children move from a sensory-motor stage, when their understanding of the world is directly linked to physical interaction, to more complex stages involving abstract reasoning. A key moment in this developmental journey is the advent of *object permanence*—the understanding that objects (and people) continue to exist even when they are not perceived. This realization (that mom is not me and she can therefore leave, but that my voice can then make her come back) typically occurs around the age of eight months and marks a fundamental shift in a child's cognition.

For Piaget, this developmental milestone signifies a form of mental evolution and the emergence of a distinct sense of self. As children begin to grasp object permanence, they understand the difference between themselves and the external world. This differentiation is crucial in forming a sense of self separate from their caregivers and the environment.

Piaget's work underscores the idea that our narrative of self is initially relational, formed through interactions with our surroundings. It continues to complexify as we grow, gradually unfolding based on our nature (genetically predisposed traits and abilities) and nurture (environmental conditions and the behavior we observe in others). Early formation of the self, based on differentiating between the self/other dyad, sets the stage for the later emergence of a more nuanced and multifaceted individual identity.

If I were to paint a different scene (which to be explicitly clear, I do not recall in the least), the baby version of me would have lain in the crib, seeing objects as amorphous even in the brightest light. She would not have had a concept of a checkered blanket or a bell or that she was in a crib. She would also not have had a concept that she was a "me" or that the warm, sweet-smelling body that held and fed her was someone separate. At first, the young organism wouldn't have had agency or volition. Her experience of the world would be reactive and not all that different from Lex's, our garden slug from the last chapter whose main objective was to maintain homeostasis. When the baby was discomforted due to hunger, temperature change (wetness), or a loud noise—she would cry. The adult caregiver would (hopefully) sweep in and make the hunger disappear and the diaper dry. Over time, the baby would learn that distress noises can prompt the caregiver to deliver relief and that the hands and boob that bring comfort are attached to a voice and a set of eyes, and a smell that is "mama." Other sets of hands, eyes, and smells belong to other entities, which—as the baby grew—would become associated with other sounds ascribed to another parent, siblings, grandparents, and extended caregivers. Becoming able to predict and direct the behavior of those entities is the young organism's primary focus and her path to survival.

Now, I said the caregiver would *hopefully* sweep in; the responsiveness of the caregiver(s) is—as far as we can deduce—the foundation upon which the young brain begins to draw conclusions about her environment. Early experiences of care and responsiveness shape the child's perception of the world as either benevolent or hostile. If someone attends to her in a moment's distress, she learns that the world is safe and good and her needs will be met. If she cries for hours and no one comes, she learns that others are unreliable, and she'd better learn to soothe herself. On the basis of these early predictions and the continuous updates made throughout the first few years of life, she forms an attachment style or an unconscious prediction about how much she can rely on others.

You may already be familiar with *attachment theory*, which has recently become quite popular in the realm of relational psychology. Based on the work of twentieth-century developmental psychologists John Bowlby and Mary Ainsworth, attachment theory posits that the responses of primary caregivers create a child's "internal working models," which dictate his emotions, narratives, and expectations in future relationships. Mary Ainsworth's seminal experiment, titled *Strange Situation,* is one of the best-replicated observational studies in the entire field of psychology across decades, cultures, and changing social mores.

The Strange Situation was devised by Ainsworth in the 1970s for the purpose of observing the relationship between caregiver and child. The experiment had toddlers, aged nine to thirty months, play in a room where a clinician could observe their behavior first with their caregiver (usually the mother), then with their caregiver and the clinician, then alone with the clinician (perceived as a stranger by the child), and lastly completely alone. Sequences were arranged so that the mother would leave conspicuously on two separate occasions, and the behavior of the child would be studied both while she was away and (importantly) during the reunion between child and caregiver. Four primary styles of reaction were observed:

- *Secure* children would explore and play when their primary guardian was present, then might become distraught when this figure left. However, they would quickly recover upon the caregiver's return and resume playing with the confidence that their primary guardian is available and reliable.

- *Anxious-avoidant* children would appear significantly more indifferent to their caregiver's presence. They generally did not exhibit distress upon this individual's departure and were reluctant to be close to them upon their return. This response initially puzzled Ainsworth and her team, who eventually concluded that the child's behavior served as a defense mechanism, masking deep-rooted anxiety over the caregiver's lack of availability.

- *Anxious-ambivalent* children, on the other hand, showed distress even before their primary guardian departed. They were volatile, exhibiting a frantic desire to resist change and often became angry at the caregiver in an attempt to control the situation.

- A fourth, *disorganized* attachment style was added later by Ainsworth's student Mary Main in an attempt to note the difficult-to-classify responses that combined both anxious-avoidant and ambivalent styles. These were children who remained mostly quiet, yet showcased tense body language and erratic behavior, belying intense *internal* anger.

While attachment styles offer fascinating insights into the relational nature of early personality development, they also raise questions about individual differences. If our sense of self develops based on our environment, why do children in the same family or neighborhood become distinct individuals with divergent outcomes? Why do even siblings raised under similar conditions often exhibit different attachment styles? Variations among siblings highlight the intricate interplay between genetic predispositions, individual temperaments, and environmental influences. They suggest that while early experiences certainly shape our sense of self, the process is deepened by our individual characteristics. Such understanding paves the way for exploring the granular nature of self—our complex amalgamation of nature and nurture—and how it emerges and evolves over time.

WE ARE GRANULAR

Though I have no claim to Piagetian levels of expertise, I, too, have observed my two children's development with the engaged curiosity of a scientist. Prior to becoming a parent, I was convinced that—while nature and nurture collaborated when it came to individual development—it was certainly *nurture* that had the upper hand. I suspect most of us want to believe something similar because it enables us to hold our parents and other grown-ups responsible for the anguish we've borne. And to be clear, they are. Environment— specifically good nutrition, lack of toxins, and the nurturing attention of caregivers—is crucial to unlocking our fullest potential; yet, what we do within these positive circumstances and how we react when things turn to the worst is sketched in the invisible ink of our genetic blueprint.

My focus shifted to examining in-born predispositions as soon as I found myself with two (very lovable) subjects to compare. While our home was certainly not a lab, I did my best to reduce external variables that would influence our children's early development based on being treated differently. They were still privy to gender-based differences and birth order, both of which spilled entire buckets of variability, but I did my best to acknowledge and diminish those, even if I could not eliminate them.

Our firstborn is a daughter: cautious, thoughtful, desirous of collaboration and warmth. Our second, a son, has been active and independent; he too loves engagement but his focus is on self-confidence rather than reassurance. I have been so humbled by *nature* and the difference that genetic predispositions make that I am loath to take any credit for the development of our children, other than (hopefully) not breaking them. My best example of individual differences is from when both kids were learning to walk at an age so young as to be mostly pre-verbal. Our daughter stood by the side of the coffee table and thought with great consternation about the possibility of letting go. After much deliberation, she relinquished the stability that the table provided, stood for a few more moments trying to balance her adorable torso, and then burst into tears at the overwhelming stimulus of sensory variability. Our son, when his time came for lifting himself up from the crawling position, stood at the top of the stairs, took one look at us who were trepidatiously eyeing the potential for harm, then gleefully kawabungaed face-first, expecting that the world would catch him. (He was, predictably, fine.) There's no one gene that makes a given child anxiously cautious and another wildly optimistic; instead, it's a concoction, a recipe of ingredients, combined by nature and baked by nurture, rising to become us.

It's been fifteen years and the kids are now almost adults, having grown into two bright and loving teens, and I can ascertain that the humans they've become trace a clear line back to the infants who arrived and especially to the temperament they exhibited as toddlers. The Latin word *temperamentum* connotes a "proportioned mixture of elements," which is pretty much how I've come to view personality— as a largely innate gathering of behavioral traits that predispose us to react in particular ways. Assuming that this assertion is directionally correct, how we measure and describe our traits to ourselves and others is where things *really* get thorny.

Personality psychology is vast, and its edges veer off into realms that become untethered from scientific measurability[1]. You've likely heard of the Myers Briggs[2] personality test, or the beloved-by-executives DISC[3] assessment, or the eerily accurate, mysticism-adjacent Enneagram. There are many different schools of personality segmentation, and I'm not going to pooh-pooh any of them, though I will caution that if a schema promises to explain

---

[1]   *(at least as far I've been able to trace)*

[2]   *Ascribed to Carl Jung, but descended from his work only in the way that the bagged fries in your freezer are vaguely linked to the fries originally sold by street vendors on the Pont Neuf bridge in Paris circa 1789*

[3]   *DISC: Assessment of (D)ominance, (I)nfluence, (S)teadiness, and (C)onsciensciousness*

everything about you, leaving little open to questioning, it likely deserves a counterfactual or two. Still, when different schools of thought coalesce on terminology that describes similar behaviors, it's worth zooming in on the common factors.

And that is exactly what the Five Factor Model (or Big Five) attempts to do. This model is based on a lexical hypothesis, which posits that, over time, languages develop specialized vocabulary to describe seemingly unique behaviors, highlighting the ubiquity of a given trait. In other words, if regular humans come up with specific terms for something they're doing, it's likely important. The formal development of the Big Five began in the 1930s, then gained momentum in the 1960s. However, the correlation of dictionary terms to behaviors proved computationally daunting, and the hypothesis lingered in a semi-abandoned state until the 1980s. That's when Paul Costa and Robert McCrae breathed new life into it, leveraging newly-available computational power to create the NEO[4] Personality Inventory. Their research provided empirical evidence supporting the model's validity and reliability, giving birth to a widely accepted framework for personality discernment.

What makes this model particularly compelling is its basis in how we naturally describe one another. When researchers applied factor analysis to personality surveys, they discovered fascinating patterns. People tend to use clusters of related terms when describing personality traits. For instance, someone dubbed 'conscientious' is more likely to be described as 'always on time' rather than 'tardy'. These semantic associations, consistently applied across individuals, pointed to five broad dimensions that we commonly use to describe each other's character or personality.

The five factors[5] that give the theory its name are Openness to experience, Conscientiousness, Extraversion, Agreeableness, and Neuroticism. (As a quick aside, while personality researchers

---

4   *The NEO was originally created as a three-factor model assessing Neuroticism, Extraversion and Openness.*

5   *You may see the acronyms OCEAN or CANOE used in reference within personality psychology.*

denote emotional sensitivity with the term Neuroticism—viewing the propensity for negative emotions as detrimental—I prefer to use Emotionality—treating general emotions as relatively neutral—in order to steer clear of the negative bias ascribed to being "neurotic.")

When I first learned about personality theory in undergraduate school, I was taught that trait dimensions are pretty much immutable: someone is an Introvert (wanting to keep to themselves) or an Extrovert (they are good with people); they are either Conscientious (meaning that you can expect them to be punctual and complete a project) or they are low on Conscientiousness (and you should never trust them with a blank check). Even back then, I suspected that such a fixed approach was missing something, but I had neither the lived nor the scientific experience to back that up.

Over the past decade of coaching entrepreneurs and trying to discern what makes one person persevere while another folds easily, I revisited the idea of individual differences, trying to discern whether there were specific predictors of success. I won't hide the ball here: there is no single trait or mixture of traits that you can test to know if a team is worthy of investment. But there *are* sets of traits that have a strong correlation to industriousness and compassion, and other sets that form patterns labeled as "the dark triad[6]" of narcissism, Machiavellianism, and psychopathy. Some of these traits are more entrenched than others, but none are set in stone.

To be clear, the Big Five are domains of behavior that describe many facets of the ways we act from moment to moment. While there is no agreeableness gene, nor an extroversion one, there are genetic markers for the behavior we describe as Compassion and Politeness (which point to Agreeableness) and for Enthusiasm and Assertiveness (which we view as Extroversion). We seem to have something akin to a natural temperament, which is the in-born predisposition of an individual to move toward or away from new

---

[6]   *Disturbingly, this leads to a "winner-take-all" mentality, sometimes yielding high-multiple investments. You can decide if that's the zero-sum game you'd like to play.*

stimuli (Openness to Experience) and our volatility or withdrawal in the face of threat (Neuroticism). If you're paying close attention, you may remember the push and pull governing our predictive models and observe that the above trait dimensions fit neatly into precisely the desires we mentioned earlier: the caution (or surprise minimization) that urges us to stay safe and the curiosity (or active inference) that nudges us to venture out and discover.

Colin DeYoung, a psychology professor and personality researcher at the University of Minnesota, has evolved The Five Factor model in precisely this direction, creating the Cybernetic Big Five Theory (CB5T), which studies personality descriptors in accord with our organism's continuous learning. DeYoung champions a hierarchical model of personality, tracing all traits to two higher-order factors: Stability and Plasticity. His methodology delineates the psycho-biological mechanisms at the foundation of individual behavior, presenting them as interconnected components of a cohesive adaptive system and allowing for both the tracing of genetic markers and the continued adaptation that active inference demands of us. DeYoung's work is remarkable for its shift away from a static one-and-done approach to personality and toward a way of aligning trait descriptions to fit within a Predictive Processing view of organismic behavior. Such new, scientifically-coherent approaches enable us to use character or personality as a predictive descriptor that can be connected to temporary states (i.e., moods) on the micro level and to autobiographical narratives on the macro.

Now, what does all that have to do with our narrative of self? The most significant factor when it comes to overall temperament is the internal stimuli that raise or lower our internal temperature—namely, emotions. Emotions don't *cause* our temperament, but they trigger or 'unlock' it. Funnily enough, the emotions we are likely to feel most easily are predicated on our temperament. Chicken, meet egg!

If you'll indulge me here for a quick aside that will take center stage later in this book, it behooves us to examine the work of Jaak Panksepp, a jovial neuroscientist and psychologist who defined the realm of *affective neuroscience* and spent his life investigating the neural correlates of emotion. Panksepp is affectionately known as "the rat tickler" because he studied the behavior of rats, experimenting on (and even tickling) them to explore how they related to enjoyment, laughter[7], or play. Panksepp proposed a distillation of basic emotional responses in mammals, narrowing them to seven categories: Seeking, Anger, Fear, Care, Sadness, and Play. He linked these with the Five Factor Model in human subjects and found a remarkably large correlation between experienced emotions (meaning affective states) and stable personality traits. This might sound surprising or obvious, depending on your own experience. The gist, which I don't want you to miss here, is that our in-born traits predispose us to experience certain affective states.

Panksepp found that Extraversion traits predispose one to greater Play. Agreeableness gives us high Care emotions and diminishes our likelihood to Anger. Openness to Experience strongly correlates with Seeking emotions and increases Curiosity. Neuroticism makes us far more predisposed to Fear, Anger, and Sadness. Our affective states (meaning the sensory pings we interpret as emotions) and our personality traits (especially the ones in the Emotionality/ Neuroticism category, which measure how sensitive and reactive we are to the aforementioned emotions) are bound together in a way that creates virtuous or vicious cycles, depending on circumstances. Traits shape our states. States, when repeated, increase the availability of particular traits.

---

[7]   *Panksepp discovered that rats emit a high-pitched squeal when tickled that is not dissimilar from laughter. What's more, they enjoy the interaction and will seek it out when given the opportunity. Further reading: Panksepp, J. (2007). Neuroevolutionary sources of laughter and social joy: Modeling primal human laughter in laboratory rats. Behavioural Brain Research, 182(2), 231-244.*

This brings us to the question that most of my clients and students care about. How can we change our traits, or at least influence which emotional states they cause us to experience?

During the onset of the Covid-19 pandemic, I noticed that individuals with high Emotionality were likely to become very preoccupied with the threat of the virus. If they also measured high on Agreeableness, they were more likely to become attuned to others' stress (whether within their family or on social media), amplifying their own anxiety and ratcheting up the overall sense of danger. This created a vicious cycle that could potentially be tempered by intentionally engaging in behaviors that amplified one's Conscientiousness and Openness to Experience. (As an aside, this is why I've come to view Curiosity as the Swiss Army knife of trait regulation.) The latter behavioral categories would encourage one to study the virus, collecting knowledge in an attempt to organize and understand the situation while remaining open to uncertainty as best they could. Translating this into the language of active inference, individuals with certain trait predispositions might have initially responded with heightened anxiety based on their priors. However, through engaging with information and adapting new coping strategies, they could recalibrate their predictive models, reducing anxiety over time.

We often think of personality traits as immutable characteristics like eye color and height, but they are actually bands of affordance as to how much of a given characteristic we can easily deploy. (Height, too, is a band; how tall a child can grow is genetically predisposed, but unlocked by nutrition and the friendliness of their environment within the timespan of childhood and adolescence.) This understanding of personality traits as dynamic, rather than fixed, opens up possibilities for growth and adaptation. It also aligns closely with active inference, reiterating how our brain continuously makes predictions and adjustments based on incoming sensory data and prior beliefs. Just as being genetically predisposed for natural flexibility does not automatically make you an Olympic gymnast, so too the genetic markers for high sensitivity do not destine you to always become overwhelmed or at the mercy of panic attacks.

Now, what about Conscientiousness? DeYoung's lab identified some genetic markers that contribute to Industriousness and Orderliness traits. Still, that trait dimension is the most socially-conditioned one and therefore, the most mutable. This is good news for those of us with a messy desk: there is no gene setting our pile of papers in stone, and it is likely that behaviors such as self-discipline, competence, neatness, and punctuality can become habit-driven adaptations toward greater personality change. Having said that, I can think of a number of clients and family members who would quickly tell me that it is impossible to alter their propensity for messiness and that I might as well be expecting them to develop a sudden ability to sing. To that, I will answer that you can likely do either, but the first hurdle is to address your ability to tolerate discomfort, meaning your Neuroticism or Emotionality.

Our traits are not static markers but part of a dynamic interplay between our genetic (and epigenetic) predispositions and the environment. They can be seen as biases in our predictive models. For example, a high level of neuroticism might bias an individual's predictions of perceived threats or negative outcomes. However, these biases are not immutable. Just as our brain updates its predictions in light of new information, we can also recalibrate our trait biases through experiences and conscious efforts. This recalibration is akin to shifting our position within the bands of affordance mentioned above.

When I started working on CRATE, I bet on the fact that not only do traits govern which emotional states we can experience most readily, but states—when experienced repeatedly—can shift our capacity for a given trait. This turned out to be true (at least as borne out by early users testing the app), so I set out to develop a framework that would allow us to change our states intentionally and with greater ease.

WE ARE EMERGENT

Most of us grow up believing that "we" sit somewhere inside our brain. We feel like there's a homunculus captaining from a command center inside our skull, using our eyes as portholes, and considering sensory readouts from a constantly flickering dashboard. He or she bravely navigates our body through space, reviewing footage of past expeditions, charting new courses, and engaging with the world. While awake, our self steers our body toward the next goal, be that a delectable meal, a desirable human, or a more nebulous objective such as career advancement. You might imagine your command center to be as buttoned-up as the bridge of the U.S.S. Enterprise or as roguish as the cockpit of the Millennium Falcon, but it was Pixar's movie *Inside Out* that came closest in its depiction of our internal command center by introducing us to several character representations of emotions, each taking the wheel at different plot points. Cute as that concept may seem, I hope the previous sections have demonstrated that we are not steered solely by Fear or Joy or Sadness at any one point. A more accurate metaphor might be a circus pyramid of emotion-based acrobats riding on vehicles made of personality traits, expressing the entangled nature of our inner workings.

Those of you paying careful attention might be thinking, "Great, so I have some childhood memories and learnings (the relational part), and I have some Curiosity riding on a scooter of Openness to Experience (the granular part), but how does any of that make me a *me*? And where does my love of chocolate or my obsession with David Bowie figure in all of this?"

You might be surprised how much of your tastes (down to whether you prefer milk versus dark chocolate or whether a particular song moves rather than disturbs you) can be traced to the genetically predisposed sensitivity of your palate and hearing, hormonal influences that steer reactions and behaviors often described as personality traits, and the mimetic desires learned from peers and loved ones. However, these characteristics alone do not forge a sense of self until bundled together and bound with the spell of your name. To do that, you need to be conscious of what *is* happening, remember what *has* happened, and have some meta-cognition enabling you to plan (and optionally narrate) what you hope *will* happen next.

Scientists don't fully agree on how consciousness arose or why we have it, but its existence is what enables us to have thoughts and to relay them to ourselves and each other in multiple forms (including this book). I'd like to propose that the thing we call *a self*—the *I* writing these words and the *you* reading them—is actually a narrative blurring. We are each composed of granular traits (biological predispositions such as how curious you are, how conscientious, how agreeable, etc.), relational states (what you have been taught by the adults who raised you, what nutrients or knowledge your environment afforded you, etc.), and emergent phenomena (the responses arising from the complex interplay between the other two, and the conscious meaning we ascribe while narrating it all). We tell ourselves and others the story of who we are and see it as one continuous whole instead of noticing all its elements. I think of this as a narrative blurring through time and conceptual space. As with our perception of time, our story of self (without which there is no sense of identity) is possible due precisely to such blurring. We are both the sea and all the drops that compose it.

That metaphoric sea—the conscious epiphenomena[8] that emerge in our minds, and which we assume to be our inner voice—is what most of us experience in narrative form. It doesn't always happen in words. Some people seem to narrate in near-full sentences; others have a mental flash of concepts; still others think in images or image maps, seeing places or experiences as if projected

---

8   *Epiphenomena are second-order effects on top of emergent phenomena. If emotions are phenomena that emerge as a response to our interactions with our environment, then consciousness likely emerges on top of that.*

on a screen inside their mind's eye, then *optionally* narrating them in words. From what I've discerned, mine is in that last category of inner experience. I have a vivid imaginal function, which likely helps with both creativity and constant distractedness. If you ask me to remember my grandmother's Bulgarian vineyard, situated in a meadow on the Danube River, I flash back first to the actual vines, overhanging with grapes, paths of yellowing grass woven between them. Then there's the big cherry tree up toward the house to the left, so massive that I remember spending an entire day living high in it, nestled comfortably in the crook of one branch, lowering and raising a roped basket with the cherries I'd picked, exchanging them for chocolate-covered wafers and bottles of water that my grandma sent in return.

My sense of self is made up of countless scenes such as these—many from very early in childhood, continuing through teen moments and adulthood, all the way to last year's holiday travel, the coaching session I had yesterday, or the coffee-on-the-couch conversation with my husband this morning. They are not narratives per se. They are scenes, freeze-frames of recollected time with as little or as much detail as the attention that my brain allotted to them based on their impact. The actual story is how I weave them together.

Like the vineyard's path, the narrative connects what has been most important, noting specific highlights and guiding me toward a specific goal. These mental destinations, or scenes, are sometimes understood consciously, but they are always first embodied and felt. Describing the scene of the Bulgarian vineyard made me feel adventurous, safe, cared for, and carefree. The moment I recollected earlier atop the Empire State Building imbued me with longing, hope and a dreamy solitude. Upon reflection, each of these scenes carries a different message. The first says: you are safe. The second: nobody gets you. How we pair these disparate learnings with the conclusions we draw from them about our relationship with the world and others in it is what emerges as our autobiographical self.

Wait a minute here, I hear you thinking! *Are you now telling me that what happens in my head is no different than Sleeping Beauty, an action movie, or a melodrama?* Indeed, I am. What's more, I want to show you how the beats of the stories we are told often program the structures and expectations of what happens in our own narratives *as well as* within our lives.

Our explanatory stories are the deepest, most primordial narratives functioning within us. They are inference models brought to life and embellished to better enable future predictions. The personality labels we discussed in the previous section are precisely such explanatory stories:

- "I stay home and read because I'm an introvert."
- "He started screaming at the board meeting because he's highly neurotic."
- "My desk is a scattered mess because I'm just not an orderly person."

On one level, the above statements accurately describe behavior and make it easier to predict how someone is likely to behave next; on another—they become self-fulfilling prophecies by invisibly shifting their function from explanation to inspiration or (self-) manipulation. A child who has grown up being told she's "the wild one" will consciously or unconsciously weave her perception (read: prediction) of being wild into her narrative of self[1]. Even a puppy who is regarded with fear because he is "snippy" will react by picking up non-verbal signals of aversion and snap at you in fear because you've just taught him something in his environment is unsafe.

Think about the stories we tell on a bigger scale: our histories, myths, and legends. Each of them carries the double-edged sword of storytelling: the light, magnanimous side where we use narratives to

---

[1] *For early sociological research, see Labeling Theory, developed by Howard Becker and detailed in his 1963 work "Outsiders: Studies in the Sociology of Deviance." More recent theory includes Carol Dweck's 2006 book "Mindset."*

explain the world, *warn* each other about it, even *inspire* great deeds when all else fails; and its dark underbelly. Where we explain, we can also obfuscate: we pretend that we know what is happening by constructing a convincing-enough answer. Where we warn, we may also threaten—keeping ourselves and others small, avoiding sharp-fanged wolves while also keeping away from those who look different. Where we inspire, we also manipulate; sometimes this is on purpose,[2] but more often it's with the best of intentions—believing that we know the right way and convincing others (and ourselves) to follow us right off the edge of a cliff.

The stories that are meant to warn are more explicit, but possibly also more treacherous. They are supposed to give us direct instructions on what to do or not to do and, therefore, teach us that given answers are right or wrong and that the wrong ones have dire consequences. Those ways of walking through the world lead to constant anxiety, not to mention the fact that some of us discover later in life that the moral messages themselves are deeply confusing. I'm not sure whether *Hansel & Gretel* taught me not to try eating strange people's houses, but they definitely made me wonder if there were circumstances that would lead my parents to abandon me in the woods.

Lastly, the blurry line between inspiration and manipulation is likely not a bug but a feature. One way or another, every story is selling us something. It is our brain nudging us to orient toward actions that will keep us (or our species) safe based on inferences about what has happened before. Curiously, that is exactly what memories are: they are not recorded to help us recollect the past; rather, we keep and update them so we can more accurately predict the future. The exterior stories, then—the ones we use for myth,

---

[2]   *Propaganda is also a story.*

entertainment, advertising, or pitches—are just an externalization (or sometimes exploitation) of that same function. Whether we are moved by Buffy Summers to give up the mundane preoccupations of high school and work tirelessly to save the world or convinced by a flawless-looking actress that the scent she is spraying will magically transport us to the French Riviera, the underlying message is not dissimilar: our regular life is lacking, and we are not enough.

Like the myth of Demeter causing winter to arrive out of grief when her daughter Persephone was kidnapped by Hades, stories serve to make sense of the world, shield our fears, assuage our worries, and soothe our anger. But while myths are symbolic, related verbally, and intended to awaken the best within us, many of our embedded stories are non-verbal, handed down by parents and caregivers who model knee-jerk emotional patterns before we have even learned how to speak. When you feel threatened, they show us, react by snapping or deflecting. When you are tired, become angry at whoever is not helping. If you are worried, pretend nothing is wrong. If you are lost, assume abandonment.

You may have received different messages depending on your upbringing and culture. Still, these unspoken if/then loops were programmed into us by example and often unintentionally. We pick them up and pass them down without noticing, allowing such defensive narratives to become the bedrock from which we (and our entire societies) make sense of the world. If we don't notice or question them, they permeate our reality, become reinforced, and settle on top of our psyche—becoming the layers of sediment that keep us from discovering who we truly are.

3

EVERYTHING AND (EVEN) MORE

Complexity and Overwhelm

"The truth will set you free. But not until it is finished with you."
— David Foster Wallace

It is mid-afternoon on a wintry Saturday in 2004. I'm sitting on the stoop of our walk-up East Village apartment, long black coat sweeping the concrete, a notebook on my lap, ideas scurrying to land before the sun descends below the horizon. Cars honk and people rush by; the neighborhood thrums with an energy that now feels like another New York—alive with momentum. Right as I stir to go upstairs, the heavy wooden door swings open behind me, and out spills our neighbor with a toddler screaming over his shoulder.

His daughter—an absurdly cute and even more absurdly precocious three-year-old—is wailing at the top of her lungs, little fists beating angrily at the air. I jump up, ready to soothe or fix or do *something*, reaching toward her imploringly.

"Sweetheart! What's wrong!?"

(Now, I know we've discussed how much of our memory is reconstructed and embellished, but I still remember what followed as if it were yesterday.) The child stops mid-scream, fixes me with massive brown eyes, sighs deeply, and says, "Oh, Dessy! ... It's complicated."

My own eyes widen and I can't muster an answer. I watch flabbergasted as father and daughter disappear down the crowded street. Leather silhouettes skate across the asphalt, a cabbie is yelling, and a pedestrian almost runs into a scooter. Smells of coffee and cigarettes mingle with the cold air. I stand there, thinking, "You're so right!" And also, "You're three! How can it be complicated?"

———

Two decades have passed since then. That toddler is now a young woman, and in the years since I have seen my own toddlers, then children, now teens, shed their share of tears in moments of overwhelm. I've also coached many adults who, at one time or another, expressed a similar sentiment:

- "It's complicated."
- "It's a lot."
- "I'm not sure I can handle it all."

Overwhelm, it seems, is a perennial problem, keeping us from smiling, sleeping, or simply being.

During a recent workshop on *Containing Overwhelm* in late 2023, a staggering ninety percent of my audience reported (via an anonymous questionnaire) that they experienced "high to extremely high" levels of stress. On a scale of one to five, forty-seven out of the fifty-two people attending said they were a four or five when it came to struggles with sleep and engaging in behaviors they considered harmful. More than half selected "drastically change my life" as their answer to my "If you had a magic wand..." question. Still, no one was actively considering changing their job or addressing the situation in ways other than trying to get some exercise[3].

A more curious thing happened the following week when I encountered several of the participants in our one-on-one coaching sessions. When I asked each how they were doing, I got versions of "Great!", "All good!" and "Yeah, everything's moving." Had they forgotten our group conversation and the experiences they shared? Or had the part of them that acknowledged how close they felt to burnout become inconvenient or unseemly, stowed away for a hypothetical *later* when they would have time to feel it... or when it would become too insistent to ignore?

We've all been there: moments when we admitted to ourselves and others that not everything is trending "up and to the right," then shoved those thoughts aside because acknowledging them would require change, and that change would necessitate confronting and dismantling the stories that aren't—or maybe never were—true.

I spent a large portion of my twenties and thirties in that psychological neighborhood and still find myself visiting occasionally. Overwhelm is generally felt in three different forms: physical (which elicits panic), mental (often resulting in some form of burnout), and social (experienced as the scorching lava of shame). All three compel sublimation or discharge. Sublimation (a form of denial) can occasionally be a useful coping mechanism, deployed when we predict that our mind cannot handle the full weight of what is occurring. Discharge happens when our tension explodes and we release our overwhelm toward someone or something else (through

---

[3]   *A few were already in therapy and/or on medication.*

verbal or physical means) or substitute the tension by overwhelming ourselves with something that is familiar and thereby feels safer. Most addictive behavior does exactly this—it is a form of signal-jamming. Though often expressed in maladaptive ways, these strategies are adaptive in that they help us survive in the moment—often at the expense of our longer-term well-being.

The trick, then, is to understand how and why overwhelm happens, and to adopt better coping mechanisms that transform its energy so that it doesn't damage us—and possibly becomes generative.

THE COMPLEXITY OF BEING

As in the case of my neighbor's daughter, we often say something is complicated when we actually mean that it is complex. Complexity is the study of systems with non-linear, random, and emergent properties, where the whole becomes greater than the sum of its parts. A fine Swiss watch is complicated; you can take it apart and (if you know what you're doing) put it right back together. A beehive is complex; the individual bees may be simple and easy to remove, but the dynamics between them create emergent behaviors that cannot be reverse-engineered.

Both our personality traits and our emotional states are complex systems. Many of the traits that capture our attention, such as beneficial ones like intelligence and curiosity, or detrimental ones like psychopathy and schizophrenia, are inherently the result of complex polygenic[4] processes. Complexity, in this case, means that each trait is influenced by many different genes in conjunction with environmental factors, rather than being determined by a single

---

[4]   *A polygenic trait refers to a feature, like height or skin complexion, shaped by the interaction of several genes. Unlike the simpler inheritance patterns described by Mendel's laws, polygenic traits emerge from the complex interplay of multiple genetic factors. These factors often mix with environmental influences, leading us to categorize them as multifactorial. Such complexity explains why polygenic traits exhibit a wide range of expression among individuals. My curiosity may present slightly (or very) differently from yours—both in terms of extent and in terms of behavioral expression, highlighting the nuanced interplay between genetics and environment in determining our personal attributes.*

marker. If these traits were dictated by simple genetic mechanisms, evolutionary pressures would have had an easier time favoring or eliminating certain characteristics. However, the reality is that our predispositions exist on a continuum, where variation is not only common but also beneficial for the adaptability and resilience of the species. Genetic diversity ensures that populations can survive and thrive in a wide range of situations, underscoring the intricate dance between nature (genetics) and nurture (environment) in shaping our characteristics. The massively polygenic essence of most key traits reflects the evolutionary advantage of maintaining a broad spectrum of potential responses in the face of our ever-changing world.

Our emotional states are another such matrix of complexity, where we, as multi-faceted systems, strive to parse a reality that is continuously becoming more intricate. This task is not merely cognitive but fundamentally biological. We must make sense of occurrences in a manner nuanced enough to identify opportunities while reacting to threats in sufficient time that they don't eat us. It's a metabolically expensive challenge, demanding the vast energy necessary to maintain our biological functions and also power our thinking. And even though the metabolic cost of emotional processing has not yet been quantified, it, too, is a crucial element of our existence. Our brain is a self-organizing system that bases its understanding on a model of reality that we continuously create and then verify against the world our senses perceive. It is impossible for us to compute all outcomes or perceive all relevant information. The resulting data would lead to a combinatorial explosion, meaning that all the available combinations would be too vast to calculate and sort by even a supercomputer. Such overwhelm would likely crash our system once and for all. Therefore, we focus on what is most salient to our survival, continuously bearing the sense that we might be ignoring something sharp or even lethal.

Imagine you're an impala[5], grazing happily in the savannah, when suddenly you hear a rustling and glimpse a dark, irregular shape behind some bushes. You freeze and stand on alert, trying to decide your next action. Chances are decent the shadow is just a tree trunk, and the rustling was caused by some wind. Bolting is expensive—physically (in terms of cortisol flooding your system to boost your muscles), metabolically (in terms of energy spent running at high speed), and opportunistically (time lost gathering nutrients, plus potential exposure to other predators). Not to mention that the other antelopes might laugh at you! And yet, that shadow might also be a cheetah, staring right at you, licking her chops. Deciding to wait for more information might be the last choice you make.

Not surprisingly, the animals that survived long enough to procreate and pass on their genes were likely the ones who ran. If you're an impala, the choice of whether to flee or keep eating was made by your nervous system with no conscious input required. This was true for early humanoids as well, but over time, there was another type of human who survived—the one who perceived the rustling and then *consciously* overrode his fear, inferring instead an opportunity to hunt. Through building tools, the latter human turned the table on predators and was able to use *them* as food, growing larger and smarter, then passing down *that* genetic message across the millennia. It is a simplification, but not an inaccuracy, to say we have evolved consciousness so we could follow two possible choices: the path of daring or the path of fleeing—and that each of us is capable of either. What decides which path is easier for us is a combination of nature, nurture, and circumstance. Either way, we are caught having to *choose*, and therein lies our main struggle with emotion. We blame the messenger, believing that the emotional pings of fear or hunger or longing are what cause us discomfort, yet the tension lies primarily at the crossroads of how we react to

---

[5]   *The antelope, not the car.*

them: do we contract ourselves and flee, or do we daringly expand and approach?

EMOTIONS AND CHOICE

The Bayesian statistician George E.P. Box aptly remarked, "All models are wrong, but *some* are useful." We don't have to be completely accurate in our model of the world—just accurate *enough*. The delta between our inference (what we think will happen) and our experienced reality (what actually happens) registers as *surprisal*, which is a fancier way of saying *emotional upheaval*. You might remember that within Predictive Processing, surprise minimization is the other side of active inference. In simpler terms: we build hypotheses of what will happen, test them, and do our best to avoid "holy crap!" moments.

Each of us must account for stimuli, process the somatic pings they elicit, and react with the right metabolic effort they demand—all in the span of 300-600 milliseconds for the simpler (or more threatening) occasions. This dance between perception and action unfolds in the corners of consciousness, marrying the immediacy of somatic sensation with liminal or subliminal response, even as the more nuanced situations snap us to attention and—for us humans—necessitate a deeper awareness and choice. Throughout these intricacies, if we *sense* that we don't understand what is going on or if our *feeling-based narratives* say that we cannot cope with what we do understand, we become overwhelmed.

Feelings and emotions are terms often used interchangeably, but they play distinct roles in this context. As Antonio Damasio details in much of his work[6], emotion represents a complex psychological state marked by physiological arousal, expressive behavior, and awareness components. In contrast, feeling is the *conscious* experience of that emotion, which you could also see as the subjective lens through

---

[6]   *Damasio, A. (1999). "The Feeling of What Happens: Body and Emotion in the Making of Consciousness" and (2003) "Looking for Spinoza: Joy, Sorrow, and the Feeling Brain"*

which we interpret our emotional states. (This, incidentally, is why I take the time to use the clumsier term 'feeling-based narrative' rather than just 'feeling.')

For example, when we see an ice cream cone, we may experience an increased heart rate, smile, and have a conscious sense of happiness[7]. Our awareness of joy is the *feeling*, while the physiological arousal and experience of our facial muscles stretching are the energy, valence, and behavioral parts of the *emotion*.

In other words, emotions are physiological and behavioral responses to internal or external stimuli, while feelings are the subjective experiences of those emotions. The two are closely related, but they are not the same.

| STIMULUS | NEUROLOGICAL RESPONSE | EXPERIENCE OF VALENCE | CONSCIOUS NARRATIVE |

emotion

feeling

As you can likely observe, this is something of a semantic quagmire that can complicate our understanding of an already-complex internal situation. To make matters worse, scientists *really* don't agree on what emotions are. I have cited Damasio's work because much of my understanding is informed by his research, and I have found his theses to integrate clearly with other discoveries, including Predictive Processing. Damasio's work rests in the relative middle between scholars like Jaak Panksepp, who was convinced that there are discrete neuronal correlates for emotion, and neuroscientists such as Lisa Feldman Barrett, who emphatically insists that emotions are constructed phenomena and that the idea of discrete emotional states is ultimately a cultural confabulation.

---

[7] *Assuming we have previously tried, and liked, eating ice cream.*

So, who is right? I'm not certain, but suspect that—as with most complex realms of human experience—the answer will turn out to be' both'. Yes, emotions (or particularly the feeling-based narratives elicited by internal somatic sensations) are constructed in our minds, dependent on language, and culturally varied (as Feldman Barrett suggests[8]). And yes, there appear to be neural correlates to brain activation when we experience baseline reactions such as Anger, Fear, or even Play (as Panksepp's experiments detected[9]). And also, yes—important for the purposes of our discussion—there indeed appear to be somatic markers (as per Damasio's theory[10]), which are felt within our body as the heralds of particular emotional states, thereby activating whatever prior assumptions we hold (to bring in the work of Karl Friston and Andy Clark for good measure). My guess is that scientists would have an easier time collaborating if they could agree that they are pointing at the same phenomena whilst using different framings to explain them.

Ultimately, whatever kinds of entities we ascertain our emotions to be, their presence and function remain relatively straightforward: we become conscious of their signals as a barometer of our well-being. We are then prompted to *choose* an action either toward or away from a stimulus. If we find ourselves numb or disconnected from our emotions (a state known as *alexithymia*, meaning "no words for emotion"), we become unable to choose, and, over time, we wither. In those cases, it's not that our weather system is absent; it's that our barometer is broken or we have become blind to its readings.

Emotions are complex, largely automated programs of active inference concocted by evolution. They help us notice what is most

[8]   Barrett, L. F., Lindquist, K. A., & Gendron, M. (2007). Language as context for the perception of emotion. Trends in Cognitive Sciences, 11(8), 327-332. https://doi.org/10.1016/j.tics.2007.06.003

[9]   Panksepp, J. (2007). Neuroevolutionary sources of laughter and social joy: Modeling primal human laughter in laboratory rats. Behavioural Brain Research, 182(2), 231-244. https://doi.org/10.1016/j.bbr.2007.02.015

[10]   Bechara, A., & Damasio, A. R. (2005). The somatic marker hypothesis: A neural theory of economic decision. Games and Economic Behavior, 52(2), 336-372. https://doi.org/10.1016/j.geb.2004.06.010

salient to us and move toward or away from it. As we bring their information into awareness, we become what is often referred to as "conscious." That sense of autobiographical, temporal narrative that we most associate with being a conscious self is, by its very essence, predicated on emotion. Visible to others[11] and somatically sensed by us, emotions are our reactions to stimuli. Feelings, on the other hand, are private and happen inside our thoughts. They are the mental experiences of body states, which arise[12] as we respond to different situations. The emotions we engage with shape the terrain of our thoughts. Marcel Proust described them as being like geological upheavals. Their peaks and valleys focus our attention, compelling us to make choices and generate narratives—positive or negative—to explain and navigate our world. In these terrains, complexity and intensity are *characteristics* of emotion. They show us that whatever has occurred is hyper-salient, and we must pay attention to it. Overwhelm occurs when we *feel* (i.e., interpret) our emotions and decide (often unconsciously) that their intensity is more than we can handle.

DIVING INTO OVERWHELM

Just as your sight, hearing, touch, taste, etc., tell you whether to approach or avoid an external stimulus, so too do emotions function as an *internal* sense, carrying information that motivates or dissuades our behavior. To extend the metaphor of geological upheavals, if I sense my stress level to be like the peak of Overlook Mountain in the Catskills (let's say I'm tasked with creating an elaborate campaign for a VR game—a vertical where I have both professional experience and personal passion), I might ready my metaphorical hiking boots, pack provisions, and head upward as soon as the sun rises. If, however, what awaits me is the equivalent of a Mt. Saint Helen-level of stress

---

[11] *In terms of tension, flushed skin, etc.*

[12] *Often in narrative form.*

(job loss or the end of a relationship), my eagerness to engage with the emotion will be mitigated by strong discomfort, which might lead to physiological pain or unwellness, and it might take days or even weeks to set off on its path—if I do at all.

We all wish we could clearly assess and respond to emotional challenges, no matter how steep. Yet our knowledge of how a given situation affects us is often naive, distorted by over- or under-estimating our capacity to withstand it. We tend to suppress or express more than is optimal. This does not mean that either suppression or expression is wrong; if a mugger holds you up, fear, anger, and even grief are all appropriate emotions, but feeling them right at that instance might prevent you from escaping. In my personal experience—and based on what I've witnessed over years of coaching—most ambitious individuals tend to overestimate their ability to contain intensity, and thereby sublimate the emotions that tell them they are at capacity.

The word *overwhelm* originally comes from the Old English word "whelm," which meant to "turn upside down" or "to cover completely." The prefix "over-" was added later, amplifying the original sense to imply completely covering or engulfing, often with a destructive force. The term has since evolved to describe a state of being wholly overcome or submerged by mental or emotional pressure. When we say we feel overwhelmed, we are expressing a feeling of being buried or drowned under too much of something, whether that be responsibilities, emotions, thoughts, or other sources of pressure.

It's interesting to note how the original physical connotation of the word has transformed into a more internal or sensory context in modern usage. Just as we can be physically overwhelmed by a flood or an avalanche, we can also be emotionally or cognitively overwhelmed by strong sensory input.

States of overwhelm are usually experienced as states of disquiet, constriction, burden, stress, and inability to cope. Overwhelm provokes fear, insecurity, and loneliness. It amplifies our sense of separateness and leaves us feeling adrift, unsupported, and laden with uncertainty. But aside from cataclysmic events, these states don't happen without warning. Usually, there's a continuum, from the little nagging annoyances to the angering or saddening moments, to the sense that life is out to get us and only bad things are happening... and all the way to states of near-capitulation when we feel we are at the end of our psychological rope. If we experience enough individual instances where our brain predicts a negative outcome, we generalize that our overall environment is adversarial and that *only* negative things will keep occurring. As mentioned earlier, there are roughly three ways in which we tend to experience overwhelm: physical, mental, and social. They often mix together for what feels like a singular and bespoke version of torture.

Physical overwhelm feels like exhaustion, capitulation, even stupor. It is triggered by massive amounts of fear, stress, or overperformance. If we don't believe we can cope with whatever is occurring, we freeze and become unable to engage in fight or flight. If our impala had delayed her decision to flee or if the cheetah had won the race and caught her, she would have frozen in its clutches, her nervous system becoming flooded and overwhelmed. There is a YouTube video[13] of this occurring, where you can watch as a predator who is about to devour its prey becomes startled by something off-camera and abandons the terrified animal. Several grueling seconds elapse as the impala lies in the tall grass, completely frozen, breathing heavily. She then sits up and begins to convulse, processing the fear that seized her system and burning off the stress hormones coursing through her body. Once all the stress has been released and fear is metabolized, the impala can rise and run off as if nothing particularly troublesome occurred. This shaking or trembling is part of the fight-or-flight response, mediated by the autonomic nervous system. It is

---

[13]   https://bit.ly/impala-video

a mechanism used by many animals, including humans, to recover from a high arousal state induced by threat or stress.

We humans don't like to show visible signs of shaking or trembling, so we usually sublimate them. Unlike our antelope, our mind overrides the natural impulse to convulse, repressing the urge and thereby forcing it to come out 'sideways.' It feels difficult, even counterintuitive, but when we are overwhelmed by physical demands, taking a few minutes to stretch or walk or run outside can do wonders. Dance is even more kinetically effective. Shaking our limbs or jumping up and down (while it might seem silly) is most in accordance with our instincts.

For most of my life, I did not move much when experiencing overwhelm because I self-identified as the cerebral type who was too busy thinking "important thoughts" to venture outside. The trouble is that when we sublimate the physical into the mental, we not only internalize the stress, we double it. A wise man (who may or may not have been Einstein) warned that "we cannot solve problems using the same thinking we used when we created them." My inner tortured artist who stayed up brooding till sunrise would have had a much easier time if she had instead taken a walk, simply gone to sleep, danced, hugged someone, watched some *Buffy The Vampire Slayer*, or even created some abstract art out of her swirling thoughts, rather than "trying to make sense of it all." We cannot solve our head with our head. Trouble is, if you tell someone they're stuck in their head, they usually give you a look as though they are ready to murder you. I've been on both the giving and receiving ends of such looks, so I'd like to examine just what happens when we become imprisoned in our minds. I would suggest that whenever we find ourselves stuck in a mental loop, unable to easily shift or consider it from a different angle, this is a good indicator that we're in the midst of cognitive overwhelm.

We've already discussed how most of us (especially within modern, western cultures) feel as if we are captaining our bodies from inside our heads, navigating and controlling the world via the power of our deductions. These chattering thoughts were first captured in the early 2000s through positron emission tomography (PET scan) by neuroscientist Marcus Raichle and colleagues[14], who were running an unrelated study on goal-directed tasks. The scientists were surprised to observe that during breaks between tasks, when they expected participants' brains to be at rest, their neurons (especially those connecting the two hemispheres) lit up like a Christmas tree. Expecting that they were observing a relatively unimportant state, they named it (or possibly misnamed it) the Default Mode Network (DMN). Active predominantly during periods of rest, when our attention is not fixed on the external environment, the DMN serves as the arena for our mind's meandering and rumination. It is within this neural network that we craft and recraft personal narratives, grasping for a sense of self and inferring meaning. Spurred by our emotions, such narratives activate our physical states, creating what is often a vicious (or at least distracting) cycle and keeping us from grounding in our actual environment.

Our incessant narrative generation and the emotional entanglement it produces can lead to cognitive overwhelm, particularly in an environment where external stimuli—and their potential narrative inputs—are both ubiquitous and relentless. While the DMN is crucial for self-reflection and planning, when its activity becomes unregulated or excessively stimulated by worry and conflict, it can itself become a cause of stress. This is where CRATE comes in. One of its functions, especially within the Regulation and Trust dimensions, is to help us modulate the DMN's activity. As we engage in structured modes of meta-awareness, we can diminish cognitive overwhelm and instead direct our mental states toward creativity and exploration.

---

[14]   Marcus E. Raichle, Abraham Z. Snyder, A default mode of brain function: A brief history of an evolving idea, NeuroImage, Volume 37, Issue 4, 2007, Pages 1083-1090, ISSN 1053-8119, doi. org/10.1016/j.neuroimage.2007.02.041.

Before we move to that approach in the next chapter, we must note one more—deeply painful—type of overwhelm inherent in the social emotion of shame. The way most of us learn to think of emotion in early childhood is often separated by several layers of inferred appropriateness (or *shoulds*) from our actual internal sensations. *Thinking* about emotion, or judging our feelings, means that we have abstracted whatever has arisen in our nervous system way before making any space to somatically process it all the way through. Up until now, we have discussed the continuum between emotion and feeling as if the two always relay the same message (or at least contain the same valence). Unfortunately for us, that is often not the case: our emotions become policed (and sometimes inverted) based on what our caregivers and peers tell us or show us to be acceptable. That judgment—internalized or inferred—shapes our primary experience. This is why guilt and shame, or their mirror image—pride and scorn—often color the majority of our feelings.

Shame is a form of narrative fracture. Something about our story of what we should do or who we should be is not adding up. The doing part is relatively easy to address. Properly interpreted, that type of emotional discomfort becomes the corrective feeling of guilt: *I shouldn't have submitted my project late. Next time, I will begin earlier and structure my time better, so this doesn't happen again.* If, however, my doing something wrong spreads to infect my sense of being *someone* wrong, the potential guilt transforms into shame and all kinds of internal tornadoes gather. *I shouldn't have submitted my project late. Why am I always a failure who can't manage her time? Next time, I shouldn't even try because all that happens is that I let others down.* The same stimulus (a project being late) can be concluded to mean two opposite things: in the first case, it's an opportunity for hopeful expansion and learning how to do something better; in the second, it becomes a verdict of fear and constriction, affirming our narrative of self as someone who cannot succeed.

Believing that we don't stand a chance is more than overwhelming. It feels like an annihilation. And this finally brings us to the center of our maelstrom. We usually regard the self as real and static. Hence, we hold on to our stories for dear life because if they aren't true, then our sense of self isn't true, and *then* we would have to undergo the kind of drastic change that feels terrifying. There's a reason Carl Jung called this experience a psychic *death*. Each of the different types of overwhelm threatens us with a form of capitulation and, as such, carries echoes of a more existential end: ours.

MEMENTO MORI

If I were to get a tattoo, it would be just four symbols on the inside of my left forearm: $\Delta S \geq 0$.

The way you read them is "Delta S is always greater than, or equal, to zero." This is the formula for the second law of thermodynamics and also the description of time's arrow. It states that entropy (delta S) never decreases. It is always either static or increasing. Entropy—the scientific concept associated with a state of randomness or uncertainty—serves as a stark reminder of the inexorable progression toward disorder.

Entropy has another name, *chaos*. In Greek mythology, Chaos had three daughters. The Moirai—or the Fates—were three blind sisters who shared one eye between them. Their names were Clotho (the Spinner), Lachesis (the Allotter), and Atropos (the Unturnable). They spent their days weaving the tapestry of being, where every thread marked a human life. Clotho spun out the yarn, Lachesis measured it, and whenever a thread didn't suit their liking, Atropos reached over with her scissors and snipped it. When I first read about them as a teen, this unnerved me greatly. How calmly, in my mind's eye, they gathered 'round the loom! How simple it was to cut a life with one small reach! How nonchalant the choices of weaving whilst blind!

Such stories of predestination are as varied as our cultures and epochs, and they have likely unnerved countless others before me.

The Moirai, the Parcae, the Norns, Karma, even *Macbeth*'s Three Witches all exist to help us navigate a terrifying truth: change happens. It waits for us and pounces unannounced, and despite our technology, data, intelligence, and connectivity, we still haven't found a foolproof way to predict or control it.

Spoiler alert: *Entropy Wins.* I used to joke I wanted that on a t-shirt, but the looks on people's faces led me to believe this would be about as well-received as wearing a bold-lettered expletive. And that's the thing—contemplating mortality feels deeply unpalatable to most of us. This visceral reaction to the concept of entropy and its implications on mortality reflects a deeper, often unconscious fear that permeates human existence and urges us to create countless narratives explaining or circumambulating it. The reality is that you, I, and everyone we love are going to die. Burying this lede is a great disservice we do to ourselves and to each other. We don't like dwelling on mortality because entropy is overwhelming, and life *resists* entropy. We are exposed to variable oscillations of our environment, many of which can prove to be lethal at any moment. Yet if we thought about them in too much detail, we would become so overwhelmed we would lie frozen like that impala in the grass, never to stand and run again.

The stark reality of mortality challenges our deeply ingrained desire for predictability and control. In the face of life's ultimate uncertainty—not knowing how or when we will die or what, if anything, happens after—we find our standard models of anticipation to be sorely lacking. Such gaps between what we can predict and the precariousness of our existence amplify our profound sense of unease. Mortality is overwhelming not only because it represents the ultimate threat but also because it is hazy, opaque, and difficult to compute. Our brains, which evolved to detect and respond to immediate threats, are ill-equipped to process the abstract but inevitable reality of our death, leading to a cognitive and emotional dissonance that becomes more unsettling the more we try to grasp it.

During the height of the Roman empire, when a victorious general reveled in the glory of his procession through Rome, it was customary for a slave or attendant to whisper in his ear, *Respice post te. Hominem te esse memento. Memento mori!* Translated, this means, "Look behind you! Remember that you are but a man. Remember that you will die!" Those words served not only as a reminder of the general's biological vulnerability but also as a psychological anchor shielding his sense of self from the ephemeral adulation of the crowds. I suspect that the current resurgence of Stoicism—the school of Greek and Roman philosophy that advocates regular contemplation of one's finitude—is occurring because many of us have found ourselves or the leaders we admire to be similar, egoically speaking, to those victorious generals. It is easy to conflate greatness with a stream of acquisitions, whether accolades, objects, or social media likes. We, too, could benefit from a counterweight to our attraction to transient heights, and while (thankfully) there are no more whispering slaves or attendants, we might wish to internalize their voices and humble ourselves to the three blind sisters weaving our tapestry.

SURFACING FOR AIR

In the process of fighting our discomfort with mortality, we shut ourselves off from emotion, barreling forward with discipline, brandishing our grit as a badge of honor, then capitulating once we run out of energy, or worse, recognizing that in the process of turning off pain, we unwittingly turned off creativity and joy.

I wish all of this were theoretical, but the theory and practice in this book unfolded through much of my flailing, experimentation, and hard-won perspective. I also wish it had taken me fewer years to realize and share with others that just because we––as conscious organisms––are complex, it does not mean our lives in turn need to be complicated. There appears to be a close relationship between embracing the complexity of our finitude and shedding complicatedness, and that is what I hope for each of us to adopt into our lives.

Strong emotions, rooted in our existential desire to survive, are so overwhelming that most of us learn early in life to sublimate their intensity lest they embarrass, derail, or destroy us. We push them down, spending our days in the delta between the loud, flashy signals of the external world and the relatively quieter ones with which our body communicates what is safest, healthiest, and most meaningful. For the most part, we dismiss our internal disturbances, hiding in overwork and over-consumption, convincing ourselves that our choices are rational, separating ourselves even further from the wisdom of our nervous system. Feel hungry? Have some sugar. Feel scared? Watch a movie. Feel worried? Buy something. Feel lonely? Scroll some images, then tap some hearts so a machine might "feed" your need for connection.

To avoid what might hurt us, we cut ourselves off from what can save us. This is how burnout happens: not from exhaustion but from internal disconnection. As Damasio points out in his aptly titled book, *Descartes' Error*, it is not that we think, therefore we are; it is that we feel, therefore we think, and therefore we are. When we interrupt this flow, we encounter not just burnout but our personal and societal existential ennui. To recover, we must come back into alignment with our psyche (i.e., our nervous system) so we can better hear and comprehend its messages and so that we can rationally *act with*—not react to—the emotion-driven narratives we call feelings.

The Jungian psychoanalyst and author James Hollis teaches that we're each subjected to a primordial dichotomy: on one side, our fear of overwhelm; on the other, our terror of abandonment. We do not wish for too much stimulus to subsume us, be it from the haphazard effects of nature or the volitions of nurture. We also don't want to be left entirely alone, even when that means all external stimuli would subside. Loneliness is one of the most psychologically and physiologically damaging predicaments. Stress is the other. Coming full circle, our body interprets loneliness as a form of stress, triggering inflammation and dysregulating cellular rejuvenation.

Hollis notes that we are caught between two existential threats, each tugging at us from opposite ends of our psyche. On one side looms the specter of overwhelm—the fear that we are small and powerless in a world that is vast, unpredictable, and often hostile to our needs and desires. This fear is etched into us from childhood, and reinforced by every experience of the world's indifference or cruelty, every reminder of how little control we really have over the forces that shape our lives.

But even as we rail against the threat of overwhelm, another risk stalks us from the shadows—our fear of abandonment. We are social creatures, wired for connection and belonging, and the prospect of being utterly alone in the world is too much to bear. So we strive and achieve, we perform and perfect, all in the hopes of winning the approval and acceptance of others. We transfer our needs for nurturance and reassurance onto anyone who seems to promise us the constancy we crave, only to push them away with our demands and our desperation.

Some of us seek out positions and roles where the validation we need is hard-wired into the structure of our lives—where we can count on the steady drip of external affirmation to keep our inner emptiness at bay. Others turn to substances or addictions, trading the uncertainties of human connection for the reliability of a chemical high, even as the satisfactions it offers dwindle with each passing day.

At the core of both these fears—of overwhelm and abandonment— is a deep longing for safety, for a world that is solid and secure beneath our feet. We want to feel held, seen, and soothed, to know that we matter and that we belong. But the harder we strive to make this longing a reality, the more it slips through our fingers, leaving us grasping at shadows and illusions.

Overwhelm results from a model wherein our organism predicts that it doesn't have the necessary resources to cope. This could be based on an assessment of current resources, or on the inability to form a dependable predictive model at all. In both cases, we default to anxiety or panic.

This is all the result of an erroneous prediction. It feels counterintuitive because, at the moment, overwhelm appears to be due to way too much intensity in the present. But intensity alone is not the problem. Think of a time when you were having tremendous fun, perhaps riding a roller coaster or reuniting with your loved one at the airport. The emotion was intense, but it was probably welcome. Or for a negatively-hued example, think of a movie scene that was wrought with loss and sadness: you likely walked out of the theater with tear-streaked cheeks, but not only could you withstand the emotion, you probably appreciated the extent to which it moved you. In both cases, your brain predicted that you had the capacity to withstand the level of emotion you were experiencing. Usually, this is based on your genetically predisposed sensitivity (remember Emotionality from the Big Five?) and the number of uncertain variables you need to process in relation to the flooding emotion. The greater your resilience and the lower the uncertainty, the more likely it is that your prediction will be that you are safe. Inversely, the more sensitive you are and the greater the uncertainty of the surrounding circumstances, the more likely that your organism will feel it lacks an accurate prediction of what will happen next—and the more likely you will get overwhelmed.

But what if we had tools to increase our resilience and decrease our uncertainty? What if we could train ourselves to make more accurate predictions about our ability to cope with intense emotions and complex situations? This was my goal for CRATE: to offer a systematic approach toward strengthening our capacity for emotional regulation and cognitive flexibility.

Overwhelm isn't *always* a bad thing. I would like you to consider that sensory data—even at the highest volume—is actually neutral information. Intensity is how our nervous system informs us that an outlier event has occurred. Suffering happens when we panic and struggle against this information, assuming it is a threat before anything has tangibly hurt us.

My coaching clients often describe overwhelm as a state of being flooded or not being able to hold on to a center. We experience that as painful and terrifying because we don't know another way. But every attempt to hold a center is a form of contraction—a clinging to a fixed narrative of self. Our internal narratives become the threads from which our reality is woven, shaping our perceptions and imbuing our existence with meaning. Rooted in our most fundamental life-preserving mechanisms, they highlight the dual capacity of our human condition: the ability to comprehend and navigate complexity and the concurrent vulnerability to being overwhelmed by it. Overwhelm and fear go hand in hand. Building a more accepting relationship with one leads the other to shape-shift into a wholly new experience.

Thus far, we have been gathering information and preparing to meet the world with a steady gaze and a grounded stance. Moving forward, we'll explore the framework I designed to help myself and my clients navigate uncertainty and head into (rather than away from) fear. CRATE aims to unlock Clarity, Regulation, Agency, Trust, and Energy at precisely the moments when they seem least accessible. It provides a way to contain our overwhelm, challenge our negative predictions, and move from a state of contraction to one of expansion and continuous flow. In the next chapter, we'll dive head-first into how this framework can help us do what scares us, make existential choices with greater ease, and ultimately, live more fully in the face of life's inevitable complexity.

4

DO WHAT SCARES YOU

On Making Existential Choices

"Until you make the unconscious conscious,
it will direct your life and you will call it fate."
— C.G. Jung

"Each of you is intelligent and impressive. At the very least, you're all impeccably dressed." A faint laughter drifts through the audience. Gentle snow falls on the evening pavement outside as I continue emboldened. "We're gathered in this gorgeous hall here in Midtown in what's arguably the glitziest city in the world. However hard you've worked, you got here. But what if..." I hear my voice become slightly shakier, less sure of itself, as I switch to the next slide, "what if Joseph Campbell was right, and the cave you fear to enter really *does* hold the treasure you seek? What if we have been avoiding our *real* quest all along?"

It's early 2019 and I have been invited by Declare—an organization focused on elevating senior women in finance and technology—to teach one of their master class initiatives. Designed as a three-session course that will meet once a month for three months, the purpose of the seminars is to help professional women gain the skills to advance further and faster in their careers. Given my background in advertising and venture, the most obvious topics I can teach all center on how to build a personal brand or ace a compelling pitch. For several weeks, I've mulled variations, jotting down ideas and looking through past keynotes to see what I can self-plagiarize. But none of it has grabbed me.

I've given more pitch and storytelling talks than I can count and have concluded that it all feels like fluff. Good stories need to be told, not made up. If we're being honest, a personal brand is just another way to pitch the product that is you. And while storytelling acumen is helpful for any professional, I've continuously stumbled over my discomfort with the concept of productizing oneself. I dislike the conflation of narrative with marketing. I've also hated the idea that we must concoct a story about ourselves rather than simply discovering, and then being, who we are.

As a result, I have arrived at what seems like a straightforward conclusion: if we know what matters to us and what we're fighting for, then we just do the next thing—hopefully the meaningful thing—and fear becomes irrelevant. The obstacles don't disappear. They don't even become less scary. They simply become less relevant to what we do next. Fear can serve as a weathervane: a strong emotion that attracts our attention toward potent energies. It usually tells us to avoid and run, but what happens if, instead, we learn how to expand and move *toward* the scary thing? Could we survive and actually learn something?

Betting on *yes*, I crafted the hardest value proposition I'd ever pitched. I called my class "Do What Scares You," and its opening session was the most stomach-churning talk I'd ever given. It required me to become genuinely vulnerable—baring myself as openly as possible—and to also admit that I have no idea what I'm talking about. It turns out this reflected not only my insecurity but my audience's anxieties as well. In my preparation, I asked my friends (most of them precisely within the target demographic of high achievers) to describe the fears they usually faced. Those fears could be distilled to three core assumptions: "I am not good enough," "I am not doing enough," and "I don't have enough." In my own internal translation, it all boiled down to: *I am not enough*. This discovery proved both astounding and a little thrilling. While I had no clue how to resolve it, it made me feel less alone, less like a freak for having exactly the same suspicions about my own career. Little did I know that by setting off to teach what I was struggling to learn, I would change my entire life and the trajectories of many incredible humans along the way.

CHANGE, CHOICE, AND (INNER) CONFLICT

Still, at that moment, all I had was the intuition that fear was important and that somehow or other it connected to the stories in our heads. I suspected that stories—or at least the emotion behind them—unlocked the path we were meant to follow *towards*–not *away from*–the scary things in our lives. Yet I also knew that the most potent narratives involved transformation, which usually came at a cost that was less than pleasant. Such narratives were not an easy sell because most people don't willingly choose to venture into their metaphorical dark woods and take on their internal monsters. Nonetheless, I decided to follow my instinct, so my core message went something like this: you don't need to make up a story about yourself. Instead, you must stand still and listen until you *discover* the story that is calling you. There are two types of stories, and we make a choice—conscious or unconscious—as to which we adopt. Some of our choices cut us off, while others connect us. Some stories (the kind we make up as a way to maintain our status quo and cast ourselves as the hero) are meant to truncate surprise, to protect and insulate us. Other stories (the ones that interrupt us, shake us up, and don't let us go) connect us to things beyond our egoic selves—be they other humans, ideas, or entirely new ways of being. The former feel safe; the latter feel scary, like entering a dark wood and hearing a rustling in the bush

.

Stories are incited by state change. Something goes from good to bad or from bad to good. In business, we are mostly pitching the latter: a given company could not exist before, but now technology/market dynamics/this team have made it possible to build something new, and this will change the world (or at least solve a big problem) and in the process make a billion dollars. On a personal level, however, we often tell ourselves the inverse: a given threat did not exist before, but now circumstances/market dynamics/other people have made it possible to lose something precious, and this will change our world (or at least cause a big problem), and in the process, we might be deprived of safety or opportunity.

We instinctively orient toward the positive stories and away from the scary, potentially negative, ones. But in doing so, we might well be choosing the cowardly option: taking the safe, well-trodden road into mediocrity instead of venturing into the wilderness along the hard, uncertain, and potentially more rewarding path. This was what I wondered about myself and my students in the class: Were we, supposedly capable individuals, playing it safe and foregoing something bigger and more worthwhile?

My dare worked. I saw the audience lean forward, confused but intrigued, and so I continued: change usually leads to choice. Do we choose to act on the strong emotion triggered within us? Do we pounce, or flee? These decisions often create conflict: sometimes with environmental threats, other times with forces that oppose us, including humans, and most often—with ourselves. How do we know what is an opportunity or a threat? How do we know if we have the strength or courage to take on whatever awaits us?

I took a further risk and highlighted the most daring story I could think of: Frodo Baggins carrying the One Ring to destroy it in the fires of Mount Doom. If *The Lord of the Rings* was just about some hobbits hanging out in a tavern in the Shire, my argument went, there would be no state change, no big choices to make, no worthwhile conflict—and therefore no transformational story. Instead, traumatized by World War One, J.R.R. Tolkien wrote of a journey whereby the smallest and least ready of heroes was called upon to rise to the most important occasion, taking on unimaginable terrors in the hopes of protecting his home and the entire land of Middle Earth. Receiving a few nods, I pushed further and asked my audience: what is *your* Middle Earth? What is the quest *you* are terrified to make, even as it calls your name?

At first there were some blank stares, so I went about it a different way. I asked two questions, both pointing in the same direction: *What do you value?* and *What are your highest stakes?* The answers came— first in a trepidatious sprinkling, then in a downpour. My audience valued excellence and loved ones. The stakes were professional achievement and personal happiness. They were ready to quest for accomplishment and recognition, but the costs were exhaustion and burnout. I could see the push and pull, the hope and fear, oscillating in the room as if they had a physical presence. Were these opposing directions a bug or a feature? As usual, the answer turned out to be both. Reconciling opposing agendas *was* the quest.

During the *Practice* portion of my first seminar, as I walked from table to table answering questions, a poised blonde woman outstretched her hand, heavy with charm bracelets.

"Excuse me," she whispered, "Can you help me? I don't think I'm doing this right." She pushed her worksheet toward me. Scribbled answers overflowed the space provided, stretching to the margins, then continuing on the back. What caught my attention was a simple state-change exercise, asking whether a recent occurrence in her life moved things from bad to good or vice versa. Her answer was the very picture of overwhelm. Whatever was going on in the woman's life, all possible narrative conclusions were hitting at once.

STATE

Where did your situation change (*things went from good to bad or bad to good*)? Circle one primary and up to two secondary state changes below, then write out what happened.

I wasn't sure what to do with that. I gestured to a corner of the table, asking if she wanted to move so we could speak in relative privacy. What poured out was the first of many similar situations. Stephanie was a seasoned investor at one of Wall Street's premier firms. She had persevered tirelessly for over two decades and was now in a position many would consider the pinnacle of a career. Her two teen daughters were well on their way towards adulthood, albeit with a few hiccups. One was at Brearley, the other—her "difficult one"—had to be moved downtown to a less prestigious school due to behavioral challenges. Stephanie had recently been passed over for a promotion and instead shifted laterally, reporting to a new, younger boss who treated her as either outdated or a threat, depending on the day.

"You said earlier, if we could tune into our emotions and embrace fear, we would orient toward the life we want." She looked straight at me, her eyes filling with tears. "But what if doing this (she gestured at the paper) just made me realize that the life I always wanted is the thing that's making me really miserable? What now?"

Her words hit me like a gut punch. Not only did I not have an easy answer, but this was the very thing I had been grappling with in my own life—the discomfort that had compelled me to eschew the easy brand-building topics and choose Fear as a direction in the first place. What if, in the process of tuning into our deepest desires, we discovered that the life we had built was not aligned with who we needed to be? What if the things we thought we wanted were actually the source of our suffering?

I took a breath and met Stephanie's eyes.

"Thank you for being brave and saying it." I placed a hand on my chest. "I get what you're feeling and hear it not only from others, but also within my own life." I considered my next words carefully. "The truth is, there's no simple answer or quick fix. Many of us feel as if we've made some nebulous bargain that ended us up in golden handcuffs. What I can tell you is that this realization, uncomfortable though it may be, is like a new door suddenly becoming visible and maybe opening just a crack. It's an invitation to get curious about what matters most to you, and to start making choices that align with the life that is calling for you, not the one that you are being told you should live."

I didn't fully know what I meant by this. In fact, it was one of the first instances in my professional life when I spoke what felt like an intuitive truth, without regard for whether it made sense, or if I would appear foolish. I answered her follow-up questions with the same honesty, then continued through a long line of participants who waited for me after the talk, wanting to tell me their predicaments one by one, or simply leaning in for a hug. When we finished, I had missed all my regular trains, so I sat outside Penn Station, watching the world go by: the humans rushing home and the humans who didn't have one. In this city, everyone was going for the hustle, but few of them—I was guessing—had a clear sense of what was at stake.

Did I?

I rode my commuter train home, turning over the choices I'd made, wondering why, *how* I had oriented toward a small suburban town, a modest house, a relatively simple existence. All of it had been in an effort to preserve optionality, to allow myself as much creative freedom as possible, while still ensuring that the kids had a decent education and a safe neighborhood. None of it had been fully intentional. In fact, the best choices I made in my life were more or less instinctual: choosing my husband, deciding to have kids, even orienting toward a small town were all antithetical to the rebel persona I held. Even moving to New York, which fit my narrative significantly better, had been—at the eleventh hour—a split-second decision. Inversely, many of the choices I'd agonized over, weighed carefully and orchestrated, all felt constrictive. My position as Managing Director, my career achievements, even my focus on excellence—they were so appealing from the outside and so limiting from within.

I flashed back to my presentation slide. Change leads to choice leads to conflict. *Doctor, heal thyself.*

INTO THE WOODS

Have you ever gone up a flight of stairs in the dark? You hold the banister and rush up, trying not to trip, but also trying to get to your well-lit room as quickly as possible. The air behind you feels cooler, and just before you get to your door, your shoulders involuntarily shudder and a tingle runs down your spine. Then, if you're like me, you feel sheepish and decide you were being irrational. After all, there are no monsters and nothing should be scary. This relationship with fear—being overwhelmed by it, then denying it altogether—plays out even without triggering the primordial instincts in our amygdala, which darkness activates. Loss aversion is the psychological dynamic of worrying that we will lose something precious to us. It is one of the most prevalent behavior motivators in the modern world. We are fearful of losing safety, approval, status, opportunity... you name it. FOMO, or fear of missing out, fuels the behemoths of advertising, finance, social media, and commerce, then slips into interpersonal relationships, including team dynamics, friendships, and even romance.

Emotions are not irrational. They actually make perfect sense, but we deny them because the decisions they point to seem to be absurd, or at least absurdly inconvenient. Conflicting emotions make us choose. They create sensory noise, cutting us off from our internal clarity, building opacity between what we know to be right to do and what we believe we "should" do. When we are free from internal conflict, our choices become obvious.

The evolutionary purpose of emotions is to transform us—to orient us in a way that shifts something. One of the reasons we strongly resist feeling them to their conclusion is because they necessitate a certain loss of control. We—meaning our egoic self or our prefrontal cortex with its narrating structures—are no longer driving. Instead, something far more limbic, more organismic and primal steps forward and says: *Yes to this! Hell-to-the-no to that!*

But what happens when that *No!* is a visceral response to our job, relationship, an identity we've acquired, or even to the life we've built? What happens at the moment when we begin paying attention to the body and there's a massive wave of energy in motion, be it goosebumps or excitement or intensity or panic? What happens is that many of us clamp down in fear. Our internalized authority—the one patterned after our parents or teachers—steps in and tells us it is simply not acceptable to feel this way. That this is not what grownups (or successful/mature/smart/insert-favorite-adjective-here) people do. We manage our own emotions in the same way our parents managed and disciplined us when we were kids, and then we orient toward whatever we label as "good," whether that's hard work, stoicism, calmness, or even spiritual enlightenment. We resolve our inner conflict through forms of narrative bypassing: a game of one-upmanship with our own organism. We paint a picture of what is acceptable and then convince ourselves we are matching it, instead of actually being present with whatever occurs inside of us.

Humans are measured by their actions. We are what we do. And like it or not, we end up doing what we feel, so at the very core of our sense of self lie our emotions. The double entendre here is both convenient and intentional. Our emotions lie in wait, in that they are the way our somatic, unconscious system communicates with our conscious, verbal, (and supposedly) rational mind. They also *lie* in that they allow us to mislead ourselves—to mistake the part for the whole: pieces of reality for the world in itself.

The reason we cannot tame or eliminate emotions is that our organisms are wired to make their choices based on them. Without emotion, we would be incapable of moving toward or away from anything; our ability to form and retrieve memories would be much weaker; and we would struggle to create anything new––be it a poem, a theorem, or even a thought. Not only are emotion and reason not separate, but reason is stacked on top of emotion (both in terms of our experience of it and when it comes to how the information is parsed within our consciousness). Given this, wouldn't it be useful if we had a way to untangle and navigate all of our emotions?

CONTAINING MULTITUDES

Golden handcuffs, comparison, misleading emotional nudges— all of that is how I got to the *Now what?* portion of my journey. I could see, first out of the corner of my proverbial eye and then with greater and greater clarity, that the choices I and others were making were far from clear. They were muddied, reactive, lacking focus, defensive, and sometimes desperate. I didn't like that.

I didn't want to keep doing it. The catch was that the biggest, most important choices were the ones with the greatest complexity or complicatedness. They felt overwhelming. They flooded my system so strongly that I lost access to that liminal, intuitive part that oriented me toward healthier, more aligned decisions.

What I needed was a way to continuously and reliably move in directions that felt authentic and expansive. To do that, I needed to figure out how to contain overwhelm. And to do *that*, I needed to go back to what my father's lab and my mother's heart had taught me: research, feel, and then iterate.

Out of this process, CRATE was born. In the face of muddied choices, it gives me Clarity. When I feel reactive, I reach for Regulation. If I lack focus, Agency helps me orient. When defensiveness makes me skittish, I find my way to Trust. And, if things really get drained, dark, or desperate, there's a path to Energy that allows me to go on.

The evening of teaching my first *Do What Scares You* seminar was the beginning of an unraveling, a remembering and reconnecting to the life that wanted to come through me, not the life that I thought I needed to live. It led me on a path of deduction, deconstruction, then finally discovery. In the process, I learned that when I orient toward fear, when I learn how to walk into the storm, trusting my self and the ground beneath my feet, not only does the fear diminish but so too does the necessity to choose. Change does not have to lead either to choice or to conflict. Instead, there is a path whereby change can introduce curiosity and then convergence—completely eliminating the need for anxious oscillation and instead arriving at Clarity. It is only once we accept the impossibility of being certain of anything that real discovery can begin.

When change happens and we encounter obstacles, a binary thought pattern becomes activated within us. *This is good or bad. I am right or wrong. I will succeed or fail.* We jump into making predictions as a way of defending against uncertainty. This first step—the *Embedded Prediction* or Story through which we engage with volatility—is the way we get hooked (usually unconsciously) into the narratives that steer us. But what if we could make the process conscious? That prediction brings forth a certain attitude toward what is happening. I think of that as the second step: our *Embodied Action*—or, the Stance we take toward our environment as we choose how to act.

However that turns out, we learn something. Ideally, that something leaves us expanded, rather than conflicted. We grow, and shift, and nudge ourselves—slightly or not so slightly—beyond our comfort zone. That final step is our *Extended Cognition*: our sense of Self grows ever more porous, having integrated pieces larger than our previous experience into our current sense of reality. This sense of Self is not something we create, but rather a process that creates and extends *us*. It is the product of dynamic emergence—the moment the agent and the arena become one.

The above three steps are the three core aspects of the CRATE framework—a way of navigating my thoughts and emotions (cognition and affect) in a way that aligned with my understanding of cognitive science, psychology, and wisdom traditions. At its core is a thesis that the self is a dynamic process that emerges from the interaction of mind and environment. I have come to believe that the ego-driven (or egoic) self is an illusion that arises from the fragmentary nature of thought, the stories we tell ourselves about who we are and our confusion around why any of it matters.

CRATE's objective is to help you contain and then integrate overwhelm, resulting in continuous flow. Rational thought, while immensely powerful, has boundaries within which it is most effective. We don't need to dismiss rationality, but we can learn when to best apply certain types of thinking, and when to transcend or integrate them into broader cognitive strategies. Integrative flow encourages the combination of our cognitive (epistemic), emotional (embodied), and social (relational) dimensions into a process of adaptation and growth. It teaches us not only flexibility but a holistic approach to navigating life's complexities.

To put these learnings together, the five dimensions of CRATE (Clarity, Regulation, Agency, Trust, and Energy) follow three aspects rooted in 4E Cognition[1]: Embedded Prediction (*what is the narrative you are using to interpret a given situation?*), Embodied Action[2] (*what is the emotion-driven shift you can enact at this moment?*), and Extended Cognition (*how can you relate to your environment while acknowledging your sense of self as containing multitudes?*). What follows is a handy table that can serve as our map while we set sail into the deep waters of Part II.

The CRATE framework recognizes that our capacity for change and growth emerges from the complex interplay of our internal narratives, our embodied actions, and our extended sense of self in relation to others. By attending to these dimensions, we can begin to untangle the knots of our conditioning and craft a more purposeful, resilient way of being.

	EMBEDDED PREDICTION *Story*	EMBODIED ACTION *Stance*	EXTENDED COGNITION *Self*
CLARITY	Constraint	Curiosity	Convergence
REGULATION	Recognition	Relation	Release
AGENCY	Affordance	Attention	Adaptation
TRUST	Temporality	Transformation	Translucency
ENERGY	Experience	Emergence	Emptiness

As we cultivate a deeper awareness of our own embodied experience, orientation, and aspiration, we break free from the

---

[1]   *4E Cognitive Science posits that our cognitive processes are deeply intertwined with our bodily experiences (embodied), our actions in the world (enacted), our environment (embedded), and our social and technological context (extended). This perspective challenges the traditional view of the mind as an isolated, abstract entity and instead emphasizes the dynamic, situated nature of cognition. This approach states that "cognition does not occur exclusively inside the head, but is variously embodied, embedded, enacted, or extended by way of extra-cranial processes and structures." Rowlands, M. (2010). The new science of the mind: From extended mind to embodied phenomenology. MIT Press.*

[2]   *I have joined embodiment and enactedness into a single aspect—both for simplicity, and because I believe that action is always emotion-driven and therefore comes from the body.*

spell of not-enoughness. By learning to listen to the wisdom of our organism and discern our relationship with its environment, we can begin to chart a path that is true to our unique combination of nature and nurture, even if it differs from the well-worn paths of those around us.

The key to navigating this process is to build a sense of trust in ourselves and in the unfolding of our lives. When we're gripped by fear, it's easy to fall into a scarcity mindset, believing that we're not good enough or that we don't have what it takes to create the life we want. But when we still ourselves, we enable trust to come through us, giving us energy and momentum and interrupting the never-ending maelstrom of doubt.

Clarity helps us identify where we stand. Regulation supports us in metabolizing the way it affects us. Agency empowers us to make intentional choices. Trust grounds us when the going gets tough. Energy provides the fuel and inspiration to keep moving forward. It is time to gather our selves and dive deep into some lived examples of how all of this can be put to practice.

PART II

CHOOSE WHO YOU BECOME

NOTE ON PART II

Theory can only take us so far. While the puzzles of our minds are endlessly fascinating, past a certain point even science can become a convenient hiding place. To test our hypotheses, we need to live by doing, feeling, and (most importantly) relating. In Part II of this book, I've attempted to bring you into my client sessions and show rather than tell the humbling beauty of relational growth. This is not a straightforward task. Not only do my coaching contracts contain a robust non-disclosure clause, there is also a personal trust that I work hard to build and would never wish to jeopardize. In the cases where I use details from actual sessions, I have both obtained that client's permission and carefully obfuscated any identifiable particulars.

The characters you will meet in the next four chapters are composites based on individuals whose narratives followed similar patterns. The emotional dynamics of each conversation are very real, while the setting, names, and personal details have been changed to ensure privacy. If you see parts of yourself in the ensuing pages, that means I have done my job well (but don't worry—it's not actually you).

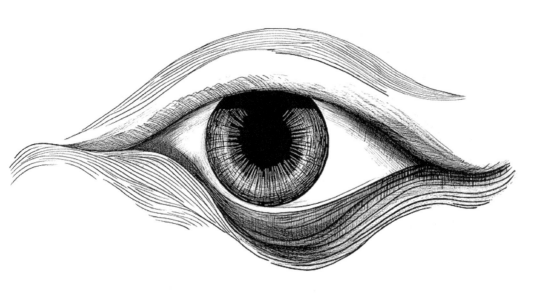

5

FINDING CLARITY

Constraint, Curiosity, & Convergence

*The first principle is that you must not fool yourself
— and you are the easiest person to fool.*
— Richard Feynman

On my Zoom screen, Carter beams a giant smile. I'm pretty sure if we were in the same room, he'd get up and high-five me. But we are three thousand miles apart—him in Sausalito with a glorious blue sky and the Bay spreading behind him, me on the snowiest day of New York winter, heater humming in my suburban study. I've coached Carter for more than two years, though I've also known him for a decade—from back in the day when we were both investors. He still is one, trying to stay above water in what might be the harshest climate for private markets since 2008.

"How's it going?" I ask, attempting to match his grin.

"Oh, you know... busy week, busy week. I've just been in meetings, and what is it today? Thursday? Yeah, I fly out on Monday to Hong Kong, and then we're gonna try to drum up some dinners there and get ahead of things for the Summit. And I just haven't had a moment, you know?"

I nod. "Yup, I totally get how it goes. But you're managing everything OK?"

"Oh, yeah!" His eyes trail off to the side. There's my opening.

"Tell me about whatever's on your mind. How can I be helpful today?"

He pauses, and I can see him shuffling through alternate topics, trying to circumnavigate the main one. A boyish mop of brown hair hangs over his forehead, making him look younger than the fourth decade he inhabits. I watch as he starts to fidget with the zipper on his fleece.

"Did the pension plan come back in?"

The escape hatch has closed, and I see the tiniest shift in his jaw.

"Nah, I mean, not yet. You know how it is—they said the timing's not quite right for them; they might be overcommitted already and..."

"It's February." My tone is calm, and I've taken care to keep things light, make it sound like his anchor investor simply didn't check their calendar. But we've known each other for too long to beat around the bush.

Carter sighs and lets his guard down.

"Yeah, Des... we both know what it means. It's a bullshit excuse. They're just gonna pass on the new fund and..." His voice trails off.

Mine is even quieter now. "What are you planning to do?"

The pension plan is one of his two largest LPs (limited partners—the type of institutional investors who put capital into private equity and venture funds). They invested the largest percentage of capital in his last fund as an "anchor," catapulting his firm into the big leagues. Losing someone like that is a hard story to spin. Up until two years ago, it was also very rare—you had to really crater a portfolio for your largest LP to pull out. Now, everyone's getting cold feet.

"I have no clue." Carter sighs. His forehead gathers into crevasses as he smushes his mouth in his fist, twisting his lips as if trying to keep them from speaking. "I can't really see a path forward."

"Well then," I say, "let's begin where there is no path."

———

Panic is contagious. This is true for crowds of humans (underscored by the legal penalties for falsely yelling "Fire!" in a crowded theater), and it's also true for most animals. A flock of birds perched on a tree will erupt into flight as soon as a few birds take off simultaneously; they don't have to spot the threat on their own. This rapid dissemination of panic is attributed to mirror neurons[1], suggesting a neural basis for how we understand others and learn from their actions, and pointing to further proof of the interconnectedness of human experience. Our neurons can reflect and even imitate what we see others doing, enabling the vicarious experience of others' emotions and creating an immediate, shared response to perceived threats. Interpreting external fear-provoking stimuli—whether they be visual or auditory—is slower than immediately feeling that emotion inside our own body. Bypassing any delay augments our brain's predictive processing mechanism; the immediacy of emotional contagion overrides slower, conscious appraisal processes, jumping us instead into the "worst case" scenario. This is very efficient, but it also leads to cognitive constraint in moments of fear. Our brain's desire to minimize surprise—or prediction error—results in a conservative bias towards safety, prompting an instinctive reaction to retreat or avoid.

---

[1] *Mirror neurons were first identified in the early 1990s by Giacomo Rizzolatti and his team at the University of Parma, Italy. They observed that certain neurons in the premotor cortex of macaque monkeys fired not only when the monkeys performed an action, such as grasping an object, but also when the monkeys observed another individual performing the same action. Further study in humans has demonstrated the involvement of specific neuronal systems in perceiving the intentions behind others' actions. However, the concept has also received criticism for its generalization and we are still in the early stages of refining and clarifying the theory behind mirror neurons. (Iacoboni, M., & Rizzolatti, G. (2005). Grasping the intentions of others with one's own mirror neuron system. PLoS Biology, 3(3), e79.)*

There's nowhere more obvious than the financial markets to watch panic spread like wildfire. Most of us have learned about Black Tuesday, October 29th of 1929, when a stock market crash precipitated the Great Depression, sending the U.S. and much of the world into a decade-long economic struggle that strained international relations and eventually contributed to the onset of World War II. More recently, we witnessed a modern-day version of a bank run in March of 2023, when Silicon Valley Bank (or SVB), a golden child of Sand Hill Road and the venture ecosystem, suddenly collapsed due to mismanagement, then panic fanned by the flames of social media and hastily exchanged digital messages. Thus far, our recent economic turns have not led to the tectonic shifts of previous eras, but they have directed the financial market toward exactly the kind of zeitgeist that Carter's been experiencing—an opacity that makes it difficult to see paths forward.

For many of us, money and relationships are the two most potent external triggers, and they're often related or even enmeshed. Both are closely aligned with our sense of security. We learn from early childhood that having enough approval and enough money is a requirement for getting whatever else we want. A tub of ice cream cost two dollars and forty-nine cents Canadian when I was seven. Getting one was contingent on ensuring that my mom was happy with me *and* that we had enough money for both the ice cream and the two bus tickets for the ride home. I didn't mind when I had to choose between ice cream or not walking, but I still remember the times when parental approval was unavailable; it truncated the possibility of any further choices.

EMBEDDED STORY: CONSTRAINT

As I watch Carter's face cloud, I flash to that memory, which seems odd at first. What does getting enough ice cream have to do with raising a large venture investment fund? Still, I've learned to trust associations, especially when they present completely unbidden. I think of these flashes as my subconscious handing me notes in the middle of class, so I follow their lead.

"What does Leah think about all this?" I ask, then see the answer immediately. "Or perhaps she doesn't know just yet?"

Carter moves to hold his forehead, then passes a hand through his hair and scratches the back of his head instead. "You know, she was traveling too, and I—we haven't had a chance to connect properly, so I was thinking maybe I'd just wait till after I get back from Asia...you know?"

I nod. The sentence bookends aren't lost on me, nor is the fact that he's hoping to find new investors and be able to repackage the bad news as not-so-bad. I weigh how much to push him toward facing his discomfort versus the risk of deflating him in a way that would be detrimental. I try for a middle ground.

"Would it help to get some clarity on the situation?"

He nods.

Victor Frankl, a Jewish psychologist who survived Auschwitz and created a school of psychology called logotherapy, is often quoted as saying, "Between stimulus and response lies a space. In that space lie our freedom and power to choose a response. In our response lies our growth and our happiness." While the quote may be apocryphal,[2] it aptly summarizes Frankl's discovery of the power inherent in making internal space, and how it enables us to disrupt entrenched patterns. This space (or *spaciousness* in Eastern wisdom traditions) is the mental distancing wherein we learn to notice the functions of our organism: the emotions that arise, the mental narratives that become activated, and the behavioral scripts that are subsequently put into play.

Clarity is the first step to opening that space. Its three aspects, Constraint, Curiosity, and Convergence, describe a path of noticing,

---

[2]   *Its provenance is complicated. Stephen R. Covey coined the actual quote while summarizing Frankl's work in a foreword to "Prisoners of Our Thoughts," by Alex Pattakos Ph.D.*

orienting toward, and then allowing (or even embracing) whatever is happening[3]. Clarity is the process of bringing into focus an internal narrative or a welling of emotion, especially when they feel strong enough to trigger our immediate reactions. Doing this serves multiple purposes: it slows down time, expands space, and introduces possibility. Making things clearer is like manually focusing your camera lens: you have to account for how much light (read: information) you have or what your focal distance is (read: the framing of your problem). The reality we consciously experience is defined by the manner in which we attend to it, so the first section of the CRATE framework begins with a very intentional focus on the constraints hijacking our attention.

Put simply, Clarity is the ability to point the spotlight of our awareness toward whatever helps us understand reality with decreasing ambiguity. How do we decide where to focus? The short answer is that we process information and then prioritize that which is most salient to our survival. The longer answer is that we make many assumptions—some of them erroneous—of what is a threat and what an opportunity. As we've covered before, we often react prior to conscious processing, then update our mental models to make it seem that we were in the driver's seat all along. That's exactly what Carter is doing—both mentally, by fast-tracking toward the next opportunity, and physically, by booking himself back to back so that his hectic schedule prevents him from slowing down and experiencing the panic beneath the surface.

I slow my cadence as I dive in. "In my experience, Clarity is the process of controlling and directing our attention in alignment with what is most salient to us. It is not the same thing as certainty, though people often mistake the two." I can see his eyes start to glaze over, but fight the urge to rush, and instead become even calmer. Those mirror neurons mean that Carter's nervous system is unconsciously

---

[3]   *You'll notice variations of this path repeating at ever-deepening levels through every CRATE dimension*

syncing with mine, so I can help him become more available to new ideas, the more open and at ease I seem. "Gaining Clarity has three aspects: constraint, curiosity, and convergence. Usually, when things feel very opaque—like there's no way out—it's because we've become embedded in an internal story of *constraint*. The world is shutting doors in our faces, and we can't figure out how to keep going. Does that ring a bell?"

I can see him start nodding before I've finished asking.

"Great. What are the most obvious constraints right at this moment?"

He starts to speak, then hesitates. Asking people to enumerate what isn't working is often painful, which is probably why we tend to avoid staring at our limitations too closely in the first place. But if we don't figure out a way to tolerate or at least acknowledge their presence, our constraints lurk, both distracting and scaring us, while we pretend that nothing is wrong.

Depending on the client, I will sometimes take multiple sessions to build their capacity to tolerate the discomfort associated with acknowledging what isn't working or available (their constraints), usually by titrating and adding a good dose of humor and affection to help them feel supported. In this case, though, we won't have another session in two, maybe three weeks, and I know this likely can't wait.

"Here's what I'm seeing," I start. "Your largest investor may not be coming back into Fund III, which means you'll either have to cut your target drastically or come up with a very impressive new story, or—"

"Or I'm dead in the water," he interjects.

"Maybe. I don't think you're there yet. But yes, that's worth acknowledging. Besides, I'm goth enough to remind you there's *always* a possibility of being dead in the water. There might be a meteor headed for Earth right at this moment." We both laugh. "So, ultimately, I wouldn't worry too much about that last part."

Carter smiles. It's not the beaming smile of thirty minutes ago, but also not the gloomy overwhelm from moments prior. I'll take what I can get.

"As I was saying, you have some headwinds both in terms of capital commitments and, more importantly, in my mind, around the narrative of an existing investor essentially losing confidence. And, if I'm reading this right, that probably happened because the performance isn't quite there yet or—"

"Yeah, what they want to see is crazy, though! I mean, the markets have been completely irrational, and we're nowhere near...."

"I hear you," I interject. "Much about the current state of the economy, the geopolitical situation—all of it doesn't feel rational. But it is what it is, and we have to work with what we've got. Reality is a mighty constraint."

We both laugh again. I've laid in a cushion of humor, so I gently venture over to the harder part.

"Are you worried Leah will be disappointed in you?"

He shakes his head immediately. I knew that wasn't likely, which is why I asked it this early. Leah and Carter have been married for eight years and together for over a decade. They have two kids and—from what I can tell at a distance—a pretty stable relationship.

"Nah, man, she'll...she'll be supportive, and she's awesome. She'll want to help and immediately start figuring out options. But," his gaze darkens again, and I can see both sadness and guilt wash over his face, "Leah has *so* much on her plate already. Media's a shitshow these days. I just...I can't be the cause of more worry."

"I hear you. You are a good husband and a good human. And if Leah's agency was imploding, I'm sure she wouldn't want to worry you either."

"Oh, I'd totally want to know! You know, RGA's too big to fail, but yeah, even *they* lost a huge account last year, and I stayed up with Leah a bunch of nights helping her think through cuts, and...but that was, that was different. Losing clients is part of doing business."

"And losing LPs is part of fundraising," I note. "I know it feels bigger and more cataclysmic, but honestly, from my days in advertising, it would be about as bad as losing a Nike account. Not that we ever got Nike...we weren't good enough for that."

"OK," I continue, "so what I'm hearing here is: you're in a bind that is scary. It feels apocalyptic, but not as bad as a meteor. The constraint on AUM is potentially pretty massive, but it's not going to be a constraint on your marriage, correct?" He nods. "And I'm also hearing that one of your biggest worries is not wanting to worry Leah. Is there more to that?"

Carter's eyebrows furrow. He spends a few moments thinking.

"I don't think I've told you this. I mean, I've mentioned how my dad was a screenwriter, but back when I grew up in the Valley in the eighties, my dad had been sweating over this action concept for years. It was like *Moonlighting* but way edgier, darker, and set in a small town. He was obsessed with it, and it was very unique, very different. Eventually, he got some names attached, and they were going to pilot, and then that strike hit in '88, and the guild was picketing for like four or five months, and Mom had to support all of us on her teacher's salary—there were five of us—and Janie was just two, and my grandma Olga was living with us, and it was just... it was very stressful." He can barely catch his breath. "And when the strike was over, the pilot didn't get picked up, and it all fizzled out, and eventually my dad just got his cabbie license, and we had to move, and that was that. Then, later, *Twin Peaks* came out, and I just saw his heart break into a million pieces, and I don't think he ever wrote or even watched much of anything after that. It's like...I don't know, man."

"It's like something robbed him of his dream," I offer.

We're both quiet for a moment. If we were in the same room, I'd reach out and hug him. I try for extra gentleness instead.

"You know, there's this Carl Jung quote that always haunts me. He said that the greatest burden a child must bear is the unlived life of the parent."

Carter looks straight at me, and we both purse our lips.

"That's real."

"Yup. And I'm sure I don't need to spell it out for you...."

He shakes his head. "I hear you. I've kinda been carrying this."

"Yup. And I'm quite curious, Carter: what would happen if you put it down?"

EMBODIED STANCE: CURIOSITY

As I noted back in Part I *curiosity* is the Swiss Army Knife of character traits. It is the one I reach for whenever I or a client or a loved one are at their most overwhelmed. It's one of the top three traits I've observed in a successful employee or founder, and, as a bonus, it is the doorway to connection, wonder, and vulnerability.

Curiosity propels us to explore beyond our immediate understandings and assumptions. It invites an active and open engagement with the world around us. By adopting a curious stance, we prevent ourselves from prematurely concluding what's going on or becoming rigid in our perspectives. Such exploration can uncover nuances we might have otherwise missed. The point of curiosity is also to foster a willingness to question and explore your current models of the world, to grasp that these models, or 'priors,' are not fixed truths but hypotheses that your brain has formed based on past experiences. In turn, this allows you to hold them lightly and become porous to new information.

Still, advising someone to get curious when they feel knotted up in scarcity and constraint goes about as well as you'd expect. If we are not approaching a problem from a new perspective (or at all), it's usually not because it didn't occur to us to do so. Rather, curiosity doesn't present as an easy possibility because it feels dangerous. We prefer to either wall off the problem, deciding it doesn't deserve our attention, or sublimate it altogether.

A useful lesson I learned from one of my teachers, the relational therapist and author Terry Real, was that in order for a relationship to change, the side wanting the change needs sufficient leverage. He taught us that whenever a coach or therapist is assessing a situation and constructing a plan of action, our first step is to form a therapeutic alliance with the client (go wherever they're standing and join them in the hole they've dug for themselves). Then, it is to look around and find the best leverage. In romantic relationships, that can come from the other partner or from external motivators such as their children's happiness or rekindling a joint narrative the couple might share. Whatever it is, Terry teaches, your leverage (the threat of what they might lose) needs to hurt more than not doing what they're currently doing. Without sufficient leverage, that boulder's going to stay right where it is.

I've climbed down and joined Carter in the hole of enumerating his professional constraints. Now, I need to find sufficient leverage to convince him to peek out of it.

"I know we don't have too much time left," I begin, "but I'm wondering—how are the kids doing? Winter break's coming up, right?"

I can see sadness flash in his eyes and regret going for the gut so fast, though we really do have only fifteen minutes. He covers it up and tries to sound upbeat.

"Oh, they're awesome! Remi's in first grade and just loving it. Ethan's still in preschool, but I'm hoping we can get him his first ski lessons this month. We probably should've started last year!"

"That's so great. Will you get back while they're still on break?"

Carter's lips purse again, and he tilts his head to one side—a half-shake that can't bear to fully say 'no.'

"You know, it's OK. Mine were small when I was in the midst of fundraising too. I know how hard it is."

He looks grateful.

"But also, I'm kind of sad because, at the time, I thought I was doing all that work so that they would have a great life, but we were all very stressed, and I'm not sure I was the best mom, honestly."

His gratitude has now turned to concern. I'm sure that my face is probably sadder than I'd like it to be as well. Our conversation's not about me, but my regret is certainly real, even if I am shining a bright spotlight there for his benefit. It's a fine line I'm walking—kids and the pain we might inadvertently cause them are some of the most potent leverage, but bringing them up can also cause defensive shutdown. I am showing my own regrets here so as to normalize imperfect humaning.

"Tell me, Carter—and I'm sorry, I don't mean to dredge up a painful memory—but when your dad lost that pilot, was it worse that you guys had to move, or was it that you had to watch him wither?"

Carter's brown eyes are glistening, so I'm careful to seem as if I'm not noticing the details too hard. His expression is pained as he shakes his head vigorously from side to side.

"No, man! Of course, it was watching how bad it was for him. I would've—of course, I wanted to stay in my old school and be with my friends—but nothing's as bad as watching your folks struggle. I thought he was awesome, you know! And then *he* didn't think he was awesome. I remember seeing him late at night sitting at the kitchen table, just kind of staring at the wall. There was this calendar from like two years prior and this nasty wallpaper. And Dad would just stare at it for *hours*. He never said a thing, but I'm pretty sure he thought it was all his fault that he had failed."

The tears come, so I watch Carter softly and also look away while he composes himself. Jerry Colonna, the OG venture-investor-turned-executive coach (I told him once he was my spirit animal, and he looked at me worriedly), is known for making clients cry with just a few well-appointed questions. He's so good at it that it's become like a magic trick—the ability to expose what someone is hiding. For my part, I try not to do it on purpose and even to be cautious, making sure the cresting of emotion doesn't start feeling manipulative.

Still, emotion is a mighty door opener. When we tap intensity and then allow it to build, it unblocks tension—shows us loud and clear there's something else beneath, and then it gets easier to get curious. The uncomfortable truth is that tears are one of the fastest ways in, especially for those of us who see ourselves as buttoned-up professionals. Anger and fear (or particularly anxiety) are more acceptable as far as difficult emotions go. If we're furious that something's blocking us or anxious about how we might present, these are seen as signifiers of a high performer. But sadness... sadness is hard to admit. It means we didn't properly guard against something or that something bigger than us got to us and hurt us. It is vulnerability, and vulnerability is often misapprehended as weakness.

I give Carter another moment, then say gently, "Yeah. I bet that must have been very hard." My voice is soft and I am careful not to come across as though I pity him. "And look at how far it got you! I remember back when you made the 40 Under 40 list and then you just kept going! You and Christian raised two funds in five years. Your Fund I's doing great, and—"

Carter shakes his head. "It's not doing that great, Des. I mean, it's not horrible, but we're not even top quartile at this point. It looks good on the outside, but—"

I see the deflation and try to nip it in the bud. This is one of the biggest reasons why we don't like to look very closely at the constraints that surround us, nor get curious about them—what we find often feels like it might swallow us whole. I try to soften things further.

"Honestly, that's a lot of my clients right now." I'm not lying. "And I have to tell you, I see a lot more of the real insides of funds now as a coach and—this is true for startups and funds and even corporations—in the right light, everything's a mess, and from a different angle, everything has plenty of possibilities." I pause, then smile a little. "Of course, some of that might just be who's coming for coaching...."

"Do you and your dad talk about stuff from back in the eighties?" I ask.

Carter shakes his head. "It's too hard. Like, he still doesn't watch much of anything other than sports or the news. He spends his time on Facebook or gardening or—" Carter's face darkens, "—or, you know, he goes and bets at the track, and now that he's getting older, he's been losing a lot. My mom worries. I had to help them last year."

I assume he means help them financially, but also know that as parents age, the necessary assistance spreads like an avalanche and just keeps growing.

"I'm glad you could help. I know I said it before, but you're a good human, and a good husband, and a good father, and also..." I pause for dramatic tension so he can see on my face that I mean this, "...a *truly* good son."

The brown eyes on my screen are glistening again, and I'm mindful to not leave him in a state that will disrupt his day or, worse—interfere with the upcoming trip, which is already going to be an uphill battle. I start to feel regret for nudging him to get *this* curious about his underlying dynamics. We've barely dipped below the surface, but for every human I've met, there's an ocean awaiting them the moment they're encouraged to dive in. Most of us are not the tiny icebergs we imagine ourselves to be; we are continental shelves, breaking off from our families of origin and floating toward others with eons of sediment in tow.

I decide to use my hesitance as a lifeline.

EXTENDED SELF: CONVERGENCE

"I'm sorry that we have just a few minutes left. I can go over by a bit, but I'm sure you're probably back to back."

Carter nods, and I imagine he's eager to get out. I roll with it.

"You're probably eager to jump to another conversation, too. It's not like this has been the funnest walk in the park." I look for a smile but don't receive one. "So let me share quickly the last aspect of Clarity, which is about finding the hidden paths of *convergence*."

I can see Carter glance to the side and wonder if he's checking his email. At the end of a call, people's attention can start to wander. This is particularly true if it was a difficult session or if they feel like they've reached an impasse. The tricky part about Clarity is that sometimes the first wave of it simply clarifies just how much we're stuck. If I were doing a longer unblock with a client (which sometimes begins our work together or can serve as an emergency intervention), I would move to another part of the framework—in this case, likely Regulation or Agency. But my situational constraints at this moment are lack of time and the depth of this topic, so I've got to trust what I have and take him out to a clearing.

"Leah probably hints at this sometimes, but the thing nobody tells you about creativity is that it's always a combination of multiple objects, ideas, or situations." Mentioning his wife pulls Carter's attention back. "I used to think new ideas were like that cartoon lightbulb moment. I'd walk around, waiting for lightning to strike or at least for the muse to poop on my head[4], but what I learned from working on campaigns was that most of it is just information-gathering and iteration. You find the things you like; you figure out how to imitate and improve on them. And when all else fails, everybody just tries to be an Apple ad." We both laugh, and the warmth returns. "The third aspect of Clarity is basically this combinatorial convergence. Nothing important happens by itself because each individual and every idea is relational. We've been taught that the best performers

---

[4] *This is based on how Stephen King speaks of his muse, not me being randomly childish.*

are brilliant and original, and there's this assumption that we're all one-man islands out there, but I've never seen that to be true. While I'm not saying we should just copy other ideas, I *am* saying that each of us rests on the shoulders of others. You are not alone in figuring this out, and it will feel harder if you keep all the responsibility and self-doubt locked up in your head."

I could go on a longer rant about how narratives of individualism keep us isolated and walled off from ourselves and each other, but I know Carter (and you) won't sit through a lecture right now. "So my point here is that once we have accounted for what's blocking us and then leaned in to understand how we got to this point, the next step is to start bravely gathering whatever pieces and humans are accessible, then see if a new opportunity presents itself out of the muck. And all the stuff we just covered—the not-so-pleasant bits of constraints that we got curious about—that has hopefully prepared you to be more honest with your partners, with Leah, and with yourself."

"OK...?" He's trying to follow me, but I can also see that he's waiting for a next step.

"So your task over the next two weeks is to look for that convergence, or as that saying goes: figure out how to make lemons into lemonade. Your constraints are threefold: a terrible fundraising market, less-than-stellar performance, and an anchor LP who's about to peace out. If you keep trying to pretend these are no big deal, you're wasting time you don't have.

"You and I both know that even in the worst markets, *somebody* is looking for an edge. If I were in your shoes, I'd be assessing all the pieces that are keeping you down and figuring out if there's a way to flip or reframe them. I see you holding a mountain of worry while pretending it's not even there—and I'm curious whether there might not be some gold deep in its belly..."

I pause expectantly. Carter swallows and tugs at the fleece zipper again. I wonder whether Patagonia planned for these to double as fidget spinners. Finally, he sighs.

"Well, yeah. The worry...the worry is about how to keep going and also about what happens when—we went through it, I don't want to have to move my family or not be able to support them or help my folks, or...."

"Or?"

"Or, I miss my big chance and end up like—"

He stops himself, and I don't push.

"You're not going to have to move, and you're not going to lose, and you are not your dad," I assure him. I don't know any of these things for certain, but I know the one thing that's different, so I say it.

"For one thing, you are not staring at the wall; you are talking about it. Convergence is not only about the matching up of possibilities; it's about combinations of humans and conversations, shared emotion as well as experience. Reality didn't end up at this point by complete accident. All the dynamics of the system you inhabit converged to this point, which—if you look at them with clarity—can enable you to understand exactly what's going and what is available if you start to rearrange the pieces. That's what we began over the past hour, and I promise that as soon as you return from Asia and you keep doing the work, the path forward *will* appear. I promise I'll be there to help you figure out the next steps. Does that make sense?"

Carter nods. His smile is faint—gentle and a little sad. "Yeah, I think that makes sense. I guess things are a *little* more clear."

We say our goodbyes, then rush to each of our next meetings.

In the evening, I ponder the conversation with tenderness and also worry. Did I give him enough clarity? Was it too much? Did I open a can of worms and then send him off having to pretend that things are alright while having a clearer picture of how they were not? The answer to all of those is: probably. But that is the case with anything important. If we expect to tie up every problem with a bow the moment we stop to examine it, we set ourselves up for failure and then learn to avoid the next real question. The big puzzles get more entangled the more we investigate them. Usually, there are no easy answers, or else—smart organisms that we are—we would have found them. As I told Carter, Clarity does not mean certainty. Understanding where we stand doesn't immediately mean knowing how to get out of that spot. It's simply putting that pin on the map, saying, "You are here." Think of orienting yourself as braving one of the scariest and most necessary steps of navigating life. From there, "all" you have do is decide where you'd like to be going.

CLARITY: BEYOND SURFACE REFLECTIONS

Whenever I explain the CRATE framework, a common question is whether the dimensions and aspects are like steps you walk through in a specific sequence or a way of identifying what's missing and then filling in the blanks. The honest answer is: both. You check through all the pieces in sequence, then fill in whatever isn't immediately obvious. In the above example with Carter, I attracted his attention to a constraint he already knew, and helped him voice it. Then, I modeled curiosity and helped him explore how bad the situation was or wasn't. Lastly, I introduced the concept of Convergence as an idea that the path forward may not be any one thing but a way of combining multiple factors, none of which are an obvious solution on their own.

To make things more explicit, let's walk through the steps involved in finding Clarity. The first aspect of Clarity—**Constraint**—can be seen as the step where we notice a *closing of capacity*. Beginning with constraints nudges us to recognize the boundaries within which we operate at any given moment. Here we can accept the limits of our environment, resources, and personal capabilities. By acknowledging these limitations, we begin to focus our attention and efforts more effectively, eliminating any distractions and unnecessary options that may lead us astray. In the context of cognitive science, recognizing constraints is crucial for efficient problem-solving and decision-making. It allows us to optimize our mental resources, then direct our cognitive and emotional energy towards achievable goals, rather than chasing what we wish were true but is not.

I have found that when we lack Clarity—whether it be in a personal or professional setting—it is because there's something we don't want to name that is "fogging up our mirror". Making the constraints explicit is a way of noticing the inconvenient bumps in the road. As the saying goes, "name it to tame it." From there, the fog begins to lift and we can lean forward to inquire into what else is available.

Next comes **Curiosity**, which is a form of *caring connection*. Curiosity drives us to explore, learn, and seek out new information. It requires an openness to questioning our assumptions, coupled with a willingness to venture into the unknown. Curiosity propels us beyond our comfort zone and leads us to challenge the constraints we've identified. From a psychological perspective, curiosity also enhances our cognitive flexibility, allowing us to adapt to new situations and then integrate disparate pieces of information into a cohesive view of what's going on. This is also the spark that ignites creativity and discovery (setting us up for convergence) and motivates us to pursue deeper insights.

I've said it in earlier chapters, and again in this one—Curiosity is the Swiss Army Knife of traits. It comes in with a plethora of questions like "Why?" and "What else is there?" and even "Is this true?" Best of all, it can take a long time to exhaust, creating a virtuous cycle of engagement, leading us to clarify the situation with each question we pose. The hidden power of curiosity is that it assumes that there *is* an answer to be found. It does not have to be an absolute or even a right answer, but being genuinely curious (rather than cynical) puts us in an optimistic mindset, wherein we act as if the universe, and our place within it, are figure-out-able.

Lastly, **Convergence** represents the process of *creative combination*. It is how we gather, synthesize, and integrate diverse ideas and situations into a coherent proposition as to what to do next. It involves finding connections between seemingly unrelated concepts. Convergence helps us create clarity amidst complexity. Its purpose is to reduce the overwhelm brought on by the combinatorial explosion of possibilities by distilling the essence of what we have learned through becoming curious about our constraints. In pragmatic terms, convergence gives us fresh hope. It enables us to align our thoughts and feelings and move forward with a clearer sense of what is readily available. It is the culmination of the Clarity dimension, where the insights gained from embracing constraints and fostering curiosity come together to illuminate a path forward. For Carter, convergence became available as he began to recognize how the past (the pain of watching his dad lose his dream and subsequently wither) overlapped with the present (driving Carter himself to avoid facing the professional dangers at hand or catastrophize and assume he was about to lose everything). While he was not yet ready to voice it exactly that clearly, this enabled him to become willing to talk about things, not just with me but also with his wife and his business partners.

When it comes to the fore, Convergence feels like multiple streams flowing into a river that then accelerates with greater force and momentum. It often feels like a bubbling up of *ah-ha!* moments, which all line up and start heading in the same direction. Curiosity (and the playful iteration that comes with it) is a fantastic way to elicit these insights and see how many of them we can gather.

It is completely OK that these three aspects won't become accessible to us immediately or arrive tied in a neat little bow, even if we step through them one by one. Convergence, in particular, invites us to find new possibilities, which is a challenge when everything appears overwhelming or opaque. In philosophical dialogue, reaching the moment of *aporia*—that sense of complete bafflement where you (to quote Socrates) know that you know nothing—is a crucial waypoint on the path to wisdom. I suspect this is not dissimilar to how Zen koans work. By examining factors bravely and rationally, we reach a point of cognitive capitulation: we admit that if there *were* an obvious answer, we would have found it.

The bigger the question, the more necessary that moment of aporia becomes. Without it, we cannot begin to fully open ourselves to intuition, creativity, and the further wisdom that our body holds. Even when we feel we've reached a dead end or an impasse, my experience is that there is likely a convergence of possibilities right on the other side. If nothing else, an attitude of "I know there's a path forward, but I just can't see it yet" prepares us for the rest of the CRATE framework, where each dimension is designed to build on the preceding one while also preparing us for what comes next. The constraints we enumerated have laid the groundwork for Recognition, which is the first step of Regulation, while also anticipating their flip side—the discovery of affordances—which will come when we get to Agency. But before we get too far ahead of ourselves let's explore Regulation through a different client session.

6

GAINING REGULATION

Recognition, Relation, & Release

"All of humanity's problems stem from man's
inability to sit quietly in a room alone."
— Blaise Pascal

"I'm *so* sorry to bother you while you're on vacation," Ella jumps in breathless, her eyebrows raised imploringly. "This is not even that much of an emergency."

I smile patiently, then lean against the tree trunk that is doubling as my backrest. The family and I are upstate, squirreling away moments of respite before the Labor Day weekend wraps, taking with it the last days of summer. Still, I've offered to FaceTime because Ella's messages over the past two days have become frantic, punctuated with exclamation marks, exploding heads, and crying emojis. Her last text also made it sound like she was set to unwind her growing startup, which seems sudden and will affect the lives of at least a dozen people.

"I have all the time in the world," I say, trying to mean it. "It's a holiday weekend, so let's just slow down. You can tell me what happened, and then we'll figure everything out together."

My calmness works for a quick moment. Ella's face relaxes and she looks both younger and more worn than when I last saw her three days ago. Then, just as quickly, her anxiety rushes back in. Anxiety is perpetually within Ella's reach. I've watched her oscillate between seeming in complete control and then suddenly careening into frantic, fear-driven activity with almost no provocation[1].

During our last session, she had just returned from vacationing in Majorca, and we spent our entire conversation discussing how good she felt and how far her business has come—from a basement store in Alphabet City where she first started selling her clothing designs to a fast-growing venture-backed startup that is hoping to redefine fashion in this new hybrid-work reality. If you'd asked me how Ella and her business were doing last Wednesday, I would have told you she seemed on top of the world. I also would have told you I was worried.

"It's Ben!" She announces, gesticulating with the phone she's holding, so I can't see whether she's about to start laughing or crying. "He's going to be the death of me—and of the business, too! I don't know what I was thinking partnering with a boyfriend! What's that saying? Don't shit where you eat, right?!"

"Right."

We've already had many discussions on this topic, and I've shared how some couples who are co-founders can be even more successful together, working toward a joint mission and outcome,

---

[1]   *Dr. Wendy Suzuki has done groundbreaking work showing how anxiety, for all its discomfort, can actually be one of our greatest allies. Her book "Good Anxiety" reveals what I've long suspected: that heightened awareness—even when it feels overwhelming—can sharpen our game, push us to prepare more thoroughly, and even help us connect more deeply with others. The trick isn't to eliminate anxiety but to learn its language and harness its energy. This is precisely why I believe emotion carries information rather than inconvenience.*

while others, of the more tumultuous variety, can risk spreading maladaptive behaviors into their work, jeopardizing both their personal and professional lives. I've told Ella a good relationship is a good relationship; if you trust someone in your personal life and have a consistent habit of communicating clearly with them, especially on difficult topics, you can certainly try collaborating; if that's missing, fix it before you go any further personally *or* professionally.

She looks at me expectantly, waiting for more, but I'm simply holding her gaze and enjoying the late summer breeze on my cheeks.

"What's that thing you told me before? I'm not gonna say I told you so, but I'm going to think it very loudly?"

I laugh. "Yeah, I say that sometimes."

"I wish you would tell me that I'm being an idiot! It would do me some good not to be coddled because I just keep making stupid decisions and choosing untrustworthy people, and now Jason is asking whether our margins are correct and when I looked closer, I'm not sure they are. So I asked Ben, and he said I was being a moron, but even if he's right and I don't get the math, my gut says things are not adding up. And now I'm pretty sure Jason and his team won't offer us a term sheet because he'll think I'm incompetent or maybe a liar—and I don't even know what's worse!"

Jason is a partner at an A-list New York venture firm that's been diligencing Ella's startup for two months now and is expected to lead her company's Series A round. He is well-respected, so a last-minute rejection from him would severely jeopardize Ella's ability to fundraise and could potentially tank her business, given how aggressively they've hired engineers. I can only imagine the level of stress she's experiencing and also know that this is just the tip of the proverbial iceberg. She's waving the phone again, and it's starting to make me dizzy. I try to work with that.

"Ella, I have a huge favor to ask. Could you please prop the phone on a table or something? I feel like I'm on a rollercoaster. I would love to see your beautiful face, and I want you to see mine... OK, good—thank you! Now, I wanted you to look in my eyes because

I mean when I say this: I will *never* call you an idiot because *no one* deserves to be spoken to cruelly, especially when they're at their most vulnerable."

Now that her hands are free, I watch as she covers her face with them, pressing fingers into her eye-sockets while her shoulders begin to shake.

"This is all my fault," she sobs.

"I don't believe you," I answer.

———

I never fully believe the stories people tell me. I also try particularly hard to disbelieve my own. We are each predisposed to bend reality and confirm the stories we tell ourselves, because we have a vested interest in things being whatever we think them to be. Even when we think everything is horrible. Even when we believe it is all our fault. The trick is that a story that's crafted to seem as though it has the full picture enables its storyteller to feel she is in control. *This is the way the world is. Here's who's right and who's wrong. Here's how I am a good person or a bad person or even a person who doesn't have a clue.* Each of these statements is a flag we plant on the surface of reality in the hopes of taming it. But the powerful (and dangerous) nuance is that a story that resonates is a story that can, and often will, become true. We find ourselves living in the reality we suspected, never realizing it is we who act to match the models that our minds predict.

To counterbalance this and ensure we set off on the path we intend rather than the one we're trying to prevent, we deploy *Regulation*, which is the second dimension of CRATE and our invitation to shift focus off of our chattering mind and onto the pings of our nervous system. Clarity has a cerebral, cognitive approach, while Regulation reminds us to check in with how our stories resonate in a felt sense. I usually reach for Regulation when my own mind (or that of a client or a loved one) is overloaded, and it becomes evident that more thinking will just spin us up like a tense coil. If Clarity is all about thinking, distilling, and considering, then Regulation's objective is to help us discern, lean into the senses, and let go.

The first part of Regulation is *Re-cognition*—meaning the re-considering or re-noticing of our narratives. This is the Embedded Prediction (Story) aspect, which shines a light on our predictive models and encourages us to challenge them.

EMBEDDED STORY: RECOGNITION

Regulation and Trust are the hardest dimensions for me to teach, likely because they're also the most difficult to master for my own temperament. Whereas Clarity and Agency can be explained theoretically, pointed to in schemas, and described with words, Regulation and Trust have to inevitably become embodied from the inside out. We can theorize about states of being calm or grounded all we want, but that doesn't help us actually live them. The more we *think* about Regulation, the more prone we become to storifying being regulated without actually arriving there. This is not dissimilar from the trope of the practitioner exiting a wellness studio toting their yoga mat, jade bracelet, and incense, yet losing their temper the moment the cashier takes too long to process payment for their matcha. Living in our heads is a defense mechanism against feeling the overload that sensory information can bring. We can decide we are calm and even acquire all the accouterments of tranquility, but without having the embodied, enacted, and extended (meaning *relational*) experience of regulation, that decision remains simply a mask that we wear.

Since recognition is still a form of cognition, however, it is only the first step inward and we must be careful not to linger there, lest we remain stuck in our heads. When working with someone like Carter (who tends to overanalyze the parts of the problem he is most familiar with as a way of coping), enumerating his constraints was a means to explicitly acknowledge what he was refusing to see. In Ella's case, I hypothesize that too much discussion about the presenting problem (the issue with her startup's margins) will just spin her up into greater anxiety. Instead, it might be sufficient to help her *feel* how entangled her narratives are, then gently challenge whether she needs to keep them this way.

"I don't believe myself either," Ella concedes immediately. "I mean, I do and I don't. I make such stupid choices when it comes to picking people or making business decisions! I just...I want someone like Ben to like me, you know?" Her face looks wistful.

"What is it about Ben that makes you want him to like you?"

"He's cool and—he was *born* cool! His whole life is like something out of *Vanity Fair*. With his mom in West Hartford and his friends from boarding school, and all the Harvard degrees! People like him are just *destined* to succeed. If he thought I was worth it, if he said my designs were brilliant, then—" her voice trails off.

"Then? You would be destined to succeed also?"

She nods sheepishly.

"I mean, I'm not a complete idiot. I know it takes more than *one* important guy liking me. But all his friends are influential people, and they all know who to call to get things done, and things are just way easier when you live like that."

"Do you really believe that?" I ask softly.

Her eyes tear up, but she still nods.

It would be disingenuous for me to argue here. Ben has been tremendously helpful when it came to shifting Ella's business from a small boutique to a technology-first concept that allows individual customization and on-demand production. His pitch combined the uniqueness of Ella's talent with innovations in 3D knit-printing and the rising consumer demand for bespoke sizing—all of which convinced investors this was a venture-backable business that could do for clothing what *Blue Apron* did for meals. It was a great story. Ben himself is a great story.

"I mean this as a compliment," I begin, "Ben is a master salesman. He's been fantastic at packaging your work. And I wonder if some of that ability hasn't also gone into how he packages himself."

Ella looks up at the phone screen, intrigued.

"There's no foolproof way to know the line between substance and dressing—at least not with your head—but I'm curious if you'll indulge me to check whether other parts of you have some information we could access?"

She nods, so I shift on the grass, trying to sit upright and hold the phone in a way that can show more of the green bramble behind me.

"I wish we were doing this in person because then I would have you run your hands over the bushes and the trees around here. Gently, of course, I wouldn't want you to get splinters, but I would ask you to feel all the textures and the difference in temperature between the sunlit bark and the shady leaves." I take a deep breath and then slowly exhale, making sure Ella is following me. "And I would ask you to inhale the mountain air and try to discern the pine from the moss and from the faint smell of wood-burning smoke that's drifting from the next property over."

Ella listens with interest, though I detect a slight confusion as to what she should be doing.

"Describe to me the textures and smells around you," I ask. "It's OK if they're not as detailed. If it smells like a normal room, you can just describe what a normal room smells like."

We both laugh, and I see her close her eyes and inhale.

"I can smell the reed diffuser," she shares immediately. "It smells of...it's supposed to be tobacco, but it smells like grass and a fresh shower with nice soaps, and someone in a tux, but really cool. Makes me think of James Bond. It's a bottle of *Coqui Coqui*—Ben brought it from a shop off Rodeo Drive." Her face lights up. "You know, that was one of my big dreams: to make it out of the Lower East Side and live somewhere fancy, like in Beverly Hills."

I note inwardly the irony of spending my teen years obsessing about moving to the East Village while Ella spent hers dreaming of getting out. But I don't voice this because I want us to stay in the senses, rather than get kicked back up to the head where dreams and aspirations live.

"Is this how Beverly Hills smells to you?" I ask.

Ella pauses for a moment. I can see memories moving across her face, then a faint smile that seems pleasantly nostalgic. "Yeah, and also leather seats and that new car smell. Or the air-conditioned feel of a nice restaurant where you walk in, and there's white marble and warm light, and you have to take a few steps down from the street level, and inside there are big linen curtains and soft velvet benches— it smells of jasmine and roses and buttery croissants."

"That all sounds really luxurious," I observe. "Is that something you associate with Ben?"

She nods, and I can see joy and relaxation spreading over her. Her shoulders are soft now and her forehead has smoothed. Who am I to say that this isn't good for her? She and Ben have made it through multiple volatile scenarios, past several occasions when I would have given greater odds to a breakup. My job is not to be prescriptive but to help my clients recognize *why* their organism is making the choices it is, and to then give them the tools to consciously opt into or out of those choices.

"How does the diffuser smell make you feel right now?"

Ella inhales again. "It makes me happy." A moment passes, then fear flashes in her eyes. "But also really nervous. Like it can all be taken from me at any moment."

EMBODIED STANCE: RELATION

The core of every dramatic story is some type of wounding. This is why I've come to believe that the essence of every uncomfortable emotion is some type of sadness or grief. Anger and fear are veneers that our sadness wears. Anger is pointed toward whoever (or whatever) hurts us, while fear urges us away from them; but if we stand still and focus our attention inward, listening to what our nervous system is truly saying at the center of our discomfort, there will be an ache, a crack, maybe even a tear in the fabric of our relationships to others and ourselves. The second step of regulating our system, then, is *Relation*—the process of acknowledging these relational woundings and the symbols they carry. This is neither easy nor pleasant. The parts of us that hurt, well, *hurt*. They also often cause us to inflict further pain on ourselves and others. At a certain point, we either build the capacity and courage to feel them, or we sentence ourselves to ignoring them, thus staying trapped and repeating the same scripts.

Ella's parents divorced when she was seven, and she got shuffled "back and forth along the Six Line," as she put it when we first started working together. Her mom had strong artistic ambitions but struggled in the competitive art market, only managing to land an adjunct position at the Parsons School of Design, which barely afforded her a tiny walk-up rental in Chinatown. Ella's dad stayed on the Upper East Side and eventually remarried, fathering two more daughters whom Ella watched have the comfortable life she could only visit every other weekend.

Ella's step-sisters are between eight and ten years younger, and she maintains that her relationship with them is "fine—we see each other on holidays, but don't have all that much to talk about." I wonder whether they would have more in common with Ben, but whenever I bring up them or her father, Ella just shrugs and changes the topic.

When people look for an executive coach, it is usually because they want to focus on their future or because they're hoping they can address the present without looking too closely at the past. Yet, as William Faulkner wrote, "The past is not dead. It's not even past." The lessons we learn, and the narratives we are handed, begin with our very first breath, whether or not we are comfortable looking back there later on in life.

As far as I have gathered, neither of Ella's parents were particularly insulting to her or even paid all that much attention to her other than to each speak horribly of the other. She has never gone into detail, but I've gathered that her dad regarded his ex-wife as "a train wreck" and "trashy," while her mother saw him as heartless, greedy, and self-interested. Whatever they said in front of young Ella, it was sufficient. The harsh judgments landed and became internalized. A child will often find it intolerable to accept that there is something truly wrong with the adults she reveres. It is safer to conclude that the terrible thing resides within ourselves—where we can lock it away or at least control it. Ella not only began to think of herself poorly, but also gravitated toward peers and mates who would sooner or later use similar words of derision about her. Like an earworm seeking to complete its melody, cruelty repeats the patterns it has known, mistaking familiarity for relief.

Our strongest mental models are formed when we feel most vulnerable. Often, it is at times when we become terrified, or feel rejected by someone essential to us, or when something dear to us is taken away. The root of an emotional wounding is not always easy to spot. The child who wants affection receives it in spades when she becomes the A+ student or a beautiful young lady; she learns, non-consciously, that affection is contingent on excellence. Another adolescent whose parents move multiple times learns that attaching to others causes the grief of separation; he becomes self-reliant, befriending his books or the technology that won't leave him. Yet another teen falls in love for the first time, and their love is returned; they are deliriously happy...until their beloved becomes more interested in the football captain. They internalize the importance of prestige and spend the next two decades becoming someone others will envy and admire. Ella, for her part, learned that stability and comfort were not available to her. She grew up (consciously) deciding to achieve comfort on her own and (unconsciously) acting as if she never trusted it.

At some early point, she also learned that the "fancier" life was for her to *visit* rather than inhabit. Echoing her mother, she told herself she had accepted this and that art and creativity were morally superior to "selling out." Yet Ben was not the first wealthy boyfriend she had dated, and—while she struggled financially when first beginning to sew her fashion designs and sell them out of that same Chinatown tenement apartment she had grown up in—her current choices of the best of the best in clothing, travel, and even scents, all compensated for a lack she couldn't admit to having.

We are born unable to regulate anything. We cry and flail and poop and are wholly incapable of caring for ourselves. If we are lucky, there are adults who assist us—they feed us and change our diapers and keep us safe until we grow old enough to do these things for ourselves. If we are *very* lucky, those adults also give us some invisible safety—they protect us from intense emotions (including theirs and our own) and then teach us how to navigate that intensity until we become capable of regulating both our inner and outer worlds, so as to maintain homeostasis. In other words, they teach us how to be at peace.

As far as I've witnessed, most of us only get smidgins of such luck by the time we reach adulthood. Even well-meaning parents and teachers spend most of their time struggling with their own regulation. They do the best they can and focus on what are deemed to be the important things: teaching us to read, write, possibly feed ourselves, maybe drive, earn a living, and become someone of consequence in the world. They rarely teach us how to feel our emotions, inquire deeply into ourselves, or puzzle out the pieces that are sticking askew. If anything, we are taught that emotions get in the way and that a sign of maturity is knowing how to ignore them, sublimate them, and forget their existence altogether. "Big boys don't cry," we are told. Also, "You should behave like a proper lady."

We want to please the adult world and become members of its secret society, so we listen. In the process of learning how to be independent, we sever our connection from the bodies that overwhelm us with their stimuli. We get serious and diligent and forget how to be curious. We lose our sense of wonder and become ever more separate from nature—both our own and that of the world around us. At the end of high school and college, sometime in our mid-twenties, awaits the open space of early adulthood, which often feels like the arrival lounge from a transatlantic flight. For some, it is crowded; for others, empty, but most of us arrive already slightly worn, disoriented, full of anticipation and vague unease.

Whether you are standing there now or have traveled much further, if you need greater regulation, the good news is that it is something you can learn—or rather, you can learn to *unlearn* the patterns that are no longer serving you. You can also build new patterns, intentionally orienting toward healthier, more secure attachments that will help you create relationships that heal rather than ones that wound. The invisible truth is that all of Regulation is essentially co-Regulation. Remember that baby in her crib who deduces whether the world is safe or unsafe based on the actions of her caregivers? You, I, Ella—all of us are her. When I see a client unconsciously act out their previous woundings in the new relationships they form, I always try to steer them to that space where the original lack of co-regulation can become apparent. Sometimes, we head in through Clarity (the cerebral side). Other times (if they're already overthinking, or if their emotions are too raw), we come straight to the felt sense of things. The intention here is not that we can undo the past. It is that we stop running and unconsciously repeating the same narrative.

"Do you also worry that *Ben* can be taken away from you at any moment?" I ask Ella as nonchalantly as possible. The fear on her face grows, and she struggles to contain it.

"I...no! He wouldn't leave me. We've been through a lot already."

"Like what? Do you mean the original fundraise or something else?"

When I first met Ella, she came in as a referral who had struggled for over a year to close her startup's seed round of funding and was having terrible insomnia. Unable to sleep or keep food down, she was subsisting on smoothies made with just water and berries and getting barely three hours of sleep per night. Eventually, Ben corralled a Friends & Family round—individual "angel investors" who bet on him and the woman he considered a prodigy, rather than relying on institutional vetting. Now, when I bring it up, she winces at the memory.

"Yeah, there was that, and also, I got... I got pretty unhealthy with my eating. I was also smoking like a pack a day, and I'm sure he thought I was disgusting, like a total train wreck who reeked, but... he stuck with me, you know?" Her face softens again, and she says almost dreamily, "He loves me."

"Remind me again," I ask, "how soon after you started dating was all this happening? I remember when I first met you, you had been together for a little over a year, right?"

She nods.

"And you'd only moved in recently, am I remembering this correctly?"

She nods again.

"OK, so you met, and Ben loved your designs, and so he came up with the startup idea, and then you both started pitching that and then you began fundraising together within, what—a few months of dating?"

She nods once again, this time a bit reluctantly. "I know! Probably not the best idea ever. But he was so passionate about me and my work, and he really believed this could be big, and I thought this was my chance...."

I raise one hand so she can see it on the phone camera. "I'm not judging!" I smile for punctuation. "I'm just going to suggest that maybe the difficulty of fundraising was because the two co-founders of the startup you were pitching had barely just met and were also *dating*. So with my investor hat on, I can see how early-stage funds would have held off, even if the idea looked good. But with my coach hat on—and particularly from right here on the grass as a human who wants to create and love and believe that dreams can come true—I *get* the leap of faith you took."

I see Ella relax for a moment. My approval, or at least my lack of strong disapproval, matters to her. It's as if she was holding her breath and now gives herself permission to exhale. I wonder if she assumes that everyone is judging her as harshly as she judges herself.

"You were having a really hard time with sleeping and eating when we met, but was that something that started before Ben, or after the two of you got together?" I can see bringing up that earlier time feels uncomfortable, so I'm treading carefully. I also know that the self-harming behaviors she mentions off-hand (dysregulated eating and sleep, smoking, etc.) are all signposts of hiding and self-loathing. In gently nudging toward them, I am trying to understand whether moving in with Ben caused or awakened them.

"It's...some of it was there. It's always there from when I was a teen and even maybe before then...but it got kinda worse with Ben." She sighs and looks away.

"Was he causing you stress?"

Ella shakes her head 'no' immediately, then actually thinks about it.

"He was great. We were really into each other. I mean, we went to Paris for our fourth date and spent a whole week there. And I remember having, like, the whole rack of lamb at *L'Ambrosie*!" Her eyes grow large at the thought, but the corners of her mouth turn in discomfort. "Not that I kept it down," she mumbles.

"Hmm...tell me more about that," I beckon. "That's right by Place des Vosges and the Victor Hugo Museum, right?"

I know that area from crisscrossing Paris on foot and visiting every playground when my kids were little, though we were certainly not in the habit of frequenting three-star Michelin restaurants. I can also see that Ella would much rather move to a different topic, so I do my best to keep the conversation light but also keep us here.

"Yeah," she hesitates, "not sure about the museum. We mostly visited perfumers. Christian Louis is a few doors down, and do you know *Ex Nihilo*? They are right nearby, too."

I do know them and also know they're not exactly nearby. It seems that something about scent is safe, while something about food, and/or possibly Ben, is not. Yet, it was Ella who brought up *L'Ambrosie* and she also mentioned another restaurant setting when discussing Beverly Hills. So, the luxury itself is appealing, but the act of consuming food might not be.

I try to get there another way. "You and Ben seem to really like nice fragrances. Is that something that brought you together?"

Ella smiles mischievously. "Oh, he corrupted me! I just knew the regular Sephora stuff. Like, I used to think Opium was high-end!" She laughs. "I remember when we first started living together, Ben actually threw out a bunch of my bottles! I mean, they weren't bottles—more like samples and travel sizes, because that's all I could afford, but like one day I went in the bathroom, and they were all in the trash." Her face falls. "It was...well, I guess they were trashy, so...." She laughs again, but this time there's no joy in her voice.

"Ella," I begin calmly, "I don't have any other clients today, so I'm not exactly watching the clock here, but I'm also cognizant that when we started this call, you were worried about what was going on with your business margins. And throughout this conversation and also during other sessions we've had, I keep hearing how Ben is helping you and making your life better but then also things he says and does—like calling you 'a moron' or throwing out your items without permission—that frankly seem insulting and condescending. I'm wondering how all of that sits with you."

The phone screen shifts again, and I can only see the top of her head and part of the ceiling. Then, a large object falls from the table, and she gets up while still attempting to answer me.

"Oh, sorry, Dessy! Hang on, please! Tricia was here earlier, helping me pull picks from the last photo shoot, and now there are all these folders here...everything's just such a mess! I *really* have to get all this crap together!"

There's frustration and also pain in her tone. I detect a slight shrillness that wasn't there before. I'm not getting anywhere, so I feel my own anxiety awaken and look around. Perhaps I'm not the right person to be helping Ella? I have offered referrals to several therapist colleagues, but she takes their numbers and does nothing with them. She also resets conversations like this one and pretends we never talked about anything uncomfortable, so I suspect that the next time we speak, everything will be coming up roses, and she will only want to discuss team issues or marketing. I'm reluctant to give up, but also feel as if I've reached an impasse. In moments like this, my only recourse is a kind of loving surrender.

EXTENDED SELF: RELEASE

"Hey, Ella," I try again, "I know we've been talking for a long time, and I can tell that you've got a lot going on. I also know we're not going to solve everything in just one hour. Honestly, if things were that easy, I'd be out of a job." I laugh, but she doesn't join. "Could you give me just a few more minutes of your attention, and then I promise we'll wrap up with some next steps?"

The phone jiggles for a moment and then I can see her face as she's holding it.

"Sorry! I have to get ready to go soon but I can call you back from the Uber if you'd like?"

I shake my head and try to decline nicely without letting my frustration peek through. "No, that's alright. This is the kind of conversation that requires our full attention. But, perhaps," I brighten up, "you can run a little experiment for me and then report back?"

She's paying full attention now, so I continue.

"When you go to dinner tonight, try to stay in your senses the way we were describing the diffuser earlier. Maybe try slowing down as you smell and then taste the food..."

Her face darkens again.

"...or pay attention to the scent in the place—the flower arrangements, candles—whatever sets the ambiance. Notice the vibe of the evening through your senses, and then text me any impressions!"

Ella nods, uncertain but seemingly willing to follow my prompt. I tell her I'll send options for our next call after the long weekend, and then we sign off. I hang up the phone and put it down on the grass beside me, staring at a pair of broken twigs, some early fallen leaves scattered between them.

I feel sad and a little bit like I've failed, or at least like I've failed to succeed. As I go back to the house, I remind myself that my job is not to fix but to offer safe harbor while also maintaining clear boundaries—that individuals will only feel as much as they can, and that building our capacity to hold intensity is a matter of patience and titration. Today, Ella withstood slightly more than previously. Next time, who knows? Perhaps we'll be able to go a little further.

—

The Extended Self aspect of Regulation is *Release*, which, if we're honest, is just a more palatable way of framing the relinquishment of control. I only understood this third step theoretically, knowing there was a turning point that needed to happen here—from control into something else resembling flow—but not actually experiencing it until I hit my own internal wall about four years ago.

It wasn't until a moment of forced capitulation that I admitted to myself that the narratives that had gotten me this far were exactly what was keeping me from moving further. The turning point came in early 2021 when—deep into the pandemic, the tension of building a startup, working to help my coaching clients, and witnessing two middle-schoolers struggling with online learning and the accompanying deep isolation—all collected into a dense ball of stress that finally hit home. Or rather, it hit my body like an eighteen-wheeler of pain. My backaches, which had gone from inconvenient to insistent, were already a daily companion. My TMJ––which stands for *temporomandibular joint dysfunction* and means that you grind your teeth so hard you inflame (or, in my case, dislocate) your jaw––was causing me near-daily migraines. And then something seized. To this day, I can't point to one conversation or gesture that caused it. All I know is that I woke up one morning and could not move. It felt like the mother of all constrictions. My entire body had tied itself up in knots and was sending cartfuls of angry letters––each from a nerve cluster on fire. My spine and the tendons around it were so inflamed that sneezing felt like medieval torture, going to the bathroom was nearly impossible, and dressing required my husband's patient assistance. It was humbling, especially when I had to crawl across the floor to get my phone, and particularly because I knew that I had (to a significant extent) caused it all. Not only does the body keep the score, it also sends messengers with pitchforks. 'Mind over matter' stopped working because matter took over mind, and because, like it or not, it was all the same thing: this organism that had dutifully carried me around while sending up regular distress flares was finally going on strike.

What I experienced was somatization—physical effects on the body resulting from mental distress. My case was acute, but manageable. Others have to live with debilitating chronic pain, autoimmune diseases, and conditions that cost them way more than a few months of discomfort or several trips to the dentist. Still, having gone through that experience at a time when I could make sense of it enables me to recognize many other instances—in myself and others—when the body makes loud and clear what the mind refuses to hear. The works of Dr. Peter Levine[2] and Dr. Bessel Van Der Kolk[3] hold countless case studies of the long-term entwinement of the anguish in our minds and the pain in our bodies. I was incredibly lucky that my teacher and somatic coach, Rachel Rider, had already taught me the skills necessary to Recognize and Relate to the narratives that were causing my tension. All that was left was learning how to shift out of them, and that came in the form of a psychic and somatic surrender.

While struggling with my incapacitated back and unable to get a peaceful night's sleep, I had a dream I was back in university, and a close friend was reading my tarot cards. I argued with her in my dream, explaining how I no longer gave credence to non-scientific modalities, yet I was happy to see her and awoke wistful for the missed connection. Then, I remembered the central card of the dream's tarot draw, still fresh in my post-slumber haze.

I've always had an affinity for myth and archetypes, so the figure of The Hanged Man, which embodies themes of surrender, pause, and a shift in perspective, seemed like an intriguing symbol served up by my subconscious. In tarot, the Hanged Man is typically depicted as a person suspended head-down, often with a serene or contemplative expression—like an inverted tree pose hung by the ankle—suggesting a voluntary act of letting go. Throughout the next few days, I spent whatever moments I could sitting in meditation and contemplation with that archetype. The pain departed, but the image remained.

I return to the vacation house and begin preparing dinner. There's a rhythm to chopping up vegetables that lends itself to

---

2   Levine, P. A., & Frederick, A. (1997). Waking the tiger: Healing trauma. North Atlantic Books.

3   Van der Kolk, B. A. (2014). The body keeps the score: Brain, mind, and body in the healing of trauma. Viking.

contemplation, so I try to become fully immersed in the moment. I have cognitively let go of my desire for any specific outcome for Ella, yet I can still feel my worry for her, curled up like a ball in my solar plexus, keeping me vigilant. I have accepted that I can't change what is and also accepted that a part of me will keep circling and iterating on it. As I chop onions, a text comes in from Ella. "Sorry I was awful. Can u forgive me? Can we talk some more? No video pls!" There's a crying emoji and a facepalm one.

I stare at my phone, wondering about the correct step to take. Coaching has blurrier lines than therapy, in that I've both befriended clients and coached close friends. While that requires extra effort in communicating clear boundaries, for the most part, I find that those relationships only build on each other, creating opportunities for deepening growth and intimacy. But something here feels off—intensely dramatic and also personal in a way that is unwarranted.

Then it hits me: Ella is re-enacting a familial dyad. She has cast me as a parental figure, both rebelling against and seeking my approval. I wish to neither reenact the role of the unavailable parent nor fulfill her narrative of judgment and inadequacy. I decide to nip it in the bud and call her back.

"I'm so sorry!" she answers. "I'm such a trainwreck. You must be so disgusted with the mess I am!"

I let her finish, then allow a beat of silence.

"I think nothing of the sort, Ella. In fact, I think you are bright and deeply talented and wish you could see what I see." Another beat. "But if you want to know what *else* I was thinking, I was honestly worried that I failed to help you because our conversation kept jumping back to the surface, and we could not address the deeper struggles you're obviously carrying."

I can't see Ella's face, but I can hear her sniffling. She attempts to say something, then just begins to sob louder. I wait, but the sobbing continues and seems to be building. Unlike some of my teachers, I'm not as talented at coaching by voice alone. While I've gotten adept at reading the tiniest nuance, I seem to be much better with visual rather than auditory cues. And yet, I have to work with what I've got and do my best to calm Ella down and help her feel accepted and loved. I decide to lay my cards on the table.

"You know, I'm not a very good coach over the phone," I admit. "If I could see your face and you could look at mine, I would be smiling softly at you, and my eyes would be beaming. I would try to wordlessly show you that I *care* and that you matter to me."

Ella is trying to stop crying, though I continue to hear sniffles.

"But all we've got is a phone call, so I am going to describe to you what I'm feeling since you can't see me. Right now, my heart feels like it is open and welling with warmth, and I truly wish I could hug you. My stomach is knotted a little. I worry for you, though I try not to, because I know that each of us walks our own path and that you will have to live with every step you must take before you get to where you need to be going. Sadly, there are no shortcuts. Still, my job is to be your sherpa; your Samwise Gamgee, if you ever read or watched *Lord of the Rings*." I can hear a faint laugh. "That's what we get to be for each other—not just in coaching, but in every caring relationship—we get to hold each other's baggage and point out the potholes occasionally, and if we're really lucky, we get to grow as we walk alongside each other. My hope for you, Ella, is that you can find this not just in a coach but in your loved ones: your friends, your mate, your co-founder...you deserve to be loved and respected by each and every one of them."

Ella thanks me profusely while I ask that she just sit with my words and allow them to sink in as much as possible. The healing part of any caring relationship is that we can borrow the other person's love for us—their calmness, their certainty, their hope, whatever it is that they can see in us—and then let it become integrated within our psyche. Paul Tillich, the German-American existential philosopher and theologian, wrote at length about self-transcendence and our relationship with a loving universe. In his 1948 collection *The*

Shaking of the Foundations, he advises his reader, "Accept that you are accepted. Despite the fact that you are unacceptable."

We will return to Ella in Chapter 8, where we can trace how much further acceptance can take us. At the core of Regulation is laying the foundation for exactly this act of loving acceptance. It is why I noted earlier that the task of regulating is always, in some way, a form of co-regulation: we can borrow internal stability from loved ones, coaches, therapists, pets, or even imaginary characters. Coming into a deeper relationship with parts of ourselves or with externalized other selves increases our capacity to hold overwhelm and introduces new mental models (mental melodies, is how I sometimes think of them) that we can now choose to complete.

REGULATION: TENDING TO THE INNER FLAME

Regulating intensity is about remembering to connect to the signals from our nervous system, interrupt the chatter of our thoughts, and build the capacity to spaciously contain or even welcome intensity. It's a matter of shedding the illusion sold to us as "control" and replacing it with "flow"—a way of going through our days with balance, openness, and ease.

Recognition is an act of *remembering the real*. It involves the conscious identification and acknowledgment of our emotions, thoughts, and bodily sensations. This first step is foundational for emotional regulation, as it requires us to become aware of our internal states without judgment. Recognition (as the term itself instructs us) is about remembering what we know, and cultivating self-awareness in a way that builds foundational *felt* awareness without getting us stuck in mental chatter. By accurately recognizing our emotions, we can better navigate our experiences, making informed choices about how to respond to our feelings rather than react to them impulsively.

In my conversation with Ella, I attempted to ground her in the realm of her senses while tracing the associations that came forth and recognizing what held importance to her and why. In understanding how deeply she sought to feel pampered and worthy of a good life, I began to get closer to the potent fear she had of losing it.

Relation is a form of *rightful recovery*. As an Embodied Action (or Stance), it emphasizes the interconnectedness between an individual and their relationships, including other people and the environment. The recovery component of relation is that we reconnect bonds that have become severed between us and our world. Our emotional intensities and responses are significantly influenced (and often triggered) by our relational narratives.

While I could not get far when inquiring into relational dynamics between Ella and her family of origin, or even between Ella and Ben, I could use *my* relationship with her (and the fact that she was continuously anticipating my judgment or scorn) to point out discrepancies between the reality she imagined and what was happening. The way Ella related to herself, her constant assumption that she was "a mess," provided an immediate opportunity to begin challenging and reframing how she related to her self.

The third and final aspect of Regulation, **Release,** builds our capacity to *relinquish the reins*. It encourages us to let go of emotional and cognitive burdens that are no longer serving us, such as outdated beliefs, unhelpful patterns, or residual emotions from past experiences. It involves strategies to embrace or at least accept distressing emotions, facilitating a return to equilibrium and freeing up our emotional and cognitive resources for more adaptive responses. Release can take many forms, including emotional catharsis, mindfulness techniques such as meditation or contemplation, physical activity, creative expression, humor, and one of my favorites: deep hugs. It is a crucial step in Regulation because it frees us to move through emotional wounds without sublimating them while also maintaining focus on present objectives and future aspirations.

All I could do in Ella's case was model Release—both by admitting my worry that I did not help her sufficiently and by voicing the care and tenderness I felt toward a self she saw as messy or unacceptable.

Being well-regulated is just the *amuse-bouche* for the much larger and deeper condition that is being in a state of Trust. If you have Trust, Regulation tends to flow on its own or can be tapped pretty easily. But if you struggle tooth and nail to find Trust, Regulation is a useful entryway on the much longer journey to inner grounding.

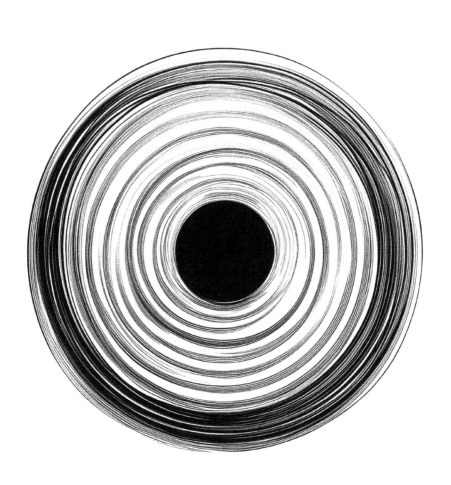

7

DECODING AGENCY

Affordance, Attention, & Adaptation

"You become what you give your attention to."
— Epictetus

path in. That was Carter's request when he called days after his return from Hong Kong. He invited me to meet at his firm's New York office so that his partners, Christian and Rita, could also attend. Obliging, I find myself waiting in a rather nondescript conference room just a few blocks east of Grand Central Station, staring out of its floor-to-ceiling windows. The team is running late, but I don't mind one bit. Across from me is the Chrysler Building—so close that I could throw a balled-up paper and actually score a basket in one of the wastebins there. Its chromed arches reflect the afternoon sun, and for one moment, I can't think of anything more glorious on the Manhattan skyline. I remember a story I heard decades ago in Ric Burns' documentary series about New York. It was 1929, and the skyline was in continuous transformation. The Chrysler Building and 40 Wall Street, two scaffolds of aspiration, rose simultaneously, orchestrated by architects who had once been partners, but had turned vicious rivals. William Van Alen (commissioned by Walter Chrysler) and Craig Severance (commissioned by his desire to piss off Van Alen) were both driven to erect the tallest building in New York—each aiming to get his name in the history books and keep the other out of them.

Learning that the Chrysler building was projected to stand at 826 feet, 40 Wall Street made a last-minute update to their blueprints, propelling their structure to breach the 900-foot mark. Severance's building seemed destined to clinch the title of tallest building in the world, yet at the last moment, Van Alen and Chrysler devised an audacious countermove. On the mist-shrouded early morning of October 15th, 1929, a derrick began hoisting tall steel pyramids up The Chrysler Building's facade. The geometric rods had been waiting within the cavernous crown, shrouded in secrecy. As the days progressed, they were meticulously assembled on the curved roof, one atop the other in a contraption that was part scaffold, part tower. Then, on October 23rd, a spire ascended from within the building "like a butterfly from a cocoon," in Van Alen's own words. Foot by foot, a steel needle weighing twenty-seven tons was pushed upward, supported by the scaffold, to elevate the Chrysler building to an awe-inspiring 1,046 feet. For the first time in human history, a structure pierced the thousand-foot mark, claiming the title of tallest building in the world.

I had forgotten all about that story until standing on this spot, craning my neck to stare up at the spire. Not only is The Chrysler Building no longer the tallest in the world (the Empire State Building stole that title less than a decade later), but it is now surrounded by many more. One Vanderbilt rises another two hundred feet right behind it, with countless others spiking up at the sky. I pull out my phone, trying to capture the way something this grand can simultaneously seem dwarfed, when I hear Carter snickering at my back.

"You know, it doesn't happen all that often that people take pictures here," he tells me by way of greeting.

"Seriously?"

"Yup." He nods, "Friends do, but usually when we take business meetings, no one admits to being impressed by anything. I think they worry they won't seem cool if they're gawking at the view."

"Instead, they come across as jaded." That's Christian, completing Carter's thoughts as usual, and walking over to wrap me in a bear hug. I notice that his temples are graying and his face looks more tired (or maybe it's worried) than the last time I saw him.

They tell me not to wait for Rita, who's still finishing the previous meeting, so we jump in, giving and receiving updates. It turns out Carter's Asia trip went about as I expected—he got some polite interest, no flat-out rejections, but not even one soft "yes." "It pretty much sucks," he summarizes. "I've given it some thought, and I don't see how we pull back our fundraising target without admitting we've failed."

Christian draws back, regarding his partner with surprise. My guess is the two of them haven't spoken as frankly without me in the room. Often, teams or couples who have worked with me for a while will wait till I'm present—whether for courage or cover, I'm never sure—before they state what's truly on their mind.

I don't know if this is too much too soon, but I do know we don't have time to waste, and if there's a team that can withstand intense honesty, this is one of them, so I decide to follow Carter's lead.

"I'm sorry," I say in agreement. "If you're expecting me to come up with a dazzling counterfactual here, I'm also sorry that I'll end up disappointing you. This is the crappiest fundraising market I've *ever* witnessed, plus you're certainly not in an enviable position with your LP and the overall performance." I pause, noting that they're both looking at me, startled. This meeting holds a record for the shortest time spent beating around the bush. I decide to make sure the clients are driving.

"Let me check in with you before I continue here. As you know, I've worked for years in pitch development and have helped raise more than a billion at this point, but I came in today as Carter's coach, not as a fundraising advisor. So, which hat would you like me to wear for this conversation?"

Carter and Christian look at each other, then Christian turns to me. "Is there a way you could do both?"

I smile and nod. "I can. And my intuition is to drop all of the supposedly expert hats and go at this with as much honesty as all of us can muster. There's no magic bullet here, but if we don't want to lie down and decide there's no possible way forward, the main thing I can think of is that we'll have to invent one. Part of why I came up with the CRATE framework was exactly for moments like these: times when we reach an impasse and have no clue which door might open, or even if there *is* a door. Having some structure—a process to follow—can give us much-needed momentum. Right now, we have to figure out what you can do, so let me tell you how I suspect *Agency* works in individuals or teams. I promise to make this the shortest and least boring lecture you've ever heard."

I stand up because I'll need the whiteboard. I don't always walk clients through the framework in "teacher" mode and I particularly try not to make it sound like a paint-by-the-numbers rubric. Still, when I work with cerebral professionals who are anxious to find a way through, I find that showing them a way to navigate calms them down, whether we actually follow the aspects as steps or just use them as signposts.

"Agency is the pinnacle of the CRATE framework, and basically the point when things come to a head. Whereas Clarity (which Carter and I discussed at our last meeting) is the beginning of the journey, and Regulation steadies you and gives you tools to withstand intensity, Agency is the point where you step into the arena. When

I give a talk on this, I usually show a frame from the *Gladiator* movie here." I draw a little stick figure with a sword and they both laugh.

"Agency has three parts: *Affordance*, *Attention*, and *Adaptation*. The path forward—which is the topic of our meeting today— is through Affordance. This is where we try to find what is both available and likely for you right now." I look up and notice that Rita is standing at the door. Tactful as always, she has waited for me to finish before walking in and interrupting. She has also overheard my words and is currently grinning from ear to ear. "I just love me some Russell Crowe," she says. "Are you *sure* you don't have any slides today?"

Rita is in her late fifties, a decade older than Carter, Christian, and me, and a veteran of Wall Street, having started her career right after the financial crisis in the early Nineties, witnessing firsthand the collapse of Bear Stearns in 2008. She is stunning and impeccably dressed, but underneath that, there's the warmth of the kind of Southerner who loves to cook delectable meals and tell stories late into the night over glasses of Mint Julep.

I shrug apologetically. "I promise to make an extra slide just for you, Rita, *especially* if you can give us a frank assessment of what's going on. What do you see as the best fundraising route for your firm, given all the conversations you guys have been having?" Her brow furrows, and she looks at me with half-serious accusation. I've put her on the spot by explicitly requesting honesty, and it's evident she's not loving what she has to say.

Rita begins by trying to lay out positives, then interrupts herself. "Oh, hell! Who am I kidding? We're all inside baseball here. Not many ways to spin this, especially in this market. I heard you talking about affordance or some such when I came in, but let me tell you, I don't think we can afford much time to linger, and if the fundraising trends continue, I don't see how we can even afford this office." She gestures vaguely at the outside buildings, and I surmise she means the location more than the digs.

We all shift uncomfortably. Hearing Rita confirm what we've been saying makes it all the more real. Still, I hew to my task, which is to help this team find a path. "I hear you," I sigh. "Not many affordances available. But one of my go-to sayings is, *Things being what they are, now what?* Noticing Affordance is about enumerating what's possible and available to us. And sometimes the first thing available is just how much the situation sucks, to quote Carter. Tension, even suckage, is not necessarily a bad thing. How we hold the tension is the important part. I don't think your situation is a matter of making adjustments or finding a better spin. I think it comes down to whether or not you're willing to make a drastic move and possibly pivot."

All three partners turn toward me—half-interested, half-alarmed.

"You said the p-word!" notes Christian, wrinkling his face in disgust.

EMBEDDED STORY: AFFORDANCE

In the late nineteenth century, Henry David Thoreau wrote in *Walden*, "Begin where you are and such as you are, without aiming mainly to become of more worth, and with kindness aforethought, go about doing good."[1] Aside from sounding inspiring, "begin where you are" is a practical dictum in both therapy and coaching, giving those in search of change some improved chances of success. Starting where you are and deciding where you'd like to be is an essential tactic for getting where you need to go.

"Carter, remember when I said that constraint was all about getting clarity through noticing all the options that are *not* available to you at a given time?"

Carter nods, raising an expectant eyebrow.

---

[1]　*Thoreau, H. D. Walden. Ticknor and Fields, 1854.*

"By the way, I totally envy people who can raise only one eyebrow at a time. That's something you can do that many others can't. Conveniently, that's exactly what an affordance is: the opposite of a constraint, an option you have at this point that others might not. So, aside from facial dexterity, what does this team have available right now that might give you a leg up?"

There's a moment of thoughtful silence, then Rita chimes in, "We all *like* each other, for one thing!"

"That's awesome and easy to see, but I'm guessing at least half of my clients would say that. What else?"

"We're great at helping our portfolio?" tries Carter.

"I hear you, but honestly, have you met any VC who doesn't claim to be exceptionally helpful? There's even that Twitter parody feed, HowCanIBeHelpful…"

For a long moment, the team is stumped. Then Christian sighs, rolls his eyes, and gets up to take the marker from my hand. "Alright, let's do this proper!"

He scrawls on the board: Market/Product/Team. "That's how we review pitches, so let's look at ourselves this way. What's going on in these?"

"Well, the market is shit," groans Carter.

"And our product is kinda meh," adds Rita.

"And we already covered that the team is great, but that's table stakes," admits Christian.

All three look at me expectantly.

I nod at them, smiling, but hold back from saying anything. Since I can't move just one eyebrow, I raise both.

Christian stares at the whiteboard for a second, then circles Product and Team in one swoopy oval.

"Hear me out: I started with these categories, and Rita said our product was uninteresting because that's what the LPs are saying right now—that our portfolio doesn't excite them enough—but we've got fifty-two investments, and you know what…?" He pauses for dramatic effect. "Every single one of those founding teams feels like they're on *our* team too. Only *two* of our companies went to zero, and in both cases, we were their first call. Dylan even called me before he told his wife."

"Exactly! And I'd wager my Sunday best I could pull up my phone and call any one of our founders, and they'd pick up by the second ring." Rita is on her feet now too, and her face is flushed. "We might not be the biggest check in, but they tell us time and again that we're the ones making the biggest difference—actually breaking bread with people and brainstorming, and hell, we just got invited to join one PortCo's offsite this past January."

"Rita, I can tell how much it matters to you that the portfolio companies feel close to you guys. Just as I can tell how true it is that the three of you like each other. I'd bet that all of this camaraderie carries over with the founders you invest in. So let me ask you this: what happens when you meet a team that doesn't click with you?"

All three foreheads furrow. The agreeableness trait in individuals or teams is quite often a constraint that's masquerading as an affordance. Everybody gets along but no one dares to rock the boat.

"You mean if none of us are willing to fight for the founders?" asks Carter. "'Cause sometimes Chris here will see something I don't. And, to tell you, Rita probably has the most tolerance—she's practically a saint!"

They all laugh. "But you mean, if *none* of us like them, or like, when we suss out that someone's dishonest or a crappy person?"

"Exactly, Carter! What happens if your next meeting tomorrow is with an AI company that's building another generative LLM, and they're going after something dicey—say generating music or gaming—and they don't care how many artists they displace or how much copyright dust they stir up... would you still invest in them?"

The three partners look at me in stunned silence.

"I... doubt it." Rita finally offers.

"I know you hadn't partnered yet at this point, but if Travis had pitched you in 2010, would you have invested in Uber?"

They look at each other, then one by one, they shake their heads no.

"Shit!" Christian finally says under his breath. "*This* might be why we're not top quartile."

We take a beat as I let his words hang in the room.

EMBODIED STANCE: ATTENTION

What appears to be an affordance can sometimes turn out to be a constraint—and vice versa. They can even change roles or transform functions from one to the other. A good way to check is to ask yourself: "If I keep doing what I've been doing, am I likely to end up where I'd like to be going?" If the answer is *yes*, the situation is affording you your objective. If it's a *no*, it is evidently a constraint.

In the case of Carter and team, their actions (sifting out predatory founders) served the unstated goal of building a harmonious working environment, but functioned in direct opposition to their *stated* goal of generating alpha-level returns. It was time to focus our attention here. The embodied stance of Agency is all about activating your *Attention*. Not only is Attention the most participatory part of agency, but it might well be the only (or at least primary) portion of conscious experience that we have any real control over. Turning your attention toward something means deciding that it is the most salient part of the information you are processing and most worth your energy expenditure. I think of it as shining a spotlight on the mental model that is most crucial to your objective and then giving it your full engagement. In this case, the team's attention naturally oriented to the unexpected discrepancy, so I did not have to emphasize it further. In situations when the client does not intuitively see what might be important, nudging them toward the greatest contradiction or the most emotionally charged topic usually offers plenty of fodder for our attention.

The silence hangs heavily in the conference room as the outside light turns to dusk. I respect that none of the participants are trying to retcon the conversation or claim they can somehow have their cake and eat it too. Often, when an objective pushes individuals to behave in ways they find distasteful, they will concoct means of ignoring or pretending this reality away. I suspect this is how many blind spots occur, and how Carter's team has gotten to this point. I decide to start here.

"I try not to have favorites, but you guys are seriously some of the most decent humans I've ever met in finance."

"Yeah, but nice guys finish last, right?" Christian sighs bitterly.

I tilt my head and regard him with warm amusement. "You know, there are multiple ways to win," I note. "Right now, I'd like us to focus our attention on the discrepancy we've surfaced. You've heard the saying, *You are what you do*, but I'd like to suggest that you are *what you attend to*. Where the focal point of your attention (or information processing) goes is the node where you can most shift the script you're playing out. We don't have to decide this right now, but I strongly encourage you guys to rank what you're prioritizing here: the integrity of humans you invest in, the impact they create, or the returns you generate. These won't always coincide, and the more you pretend that they're the same, the further you will drift from achieving one (or even all three) of these objectives."

Carter nods and props his elbows on the conference table, holding his temples. "I get that you're right." He sighs. "Last time, we were talking about my dad and how he lost that series pilot, and it devastated him. Thing is, he probably told himself and Mom that supporting us was the most important thing, so he changed jobs, and we moved, but—honestly—I think working on that show may have been what mattered most to him, both personally and creatively. He refused to admit that, and so he's never really made it back from that strike." Carter shakes his head and holds the bridge of his nose. I watch as Christian moves back from the whiteboard to rest a hand on his partner's shoulder.

"OK, you guys!" Rita's voice snaps us back, melodious yet decisive. "No one says we gotta sell our dreams down the river here. What did we say when we started this? We'll keep going as long as it's fun, right?... So? Are we having fun?"

The guys look at her, then at me, and shrug.

"I mean... yeah... except for fundraising, right?" offers Carter.

"Well, we love doing this and working with each other, and we haven't lost people's money. We just haven't made them as much as they've wanted," adds Christian. "And I'd say we're pretty decent at what we do—we just don't have product-market fit when it comes to where institutions want to invest right now."

All three of them are nodding. I decide it's time to chime in.

"Let me ask you another question: if you had to sacrifice the caliber of your portfolio founders or the way you all relate to each other, would this"—I gesture at the three of them—"still be fun?" They immediately shake their heads, so I continue.

"When Carter first came in, I was staring at the Chrysler Building out there, thinking about the mad race in 1929 when it was first being built—how they competed with 40 Wall Street for who would be the tallest building, and the obsessiveness that all the guys involved put into outmaneuvering each other." I walk over to the window. "And the biggest irony is that even though Chrysler and Van Allen came up with the idea of the spire and won, nobody actually noticed until many weeks later. Do you know why?"

They shake their heads again, and Carter looks at me, puzzled.

"Because the spire went up on October 23rd, 1929, and then the next day was October 24th—also known as Black Thursday. That was the day the stock market crashed and sent the economy into freefall, precipitating The Great Depression. Chrysler and his architect were on top of the world—literally—and then the bottom fell out from under them."

"Jeez Louise!" says Rita.

"What's that Lennon saying?" Christian laughs, "'Life's what happens while you're busy making other plans?'"

I nod. "My point here is, none of us know what will happen with the market, or the whole world for that matter. You can figure out how to please the next LP today, but that won't guarantee that whatever you do will be what they'll want tomorrow. If you're optimizing for maximum fundraising and returns, be clear about that and we'll have to sacrifice some of the other choices. If what you want is a certain type of portfolio founder, then be clear on *that* and let's figure out who out there wants to fund *that* vision!"

"OK, so are you saying we change our pitch and lead with how decent our founders are?" Christian snickers. "'Cause I don't think that's going to play too well..."

"We'll be the laughing stock of the Street," Rita says. "I can just hear the verdict: they couldn't hack it, so they turned *impact*." She spits out the last word.

"Right! Or that ridiculous euphemism—*double bottom line*!" Christian and Rita are both laughing now. Carter smiles too, but I see sadness in his eyes.

"Hang on! Allow me to orient us for a moment," I offer. "I'm not suggesting you pitch the firm as anything that feels disingenuous or laughable. That said, I'd like us to attend to one more discrepancy I'm seeing, which might well hold the unlock for your predicament."

I have everyone's full attention now and worry I may have oversold the weight of the potential revelation. The thing is, I'm realizing that I haven't seen the team disagree on anything over an hour-plus of weighty conversation. I have seen their care for each other, a fair amount of self-congratulatory assertions, and an overall narrative that nothing of what's happening is their doing: it is not their fault that the market is hard, or that LPs don't see their value. It's them against the world, which tends to build camaraderie and feel really good, but it also keeps the truly new options from becoming visible.

"When you brainstorm with founders—whether it's before or after committing to an investment—do you all tend to get along similarly to the way this conversation has been going?" I ask. They look at each other, then shrug and nod.

"I figured. And when you're debating investment decisions, can you think of a time when one of you seriously disagreed with the others?"

They think for a moment, then Christian says, "Not really. There've probably been times when it starts that way, but we quickly see each other's point of view."

"I figured that too. So now I'm going to tell you what I think is part of the obstacle you're encountering: you prioritize harmony and accord over truth."

They look at me startled.

"Wait, what?!" Rita is up from her seat again and she seems ever so slightly angry with me.

EXTENDED SELF: ADAPTATION

"I fell in it too," I admit. "Everyone here gets along so well that I wanted to find a copacetic path forward where we could all keep nodding or shaking our heads in unison, and we could all agree on what was right and what was wrong. But I can tell you, in advertising and in any creative profession, design by committee is the kiss of death: if you wait for everyone to agree what the message should say or what font to use, it will be the blandest, most inoffensive ad you can imagine, which also makes it the most boring and least memorable.

"And that's the thing about investment decisions too: if you're optimizing for agreement, you are missing the special things that each of you can see and the others can't. You are robbing this firm of the biggest advantage that a smart team of divergent opinions can afford by turning yourselves into a homogenous group."

No one says a word, so I continue. "My guess is that you are also unconsciously selecting for teams like yours: founders who are reasonable and agreeable and optimize for group harmony. But those are not usually the big disruptors..."

"...or the big winners." Christian finishes my sentence.

"So, are you saying we start investing in assholes?" asks Rita.

"I'm saying it's a false dichotomy," I state calmly. "I suspect that if you stop optimizing for agreement, you will find that you are just different enough—that your views of the world and of humans and what makes them successful are divergent enough—that one person's asshole will be another person's ornery genius. I mean, think of Tony Stark: he wasn't everyone's cup of tea...."

We all laugh.

"Yeah, and he built Ultron and cost *how* many lives?" Carter perks up, and I note internally that this is exactly why we became friends in the first place.

"Didn't he also—" Rita begins, but Christian interrupts.

"Hey, no spoilers!"

Everyone is laughing now and the energy in the room shifts as I watch the team get a first glimpse of a path forward. It's only the beginning, but I can sense that they're becoming clearer on what they are and are not willing to shift. I stress that I am not suggesting that they invest in unscrupulous founders or that they compromise their sense of integrity. I suspect—but don't tell them—that if one were to place them on a continuum of tolerance, Carter would be the closest to an impact investor and Rita would more likely orient toward profit over humanitarian concerns. If they can learn to tolerate each other's genuine disagreement, I suspect the investment choices this team will make will become far more competitive. This is the point where *Adaptation* picks up the result from the *Convergence* aspect of Clarity and starts experimenting—where Clarity and Agency merge and begin to work their magic.

So, how does Adaptation work, and how do I teach it to an individual or team in just one session? I can't telepathically beam the experience of willful experimentation into their heads, but I can point at it and also point out that it is a process rather than a place of arrival. In recognizing that they were no longer obligated to agree with one another, that this was in fact keeping them from where they wanted to go, I gave permission to Carter and his partners to show up more authentically, and to ask themselves whether they genuinely agreed with an opinion or were just going along to get along.

"This last bit is going to continue for a while," I tell the team. "It's like learning a new dance together, and there will be an inevitable stepping on toes. But I called this last aspect of Agency *Adaptation* because it is a work of iteration: a pragmatic acceptance of what is, together with an artful authorship of what could be."

"So the big revelation is that the way to get agency means we have to accept things?" Christian's voice is warm, but I can tell he's a little exasperated. He leans forward, his brow furrowed. "You're basically saying we need to just accept things as they are. That doesn't sound like much of a strategy."

I shake my head, smiling. "Not exactly. Adaptation isn't about resignation or passivity. It's about facing reality clearly, so that you can make more informed, intentional choices about how to respond. It doesn't mean agreement or acquiescence. Instead, Adaptation picks up the convergent ideas you get in Clarity and then integrates the ones that work while also discarding the ones that don't. Disagreement is an important part of that."

Rita nods slowly, a glimmer of understanding in her eyes. "Kind of like how you have to accept the materials you've been given and discard the ones you don't need, before you can create something new from them."

"Exactly," I affirm. "Acceptance and refusal merge as parts of Adaptation. This is the first step in authoring a different story."

I'm always careful when using the word 'acceptance' with individuals in startup land or finance; to them it usually translates as 'capitulation', then bounces right off. Yet the reality is that Adaptation—both in real life and as an aspect of Agency—requires that we give ourselves permission to see past our own defenses, so that we can begin to author something new that can be born on the basis of what currently is. In that, there is inevitable tension: you have to both accept what is present *and* be willing to push past it.

I can see the wheels starting to turn in Carter's mind.

"What if..." he begins, "...what if we used our remaining Fund II capital to place some smaller, more targeted bets on teams that are tackling really audacious problems; the kinds of founders who might ruffle some feathers, but who have the vision and drive to create something truly game-changing?"

Christian jumps in, his eyes widening. "We could frame it as an exploratory thesis—a way to expand our reach and learn about new markets—without the pressure of a traditional fund cycle."

"And we could use our diligence process to get a deeper read on team dynamics," Rita adds, "to make sure we're backing founders who can handle the heat and stay focused on execution, even if their personalities are a bit more...intense."

I sit back, watching the energy and ideas start to flow, as the team begins to embrace a more adaptive, experimental approach to the challenges and opportunities before them. We are way over time now, though thankfully this is everyone's last meeting. By the time I begin the walk back to catch my train, Carter's firm has a plan of iteration and, more importantly, a new way to walk it. I stop before entering Grand Central and finally snap that picture. The Chrysler Building seems tiny, surrounded by larger skyscrapers, yet its chrome roof sparkles brightest in the evening sky, all Art Deco and one of a kind.

AGENCY: STEPPING INTO CHANGE

Agency comes with a lot of responsibility. Not just the obvious weight of our actions—which being an agent in the arena entails—but the responsibility to acknowledge and accept what is present in and around us as truthfully and authentically as we can. This is why it's a good idea to go through Clarity and Regulation first: we need to prepare ourselves to see how the situation we say we don't want is somehow already serving us, whether we're eager to admit this or not.

At the heart of the CRATE framework, Agency emerges as the pivotal dimension where insight and understanding transform into purposeful, creative action. It's the dimension where we claim our power to shape our lives and our world, not by controlling every circumstance, but by authoring our response to the ever-changing tides of challenge and opportunity.

Affordance is about recognizing the possibilities and pathways available to us in any given situation. It's the challenge of reading the horizon with clear eyes, and attuning to the invitations and opportunities that are present, even amidst previously established constraints. When we cultivate a keen awareness of affordance, we begin to see the world as a field of potential, alive with open space wherein we can learn, grow, and create. In the case of Carter's team, their camaraderie and the rapport they clearly had with each other and their portfolio founders was an affordance from which they could grow and experiment, without scrapping the chemistry that helped them survive for this long.

Attention, in turn, is the power to direct our focus toward what matters most. In a world of endless distractions and competing demands, the quality of our attention determines the quality of our choices and actions. As the heartbreakingly earnest philosopher Simone Weil noted, "Attention is the rarest and purest form of generosity." By training our attention through practices of mindfulness, discernment, and intention-setting, we harness the full power of our mind and point it in service of our deepest aspirations.

I think of Attention as the magnifying glass that focuses the vast light of all possible information available to us. We filter and focus attention to light the fire of action, concentrating on what we most need to ignite. When individuals and teams are scattered, when their output seems haphazard despite their frantic activity, this is usually the piece that is missing. By focusing Carter, Christian, and Rita's attention on how they evaluated investments and whether or not that was serving them in the long run, I attempted to check whether the targets they were aiming for were actually the ones they were going hit.

Adaptation, then, is the culmination of Affordance and Attention—the capacity to weave the threads of possibility into a new tapestry of meaningfulness. Adaptation requires courage to experiment while trusting our intuition, so we may create something new and valuable from the raw materials of our happenstance. When we approach our challenges with the spirit of an artist, we open ourselves to surprising insights and solutions. In Carter's example, Adaptation required the team to begin iterating their way toward more disagreement and less obvious investment choices. It also meant accepting that what the market rewarded right now were riskier, less feel-good choices and toeing the line to discover whether the firm's partners have the stomach to make them.

The aspects of Agency invite us into experimentation. They remind us that, even in the face of uncertainty, we have the power to shape our story, choose our stance, and become the co-authors of our fortune.

Claiming our Agency is not always easy or comfortable. As Carter and his team discovered, it often requires facing hard truths, reckoning with the less visible sides of our patterns and personas, and making tough tradeoffs between competing values and priorities. It demands that we take responsibility for our choices and their consequences, then embrace the vulnerability of charting a new course.

As we build our capacity for Agency, we discover a profound sense of resilience and inherent creativity. We find that we're no longer at the mercy of external circumstances or internal reactivity, and that we become able to meet change with openness and courage. Agency is not about achieving perfect control or certainty, but about engaging skillfully in the unfolding mystery of our lives. It's about welcoming both the affordances and constraints of each situation, attuning our attention to the invitations that reality presents us, and, as Rita put it, creating something worthwhile from the materials at hand.

As we explore the last two dimensions of the CRATE framework, we'll discover how Agency sets us up for the deeper efforts entailed within Trust and Energy, laying the groundwork for personal and collective transformation. We'll see that the powers of affordance, attention, and adaptation rest at the heart of what it means to be human—and how, by stepping into the arena with these powers in hand, we activate a future worthy of our aspirations.

8

BUILDING TRUST

Temporality, Transformation, & Translucency

"The name of the story will be Time,
But you must not pronounce its name."
— Robert Penn Warren

Ella's appointment is during my bedtime. Not that I actually go to sleep at 8 pm on a Tuesday, but this is the time when tasks are usually finished—when I curl up under a blanket, ready to read or write or cuddle up with family. Mornings and evenings are the bookends to my conscious experience. Over time, they set the underlying hum to one's life, so I've learned to treat them with reverence, generally ignoring texts unless there's an emergency and definitely not scheduling client calls unless there's an even bigger emergency. (Unless the ghosts in my machine decide that a late session would be no problem three weeks hence, and then "three weeks hence" becomes "tonight.")

At some point in what seems like the distant past, Ella and I settled on this unorthodox hour because she begged me to meet with both her and Ben, and it became somehow impossible to find a spot on his calendar before sundown.

"It's really important that you look him in the eyes," she said. "You know, as a professional—I need to know if he's lying to me."

I tried to explain that being a coach doesn't make me a professional lie detector, but she persisted and I acquiesced, so now here I am, moving desk plants out of the way to add an extra lamp and set a bright, welcoming ambiance for what I'm hoping against hope will be an easy conversation. As soon as Ella joins the Zoom call, however, that hope evaporates like steam. I take a sip of my lavender tea, anchoring myself in its aroma while the screen across from me fills with two well-manicured hands holding tissues, maneuvering the laptop camera back and forth.

"Can you see me OK?" Ella asks, her voice anxious and breathless.

"I can see your hands," I say, bemused. "Take your time! I want you to be comfortable."

When she pulls back, I study her face, which looks miles away from any comfort. Her eyes are bloodshot, though she's wearing fresh eyeliner, neatly applied. Ella fusses with her screen some more, then eventually settles in and offers an obligatory smile that looks more like a tense baring of teeth.

"Oh, hey! I... I'm sorry. Thanks for taking this call so late. I...." she cranes her neck off camera, and I'm guessing she's looking for her boyfriend and co-founder.

"Is Ben running late?" I inquire cheerfully.

"He..." She cranes her neck again, this time pulling half her torso out of the chair. "He's here. He said he would be right here, but...Ben!!" Her voice rises sharp and loud, piercing my eardrums. "Bennn!! Are you coming?!" I turn down the volume and consider switching away from using earbuds. There's some muffled back and forth, then Ella mutes herself, gets up, and walks off-camera. I wait patiently.

The Soho loft Ella and Ben occupy in Manhattan spreads openly before her laptop. I normally see the back of her home office where she takes work calls, so I study this living room with curiosity. It is vast—either half or an entire floor, I can't fully see—with arched windows on one side and prewar moldings framing the ceiling. There are several couches with clean Scandinavian lines and velvet upholstery—one in dark turquoise, one brownish camel. Above them are two framed art pieces, each lit intentionally. There is a Richard Prince, a perfect rendering of an Agatha Christie pulp cover, "The Mystery of the Blue Train." It depicts a redhead with her head thrown back, struggling to free herself from a rope wrapped around her neck. Behind her, floating gloved hands pull the ends—either murderous, puppeteering, or both. As with much of Prince's art, there's a cheerful violence to the painting. Across from it is an even bolder piece: a Damien Hirst skull, a large purple and gold canvas that looks like the inverse of a photograph. It is missing several teeth, and its eye sockets stare at me, confoundingly friendly yet ominous.

Eventually, Ella and Ben return to the screen. Ben is holding a large bowl in one hand and chopsticks in the other, sneaking noodles into his mouth even as he walks.

"Really sorry!" Ella begins, exasperated. "We're ready now."

She gestures toward Ben, then realizes he hasn't taken the chair she prepared next to hers. Instead, he is half-sitting on the arm of the camel sofa, oriented toward the screen, yet six feet behind.

"What the f...." she stops herself and holds her mouth for a moment, then tries again. "Ben, aren't you going to join us?"

"I'm eating!" Ben waves the chopsticks, then rolls his eyes—possibly at me, though I can't fully tell, given the distance. "I haven't had a bite since this morning. Do you want me to starve here?!" He's acting annoyed but also grinning. His eyes sparkle with the mischievous air of a boy who just snuck in a frog at the dinner table. Ella seems ready to cry, so I attempt to defuse the situation.

"Given the timing of this conversation, I think I can make an exception." I smile calmly. "Usually, I'm not a big fan of splitting our attention between food and the work at hand, but life happens, and I certainly don't want Ben to associate me with hunger pangs." Ben and I laugh while Ella purses her lips, incensed.

Coaching over Zoom certainly has its opportunities and drawbacks (or constraints and affordances, as we can begin to frame them). On the one hand, I usually don't do my best work without being able to see the full body of the person I'm coaching—how they carry themselves as they walk into a room, or the manner in which they hang or throw their coat. On the other, videoconferencing feels akin to a house call, especially when people don't blur their background. I can learn a lot from the environment they inhabit (even if it's a coffee shop they've chosen), and I can study the micromovements of their face more closely, in a manner that would be either difficult or creepy in person.

As the current scene unfolds, I realize how glad I am that I made an exception to do this evening session. An at-home dynamic that would usually be invisible in a work setting opens the window into Ella and Ben's relationship, and tells me more in five minutes than I have learned from dozens of sessions alone with Ella.

First, there's a lot of honest but distorted attachment between the young couple before me. They love each other, or at least they relate to one another as each other's mate with all the possessiveness and manipulation that can entail. My psychology mentor, David Pezenik, liked to say that individuals often wear their identity as if on a t-shirt and that if we pay close attention, we can read what each t-shirt says. In this case, I don't need to see Ben's Alexander McQueen skull t-shirt to know it reads "I am trouble." Nor does the understated burgundy top Ella is wearing camouflage her invisible t-shirt that reads "I'm in trouble."

As often happens, they have matched themselves perfectly. Whatever they are enacting right now carries the ghosts of thousands of past moments that taught them early on what it means to be in a relationship with another. As you may remember from our discussion of Attachment Theory in Chapter 2, each of us forms early predictions about how the most important humans in our lives will treat us, and we then build coping strategies for the pain we expect them to inflict on us. You don't need to have studied Bowlby and Ainsworth's theories to immediately notice that everything about Ella's stance toward her partner was wrapped up in anxiety, while much of Ben's cool-guy posturing served as a useful shield of avoidance.

Second, the distance between Ben and Ella feels like a character of its own. I don't just mean the distance between the chair and the sofa, but the light years that separate the reality that Ben inhabits from Ella's. His body is languid and cheetah-like, and he moves through space like a well-fed predator. Whether this is due to the Connecticut upbringing that Ella envies, or whatever boarding school taught him, I would wager that Ben has never really felt in danger, even as he wreaked incessant mischief. Conversely, Ella grew up feeling that her place in the world was always precarious. By the time she went to Pratt, her talent had become evident to the adults around her, yet she had to work doubly hard to get noticed, and it was as if the world had intentionally turned a blind eye to her existence. The primary distance between them is that one person believes that doors always open, while the other knows viscerally how it feels when they close.

Both of these factors run deep enough to distort their relationship, but I intuit there's something else on an even less conscious level, so I decide to explore.

"Let's give Ben a moment to finish his takeout," I continue. "I'm curious, Ella, what is running through your head right now?"

She looks at me confused, so I gently direct her. "Can you take a deep breath down to your belly button and just listen while you exhale slowly? Just let me know what it is that you can feel or hear inside you."

Ella looks like a deer in headlights. She really doesn't want to go inward right now, yet she's also not the type to openly say "no," so after a brief pause, she relents and breathes in. I watch the pain hit her before the inhale is finished. Her jaw clenches, and her eyes squeeze into a wince. She tries to push it away, her head moving into a barely perceptible shake.

"Take your time, Ella. You're safe here."

As soon as she registers my voice, the tears spill over. I often suspect that the reason we refuse to be kind to ourselves is that such tenderness would give us the safety and permission to actually feel what is happening inside of us. I can't even count the times I have said to a client or a loved one that it was OK to feel and then watched the floodgates open. I have also noticed how hard it is to allow my husband to hold me at those times when I feel most vulnerable. It's as if life's hardship flays our skin, and we walk through the world raw and exposed, willing ourselves to callus, fearful that if we took momentary shelter, we would betray ourselves and have to acknowledge how devastating it feels to have a wound seeping inside us.

Ella attempts to dismiss her tears, then when she fails, her anger jumps in to protect her.

"I can't DO this anymore!" she almost screams. "I've had it with this bullshit!"

Behind her, Ben is wide-eyed, noodles frozen mid-air, uncertain of what just transpired yet caring enough to assume it is somehow his fault. I give Ella a moment to collect herself but don't push her further. Instead, I address Ben directly.

"You might want to put those chopsticks down," I say with a slight smile. Part of my objective today is to establish rapport with Ben without making Ella feel othered. She and I have built trust over the many sessions when I've shown her that every part of her is welcomed in the mental space we've created together. Ben, on the other hand, has done everything in his power not to be here. He doesn't trust me yet, and I'm not sure he fully trusts Ella, especially in this context. Given that she asked me to be her lie detector, the lack of trust appears to be mutual. Based on everything I've learned from working with highly intelligent and highly insecure individuals over the years, I would bet that much of this stems from the fact that Ben and Ella don't trust *themselves* either.

EMBEDDED STORY: TEMPORALITY

Hang on a moment, you might be thinking. *You just told me how Ben walks through the world as if he owns it. I get that Ella is insecure, but why would Ben not trust himself? Aren't guys like him certain they're the cat's meow?* The deeply ironic thing about trust is that it is impossible to get it by trying to convince ourselves that we have it. Ben and many other high-performing, high-status individuals constantly test others and their environments in an effort to prove to themselves that they truly are at the top of the proverbial food chain. The catch is that if they need to prove it this often (or at all), it's because somewhere in their subconscious (meaning, their limbic system's modeling of the world) they don't believe this to be a hundred percent true.

My suspicion is that unless a child learns how to be securely attached to their caregivers, they have a difficult time building a secure attachment to their sense of self as it evolves throughout the years. This is because our sense of self grows out of our relational interactions with the world. We figure out if we are worthy by whether or not our caregivers and peers treat us as such, and *also* by whether their response to us matches the reality we observe. Ella's parents treated her as secondary to their problems, so she learned that she was unimportant. While she has achieved a lot in her life already—in an effort to move as far from her experience of childhood as possible—she is still calibrating for her importance in others' eyes (in this case, mine and Ben's) and thereby preventing herself from establishing a sense of inner trust and worth. Ben, on the other hand, likely had much doting, or at least permissiveness. From what Ella has told me, his mother treated him and his two brothers as golden boys and heirs to a great empire. Since there is no actual empire to speak of in this case, Ben likely understood (on a subconscious level) that the worth bestowed on him was undeserved; he wants to believe he's all that, but I suspect that somewhere within, he is not so sure. The result is that he keeps Ella (and, by proxy, me) at arm's length. It is always easier to seem cooler at a distance, so many humans keep others and themselves far from their innards precisely for this reason.

Trust is always relational. It hinges not only on external relationships but also on how close we feel to parts of ourselves. Unfortunately, lack of trust has a very Catch-22 nature, which makes it difficult to find a foothold. Here, too, I've learned to grab onto a version of "begin where you are," which in this case means beginning where you are in time.

Temporality is the first aspect of the Trust dimension of CRATE, and it is just a fancy way of saying that time changes everything, both in the sense that we change over time but also (often more importantly) that the ghosts of our past, which we carry through time, have the power to distort everything that occurs in the present.

Ella lives just six blocks from the Chinatown studio where she grew up, and also a world apart. More than a decade has passed, and she has come a long way, in terms of career, finances, access, and even prestige. Yet at each moment, she behaves as if she's only one slip away from being alone in a tiny tenement apartment, or worse.

"It's OK to be angry," I tell her. "You've been through a lot and things keep not working out quite as planned. That will get to anyone."

She nods and reaches for the crumpled tissues from the beginning of our call. I'm guessing they are doing double duty tonight, both as absorbent and distraction. I give her some time, then continue my focus on Ben.

"Ben, do you have any idea why Ella is upset right now?"

He starts to lift his arms in a giant shrug, but I cut him off. "I can see you're a smart guy. How about taking a guess?"

The flattery works. I watch him look to the side and consider the situation. Then I see him shift and look up at the ceiling. I'm guessing he's not liking the answer that just presented. His head is trying to physically move away from the feelings in his body, so he stands up, taking a much stronger, better-defended stance. I won't be getting in just yet, so I switch again.

"Ella, if your tears could speak, what would they say?"

She thinks for a moment, then answers very clearly.

"They would say that I'm tired...*exhausted*...and I've had it with being taken for granted! Also, every time I ask Ben for something, he acts like it's the biggest imposition. Like he's got so many more important things to worry about than being here and having a real conversation about our relationship and our startup and our *future*!"

"How am I not wanting to have a real conversation?!" Ben steps forward. "Almost every day, you lay into me, either during work or in the evening when you're tired and holding a glass of wine. I put up with it, I try to understand, but this is completely idiotic! It's like I can never do anything right."

Ella starts sobbing again as soon as Ben raises his voice. She has covered her face, and her shoulders are closed in. Her response is far more intense than the situation that provoked it, so it's likely she's reacting to a lot more than the present moment.

As you might notice, I am not explicitly referring to the CRATE framework at any point in these conversations. That is because the situation is already tense, and bringing in any abstractions will provide an escape hatch that would only be detrimental. Instead, there are occasions when I can work to build trust with two partners (whether a romantic couple or co-founders) by asking each of them to relate their perception of what is going on right at that moment (back to *Temporality*), thereby creating a container in which they can fully hear each other's narratives. Seeing one another be vulnerable prompts them to begin opening up, not just to me but to each other.

Ella carries a truckload of pain, which Ben might be (and likely is) making worse, but it would be unfair to put all of the responsibility on him. The fact that he's shown up tonight and hasn't yet made any movement to storm off tells me that he cares and that he is doing his best—insufficient as it may be—to be present for Ella.

In my Relational Therapy training, the psychologist and author Terry Real (whom I've mentioned before, and from whom I also learned the question "If these tears could speak…") taught us to always look for where the feet are pointing. He said it didn't matter how much someone says they are committed to their relationship—if their shoulders or feet are pointed away from their partner while in conversation, chances are they are looking for a way out.

Ben has moved *closer* since Ella started crying. Yes, his shoulders are squared, and he is in "defensive guy" mode, but he has physically moved toward, not away from the emotion that is discomforting him. I need to help him show Ella that he cares.

EMBODIED STANCE: TRANSFORMATION

Seeing the path to change becomes possible once you understand the foundation of our human system. We make unconscious predictions that attempt to steer us toward homeostasis. These predictions are often orthogonal to our desires. We then become overwhelmed, stuck at the crossroads between conscious and unconscious choices. To get ourselves unstuck, we have to either teach our limbic system how to make new predictions or stop fighting the ones we have with our thoughts and actions. As usual, the actual path forward requires a bit of both.

The key part of this thesis is that our unconscious predictions are doing their absolute best to steer us toward homeostasis. Ella's anxious attachment (or relational stance) is a set of behaviors all doing their darnedest to ensure she is not rejected. To an anxiously attached person, the least homeostatic thing is to be rejected and cast out. This is why she has never set clear boundaries with me—said outright when she doesn't want to discuss something—and instead will be late for sessions or suddenly need to depart for an important meeting, or forget specific objectives we have set. My guess is that she's doing the same with Ben; she likely does not set boundaries with him but tries to steer him (consciously or unconsciously) toward getting what she wants without outright stating it and risking being rejected.

Ben's avoidant stance makes it likely that he finds Ella least tolerable when she appears weak or manipulative. His homeostatic impulse is to never be found wanting, so he is likely oblivious to any requests that are not stated clearly and undeniably. He lashed out just now because Ella's emotional outburst likely registered as opaque to him, and so he wanted to metaphorically shake her and have her stop doing what, in his view, is an irrational overreaction. Avoidant individuals often create precarious paper castles wherein everything makes sense as long as they can keep every person or counterfactual at a distance[1].

"Ben," I try again, "I heard you say this situation is idiotic. Can you tell me more about why you chose that word?"

His arms shoot up in exasperation again. "Because it's totally ridiculous, that's why! I seriously can't get anything right with her. Whatever I try comes out sideways or gets misinterpreted, and I end up looking like a total moron."

---

[1]   *In both the anxious and avoidant patterns, I speak from first-hand experience. As a human who had fearful-avoidant tendencies, I have had to discern (and hopefully reconfigure) the "best" of both sides, which gives me visceral empathy for how each pattern is doing its best to keep us alive.*

"Hang on a second! Let's be real here. Do you see how being late for this call may have caused Ella to feel exasperated?"

His arms flail again in outrage.

"Exasperated?! She just sprang this on me when I walked in tonight. I had totally forgotten we had some weird coaching call at eight o'clock in the evening. Who does that? I thought I was coming home to chill and eat, and now I have to deal with this bullshit!"

I watch Ella's face crumple as he speaks and decide to follow a hunch.

"It must be very difficult to feel like you can't get things right," I agree. "Do you ever lash out at Ella about this?"

Ben looks at me startled, then confusion sets in. "What do you mean 'lash out'?"

"Do you ever call her a moron or an idiot?"

His confusion deepens, then turns to horror.

"No!! Good god, why would I? Did she tell you that?! I mean...I am...*I* feel like an idiot, and this whole thing makes me want to punch a wall, but I would never call Ella names!"

I see Ella look up, turning partially toward him.

"But that's how you make me *feel*. Whether or not you say the word, you're making me feel like a stupid moron right now!"

More horror on Ben's face. He is now struggling between genuine worry not to upset his partner, and the self-defensive posture of not wanting to be in the wrong or get overly involved with her intensity. There's also likely a part in him that's horrified of his image being tarnished. The two of them are surrounded by funhouse mirrors of emotional distortion, each seeing their worst fears as apparitions in the other. It is my job to hold the unwarped mirror and bring some reality back in.

"OK, you guys," I sigh, taking off my glasses and pretending to clean them for a moment. I'm intentionally stretching out time so they can both jointly experience vague confusion and wonder what I'm about to say next. Getting people to be in curiosity or laughter together is an effective trick of shifting them into a joint stance. If neither of those works, even making them mad at me would still be a possible path toward helping them unite.

The curiosity nudge works. Ben is now next to Ella and he sits on the empty chair, not because he wants to, but because he wouldn't be able to clearly see the screen otherwise.

"Let me tell you what I'm seeing," I begin slowly. "I'm watching the two of you speak past each other as if you were in different rooms. I also observe the rawness of Ella's emotion and I'm reminded of the way that time can seem to collapse in on itself in moments of vulnerability. The past bleeds into the present, old wounds become reopened, and we find ourselves reacting not just to what is happening right now but to all the accumulated moments of pain we've experienced before."

Ella hides her face in her hands again.

"Can either of you tell me whether you discussed the timing of this coaching session in any concrete manner? Ella, when you were looking for a time on Ben's calendar, did you actually consult him about it? And Ben, it sounds like you heard at least in passing that we were speaking tonight. Did you note that something like this could be important to Ella, or did you just brush it off?"

They both sit in sheepish silence. Then, eventually, Ben speaks quietly.

"I think she told me. But...yeah. I mostly just kinda ignored it."

"Does that happen often? Like, when Ella asked that you go over your startup's margin calculations with her—did that register as something important, or did you brush that off also?"

I see anger flash on his face and also worry. There is definite concern about his reputation and about what Ella may have told me in regard to this topic.

"I don't understand why she doesn't just trust me with the P&L calculations! I have a friggin' MBA and have built financials a gazillion times. I don't understand what is so complicated about all this and why I have to defend my work!"

His voice trails off, and I let him sit for another few beats before answering.

"I wasn't there, so I don't know if Ella said that she doesn't trust you or that you had to defend your work," I state calmly. "But I do know how it can feel to have our work questioned. I've been there. Especially when writing investment memos and also right at the beginning when I was starting CRATE, and everyone looked at me to have a business plan figured out and I didn't even know *what* we were really building." I take a breath and then continue more ponderously. "I can tell you, though, the less sure I was of what I was doing, the more incensed I became by other people's questions about it. There's something pretty natural in feeling uncomfortable when we know we aren't completely sure. Like, if I told you right now that I thought you had weird blue hair, would you get mad at me?"

Ben looks at me quizzically, not sure what he should answer, then shakes his head.

"Right, because you know for pretty certain that your hair isn't actually blue and that if I'm insisting that it is, there's probably something wrong with my vision. Correct?"

He nods.

"But if I ask you whether you're certain if your margin calculations are accurate, MBA or not, given how early your production lines are I am guessing you can't be *that* certain, or you'd be bullshitting me...or yourself."

Ben leans back in the chair and looks off to the side. I'm guessing he doesn't like what he's feeling, but he's not fighting it as hard. I switch over.

"Ella, I'm curious. When Ben got upset about the margin calculations, did you guys try to work on them together, or did you keep asking him more questions?"

She shifts defensively, and I can see tension and even annoyance on her face.

"He always treats me like I'm dumb!" Ella explodes. "Like his amazing Harvard degrees mean that he is always perfect, and I'm just some ditz who can't possibly understand numbers."

"What the hell are you talking about?" Ben's voice is frustrated and loud and I observe him try to rein in his temper, knowing that I'm watching. "You asked me ten times if I was sure the calculations were right, and I kept telling you that I *thought* that they were but that we have no way of knowing for sure until we run several batches of the knits and actually sell some. How on earth am I supposed to know customer acquisition costs before we've sold any product to actual customers?!"

"OK, but you were assuming numbers that were way too favorable and Jason said it looked fishy!"

"Jason is an investor. *Of course* he's gonna push back. I thought you wanted to fundraise?! How the fuck are we supposed to fundraise with weak numbers?"

Ella tries to answer, but her anger hits an internal wall and turns to tears. Her sobs seem frustrated, forlorn, almost desolate. I watch Ben's torso soften, then regret moves across his face. He leans in and puts an arm around her.

"Thank you, Ben, for doing that," I say gently. "It's a profound act of courage to be able to stay present with intense feelings, to resist the pull to shut down or lash out, and to instead turn towards a loved one's experience with openness and care."

He looks at me quizzically. His eyes are glistening, and I see an opening.

"Can you tell me what prompted you to comfort Ella just now?"

There's a long pause.

"She's in pain." His voice is hoarse. "I don't want her to be in pain."

"Why is that?" I ask very softly.

"She...deserves better." I think he wants to say more, but his voice wavers, and he stops there.

"You are right." I nod. "Both Ella and you deserve a better way to relate to one another. I'm watching it happen right now." I turn to my left. "Ella, I see how difficult it is for you to trust—either Ben or yourself. But I also see that you want to get there. And Ben, I am watching you override your own defensiveness and try to earn Ella's trust, even if parts of you think some of it is unnecessary. In doing things even *a little* differently, we each start to create a new relationship, not just with ourselves and each other, but with time. You are doing this right now, and the landscape of what is possible between you becomes wider. The two of you don't have to stay at the mercy of your conditioning. You can help one another make new choices and, by doing that, begin to heal together."

I invite Ella to take a few more breaths, to feel the ground beneath her feet and the sensation of the air on her skin. I ask them both to bring gentle attention to the feeling of Ben's arm on her shoulders and to contrast that with the tightness in their jaws, the pounding in their hearts, or the thoughts racing and being pushed away. I encourage them not to judge or resist these sensations, but to do their best to stay with them; if they cannot welcome them just yet, to at least not forbid them from being.

Slowly, almost imperceptibly at first, I sense a shift in Ella's face as she relaxes a little. Her breathing deepens and steadies, her shoulders drop infinitesimally. It's as if, in being witnessed and held in her vulnerability, she's building a new model of what it's like to be noticed and fully seen without being rejected.

This, to me, is the beginning of Transformation—the process by which we transmute the lead of our past into the gold of our present and future. It's not about erasing or denying our wounds, but about integrating them into a larger story and orchestrating ways in which we can viscerally prove to ourselves that other, less threatening realities are also possible.

Of course, this kind of shift doesn't happen all at once, and it's rarely a linear journey. Transformation is often a spiral path, one that brings us again and again to our deepest knots and blindspots, but in a new way, inviting us to meet them with ever-greater levels of awareness and love. William Blake depicted this in a painting of Jacob's Ladder as a spiral stairway, heading upward. I'm not one to peddle ascension metaphors, though I feel compelled to note that the narratives of transformation that I have encountered all function in some spiral shape—seemingly re-treading patterns while never repeating them exactly the same way, and always moving further inward. In moments when we're able to catch a glimpse of ourselves beyond the distortions of our conditioning, we gain the potential for radical change. We remember that, no matter how entrenched our patterns may seem, there is always the possibility of choosing differently, of stepping into a new way of being with ourselves and others.

As Ella's eyes meet mine through the screen, I see a tentative but unmistakable opening to a different kind of relating with others. It's a look I've come to recognize—the dawning realization that change is possible, that the past need not dictate the present, that a new story is waiting to be written. I've always loved the idea that *hope* is a verb: an act of the imagination.

"Thank you," Ella whispers, her voice still thick with emotion but also clearer. "I didn't...I had no idea how much I was carrying here."

I smile and nod, honoring the significance this has for her and also knowing it is just the beginning of a shift that may reverse itself just as easily.

"You're welcome," I say softly. "And thank *you* for your courage, for allowing yourself to be real, and for considering a new way to relate to Ben."

She hasn't fully done that last part, but I highlight the opportunity and watch both their faces light up.

"It's not like I have much of a choice," Ella laughs. Her voice is still sad but also lighter.

I glance at Ben, who's watching Ella with a mixture of trepidation and tenderness, his own defenses starting to soften in the light of her vulnerability. I let the moment settle, allowing it to reverberate in the breaths between us. These shared, synched-up breaths are the true work of transformation—not the momentous epiphanies or dramatic breakthroughs, but the small, daily acts of turning towards ourselves and each other with honesty, compassion, and a willingness to begin again. It is the slow, steady work of unraveling the knots of the past and weaving a new tapestry of meaning and connection in the present. I know this might sound extremely cheesy, but I'm quite certain that we transform relationally through loving and feeling loved.

Ben and Ella's work has continued, and I am certain they have much more to learn from one another. But that's the thing about transformation: in the best case, we are continuously arriving at a new place, never quite resting there for long.

EXTENDED SELF: TRANSLUCENCY

When we step into that space between stimulus and response—the one to which Viktor Frankl first introduced us—we open up the possibility of re-encoding our next prediction, and reality becomes more transparent. Ella kept interpreting Ben's anger as being directed at her because, as far as she had known throughout her life, all the humans who mattered were somehow angry, and it all affected her. Her parents had been mean toward each other, but their young daughter internalized it as being about her. Ben was angry at a situation or himself or the world or maybe even sometimes at his partner, but to Ella it all blended into one overwhelming anger whose arrow always pointed at her core.

Translucency, with regard to its ability to shape our sense of an extended self, is about seeing through the veils of our conditioned beliefs and beginning to notice what is actually occurring, as well as what we are bringing to it. As we practice translucency in our relationships, letting ourselves be seen and known and meeting others with open curiosity, we begin to see how much of our sense of self is crafted in the relational moments with another. We recognize that the self we take to be solid and separate is actually a fluid, contingent construct, interconnected with all that has happened, is happening, and could happen to us.

This is my understanding of translucency: a radical clarity that reveals the open possibility at the heart of all forms and the open awareness that is available to each of us. In this light, we see that our stories of limitation, desire for control, and certainty are all movements of a mind that is struggling for homeostasis and predicting its lack. We see that reality is not a fixed set of objects or outcomes to be grasped, but a continuously unfolding dance of appearances arising in open, boundless space.

As we cultivate such translucency, we learn to hold our beliefs and narratives more lightly and recognize them as provisional maps rather than ultimate truths. We become more attuned to the subtle textures and tones of our present-moment experience and less captivated by the mental commentaries that overlay it. We see through our habitual reactions and defenses into the vulnerability and tenderness that lies beneath.

This can be a powerful shift in perspective and can feel disorienting at first. In seeing through our familiar reference points, we may feel groundless, unsure of who we are or what is real. But as we stay with this not-knowing, as we keep softening into the translucency of each moment, a new kind of stability emerges, one not based on fixed positions or possessions but on an unwavering trust in the wisdom and workability of all that is occurring.

In this space of translucency, we discover a freedom and flexibility we may never have imagined possible. We are no longer so caught in the drama of our personal story or the need to defend a particular self-image. We can welcome the full range of life's experiences with greater equanimity, knowing that none of them can ultimately touch or diminish our core.

Translucency, then, is a portal to a profound kind of trust—trust in the inherent rightness of reality, just as it is. This is not a naive or passive trust, but a courageous willingness to meet life on its own terms, to surrender our agenda of control and embrace the unknown. It is a trust born of direct insight into the nature of things—a knowing that is embodied beyond concept or belief.

———

They say all research is *me-search*, and, in hindsight, I suspect that the whole reason I started the CRATE platform was to solve this T-part of it for myself. I didn't know at the time that this, *Trust*, was the most foundational part of the entire framework for me and the key that would unlock the rest, not only for my work but for my path in the world, when I eventually glimpsed it.

When I started working on the puzzle of how to help myself and others live more comfortably with our emotions, it seemed intuitively clear that there would be some relational, safety component to our wellbeing. I knew that trust was integral to our narrative of growth (after all, every hero has a sidekick or three), but I didn't know what it was in there that compelled me so powerfully and why it seemed so vitally important and resonant.

For most of my adult life, I lived believing I was a walking brain. I genuinely thought that my body was here just to move me around, and that any time it showed weakness (such as exhaustion or pain), it was a matter of willpower to persevere and make it conform. That line of thinking enabled me to work eighty-hour weeks in advertising, function on three hours of sleep, starve myself down to questionable health, and (later) tandem-nurse a newborn and a toddler while also running an overbooked creative consultancy. None of these choices are ones I would wish on my children, clients, or anyone else. In hindsight, for every seeming tactical advantage they provided, they held me back by substituting mere appearances of achievement for actual confidence and creativity.

The problem with wanting to be perfect is that you get *stuck* in trying to be perfect. You beat yourself up when you fall short by the tiniest bit, and the narrative of *not good enough* starts to permeate not just your projects but also your relationships, your days, and your life. At least, that's how it worked for me. We've discussed at length the concepts of expanding or contracting choices, but another way to reframe this is to view our behavior as a way of responding from a place of scarcity or a place of flow. I use *flow* rather than *abundance* because until very recently, my internal *not enough* stories continued to be alive and well, even if their teeth were getting progressively less sharp. I stepped into the concept of *abundance* like an awkward teenager on her first day at a new school. *Do I have enough food? Check. Enough safety, meaning, support? Check, check, and check. Do I have abundance? Uhm....*

It wasn't until I felt enough love—not just from others, but from myself toward myself—that the last box was finally checked.

How did that happen? What shifted, and how can it shift for you, should you need it to? I've pondered this discomfort, feeling woefully insufficient at being the kind of person who is properly grateful. But it's not that I am not cognizant of my tremendous fortune, nor that I'm unaware of the sacrifices that my parents made immigrating to Canada and enabling my children and me to have a life where abundance is even possible. Still, narratives of scarcity are downright epigenetic, at least on a psychological level. When the adults around you treat a banana as a treasure worthy of being a Christmas present, and you grow up choosing between taking the bus or having ice cream, this translates into every positive thing being assumed to have an invisible cost, and an internalized message that you somehow have to earn every last crumb, because otherwise, someone might decide to take it away.

I write this while knowing that my childhood was not one of particular lack. Yes, we were an immigrant family, but we never starved nor had to worry about housing or healthcare[1]. I share it to illustrate how the lessons we learn while young reverberate through the chambers of our lives well into adulthood. Whether we trust that the world and our role in it will be one of lack or one of plenty depends in great part on what we learn about these things early in life. Still, it does not mean we are stuck there. Neither I nor you nor Ella nor Ben are sentenced to thoughtlessly repeat our patterns. The very fact that you are here reading these words introduces a wrinkle in the temporal narrative of your life, opening you up to transformation and translucency.

What does that feel like when it works? There's a homeostatic feeling that awakens in my body when I am truly well. It's a feeling of joy or even glee. It's as if my cells all wave at me, going, "Wee! You're doing a great job. Keep going!" I suspect that's the jumping-for-joy feeling we encounter when we are young, and then later mostly forget or encounter only in fiction. I found myself experiencing this a few years back while on a quick getaway in Woodstock with my parents, children, and husband. It was a confluence of pieces fitting just right: the weather was gorgeous, the surroundings were lush and inviting, the food was delicious, and I was watching people I love being happy in each other's presence. On the second day, while moving to open the glass patio door and seeing the sunrays fall across my hand, I was stopped in my tracks by a thrumming feeling of pure awe and joy. *So this is what it means to be thriving?* I thought. I wanted to hug the world and thank it, yet immediately felt worry cloud over me. *What happens*

---

1   *Thanks, Canada!*

when we get back to the city and all my work has piled up? How much will I miss my parents when they return to Canada? Why can't every day be like this? And what about all the people who are suffering and don't get to experience even one moment this beautiful?

Care, the category of feelings that includes nurture, attachment, and belonging, is one of the most integral parts of our homeostasis, yet also one of the most volatile. Our brains have separate parts that activate: parts that urge us to seek and collect our young when they are lost, parts that react when a loved one calls for us, parts that activate when we communicate or play with them, and an entirely other, possessive part that activates when we think of all the members of our in-group as relating to our internal narrative: *our* children, *our* parents, *our* mates.

It is that last part, the narrative of *our* happiness, that we seem to be most attached to—a desire so prevalent in the United States that the Founders wrote its pursuit into our constitution. The thing that has dawned on me as I experience more and more of these homeostatic moments is that we can't call up that feeling by orchestrating it. We don't get to it by gathering achievements, purchasing handbags, or even setting up picture-perfect moments where the weather, the food, and loved ones gather just so. We don't get to it through a narrative because it isn't narratively driven. Our sense of well-being is limbic, visceral, pre-cognitive. It registers in nerve cells rather than words. It's not something we decide but something designed to direct our decisions. "This is good for you; keep going," it says—reminding us that we are the ones on stage taking direction, not the ones running the show. *Trust* is becoming willing to listen and take its direction.

As I've deepened into my own state of translucency, I've discovered that trust is not something we need to cultivate or acquire but an expression of what we most fundamentally are. In touching the boundless awareness at our core, we rediscover a primal confidence and ease, a sense of being at home in the world. We see that the ground we have been seeking has always been beneath our feet, holding and nourishing us at every moment.

From this ground of translucency and trust, we can learn to engage the world with greater clarity and agency. We can navigate life's challenges with a sense of spaciousness and perspective, less driven by fear and more responsive to what is needed now. We can show up in our relationships and communities as an authentic presence, in service to something larger than our egoic self.

TRUST: GROUNDING AND GROWING

Trust is the foundation upon which we build our capacity for resilience, connection, and growth. It is the inner knowing that allows us to face uncertainty with courage, relate to others with openness, and embrace change with curiosity. Cultivating trust is a process of remembering our core, a journey that involves reclaiming our inherent wholeness, repairing past ruptures, and learning to stand still and simply *be* in the present. The three aspects of Trust—Temporality, Transformation, and Translucency—provide a roadmap for this journey.

Temporality is about developing a new relationship with time. So often, our past experiences of hurt create lenses of fear and doubt through which we view the present and anticipate the future. By bringing care, awareness, and even acceptance to these temporal distortions, we can begin to untangle ourselves from old stories and reactive patterns. We learn to discern what is actually happening now from the echoes of our past. We practice meeting each moment with curiosity, trusting in our capacity to respond wisely to whatever arises. As we solidify our presence, we discover that trust is not something to be earned or proven but an inherent quality of our being that we can simply relax into.

Transformation points to the alchemical power of vulnerability. When we have the courage to face our fears, feel the full intensity of our emotions, and thereby reveal our authentic self, we create the conditions for tangible change. Trying to get out of an emotion is nowhere near as effective as having the courage to go straight into its core. When we do this and allow ourselves to be witnessed by others while doing so, we are inevitably transformed. Old identities and defenses melt away and new possibilities emerge. We discover that we are far more resilient and creative than we could have imagined. We learn to trust the wisdom of our bodies and the regenerative power of connection. Transformation requires us to relinquish control and embrace uncertainty—to trust the process, even when we can't see its outcome. It turns out that our true path forward is always entangled with that which we are most afraid to face.

Translucency, in its deepest sense, is the process of seeing through in order to see within. As we practice letting ourselves be fully seen and known, we begin to peer through the veil of our own conditioning and realize the inherent interdependence of all phenomena. We discover that the self we take to be solid and separate is actually a fluid, contingent construct, forever interconnected with the whole of life. In this recognition, we find freedom and flexibility and are no longer caught up in the drama of our narratives or the need to defend a particular self-image. We learn to hold our stories and beliefs more loosely, resting in the openness and clarity of our nature. This is a radical translucency—a seeing through the appearance of division to the boundless awareness that is our shared ground. As we embody this translucency more fully, we become a conduit for the wisdom and compassion that can become available to us, offering our intellect in service to the generative impulse inherent in all living organisms.

Cultivating trust is an ongoing practice, one that invites us to keep turning towards ourselves and each other. As we do this, day by day, moment by moment, a fundamental shift occurs. We discover an unshakable okayness at our core, a goodness that cannot be earned or broken. We recognize the web of relationships that hold and nourish us, and our own capacity to contribute to the healing of the world. We come home to the wholeness of our being and the vast love that surrounds and sustains us.

In the end, trust is an act of courageous surrender: letting go of the illusion of control and leaning into the intelligence of our organism. It is a radical commitment to the truth of our interconnectedness and the power of our presence. As we anchor ourselves in trust, aligning our thoughts, words, and actions with our deepest values, we become a force for healing. We bring our gifts and our wounds, our passion and our vulnerability, to the great work of co-creating a more connected and generative future.

Trust, then, is not a destination but a way of being—an embodied stance of agapic love. It is the space from which we grow into our fullest potential and the wind that guides our sails home.

9

DRAWING ENERGY

Experience, Emergence, & Emptiness

"Everything is energy and that's all there is to it.
Match the frequency of the reality you want and you
cannot help but get that reality. It can be no other way.
This is not philosophy. This is physics."
— Albert Einstein

"Hey, lady! You fall asleep?"

The deli clerk is regarding me with a mixture of concern and suspicion, and I don't blame him. I've been standing immobile in front of an open refrigerator lined with kombucha bottles, staring at the same spot for what might have been a minute or possibly ten.

An hour from now, I must face a group of young adults—a class of neuroscience students at NYU—and tell them all about emotion, or rather, explain to them what emotions and feelings are and why they should care. The thing is, it doesn't matter whether we care how emotions work. By now, I've hopefully shown you how we get whipped around by our nervous system, excited or terrified, pushed and prodded. We can pretend it's no big deal, and that we somehow have the upper hand, but emotions do their thing and steer us around, dictating most of our choices whether we like it or not. Conversely, we may care deeply about how emotions work, about the makeup of our nervous system, the dynamics of our predictive model, and the narrative confabulations of our minds. We might have studied all of it for years and *still* find ourselves standing frozen in a West Village deli, staring into empty space, trying to find a center amidst the nervous energy threatening to overwhelm us.

I pick a kombucha bottle at random and purchase it apologetically. Then I walk over to the Arts & Sciences building, make it past security and up the elevator, and next thing I know, I'm presenting a guest lecture to a sea of unimpressed faces wishing they could be checking their phones or grabbing an afternoon snack. I am nervous in a way that much larger auditoriums filled with professionals have rarely made me feel. The stakes here seem higher. Perhaps this is because I have always had great reverence for academia, or because I remember the difference that individual lecturers made in my own life. My head is filled with the weight of this moment, the importance and responsibility of conveying just how much our minds can open, and thereby change, when we become aware of the ways they function.

My delivery is breathless and stilted. I struggle to remember what should be on the third slide and feel a constriction begin to form in my chest, all graspy and trying. I see a student yawn, another one look to the side. My own limbs feel leaden. I'm terrified that I've failed already, less than ten minutes in, and that not only will I not get to come back, but I will be doing these young humans a disservice and fail to show them the power inherent in connecting to their bodies.

But wait! That's right—I have a body too! I pause. I take a deep breath and exhale very slowly. *This is not about you*, a thought resonates loudly inside me. *Step out of the way and let the energy pass through.*

"But this is not about me," I hear myself say, "or even about impressive scientists like Jaak Panksepp, Antonio Damasio, Lisa Feldman Barrett, or anyone else we could mention here. Understanding emotions is about *you*. When you become aware of your own experience and learn to allow whatever is occurring, when you can feel your self moving all the way through with emotion and into the action it unlocks, you 'unclog your pipes'. You stop fighting yourself and tap into the energy dynamics of your system, becoming far more productive and resilient."

Every student in the class is looking up at me. As I'm about to learn during our Q&A session, productivity and resilience are the greatest pain points these young humans face on a daily basis. They are sleep-deprived, stressed, overwhelmed, confounded. And I have just told them there might be another way to be.

EMBEDDED STORY: EXPERIENCE

We have now reached the final dimension of our framework, and it is worth acknowledging that Energy is somewhat different from the other four parts of CRATE. While Clarity and Agency can be seen as the flipsides of cognitive energy (figuring out where you are and deciding what you want to do about it) and while Regulation and Trust are all about relational energy (learning to connect to ourselves and others), Energy itself is the unifying factor that grounds all of the above. It's the largest box nesting all the others within it and making explicit the phenomenon to which they're each pointing.

If you study the framework table again (included once more for your convenience), you may notice that each aspect is saying a similar thing using different terms—or rather, looking at the same occurrences through different framing.

	EMBEDDED PREDICTION *Story*	EMBODIED ACTION *Stance*	EXTENDED COGNITION *Self*
CLARITY	Constraint	Curiosity	Convergence
REGULATION	Recognition	Relation	Release
AGENCY	Affordance	Attention	Adaptation
TRUST	Temporality	Transformation	Translucency
ENERGY	Experience	Emergence	Emptiness

For instance, the Embedded Story aspects of Constraint, Recognition, Affordance, and Temporality are each paths into noticing our Experience. Whether we're naming the obstacles, remembering patterns, seeing possibilities, or becoming aware of ourselves in time—all are ways of stilling ourselves and understanding *I am here.*

When it comes to the first aspect of Energy—our *experience* of what is happening and how we sense it—we use the term *energy* to describe things like vitality, motivation, creativity, or emotional charge. The work of biologist Michael Levin[2] offers an even more tangible way to understand the energy that flows through us and shapes our experience: emotions—the very phenomena we're trying to navigate—may be rooted in information-bearing bioelectricity. Our bodies use electrical fields that process and store information, much like a biological computer. This bioelectric signaling is likely the physical basis for our emotions, serving as the body's primordial language for approach or avoidance decisions. Such a view of emotions aligns well with Antonio Damasio's somatic marker hypothesis. He proposed that emotional processes guide behavior through bodily

---

[2]   Levin M. *Bioelectric networks: the cognitive glue enabling evolutionary scaling from physiology to mind. Anim Cogn. 2023 Nov;26(6):1865-1891. doi: 10.1007/s10071-023-01780-3*

states (or markers) associated with particular experiences[3]. Pairing the two, we might extrapolate that these somatic markers have an energetic component, with the bioelectric fields described by Levin forming the most basic physical substrate of our emotional signals. This hypothesis encourages us to view emotions as whole-body phenomena, deeply rooted in our biology and crucial to our decision-making processes. If this proves to be the case, it would give us a more foundational way of understanding the energy that flows through us and pave the way toward more concrete ways of measuring and interacting with it.

When observing my own experience and that of my clients, I've noticed there are generally two extremes at which we become conscious of our energetic state: high friction (leading to overwhelm) or high engagement (leading to flow). When situations feel difficult and painful, or become positively all-consuming, they attract our attention and make us want to understand what has happened so we can avoid or repeat it.

Both overwhelm and flow are two ways that our organism's energy can present. They are energetically-charged states that draw our attention, albeit in opposite directions. Overwhelm is characterized by a sense of resistance, struggle, or depletion. We might feel physically drained, mentally foggy, emotionally raw, or creatively blocked. In these moments, even the simplest tasks can feel like an uphill battle. We find ourselves questioning the value of our efforts, wondering if the energy expenditure is truly worth it. Such high-friction states draw us into a vicious cycle of energy expenditure: effort to fight resistance, perfectionism to counteract anxiety, and obsession to keep ourselves going past our natural boundaries.

On the other hand, flow states, as defined by the psychologist Mihaly Csikszentmihalyi, are marked by a sense of low-friction

---

[3]   *Damasio, A. R. (1996). The somatic marker hypothesis and the possible functions of the prefrontal cortex. Philosophical Transactions of the Royal Society of London. Series B: Biological Sciences*

engagement, timelessness, and intrinsic motivation[4]. When we're in flow, we are still expending effort but in a manner that helps us feel energized, focused, and fully immersed in the present moment. The evaluative, judging mind takes a back seat, allowing us to simply be with whatever is occurring.

In this non-dual state of awareness, the usual distinctions between self and task, effort and ease, dissolve. We're no longer fighting against our experience, but aligning with it. This makes us feel like we have more energy, not because our physical (metabolic) energy is actually increasing, but because it is moving through us with much greater efficiency. We get more bang for our energetic buck.

The quest then becomes to cultivate more moments of flow in our lives, not just in our work or creative pursuits, but in our everyday being. This is easier said than done, especially when we're running low on resources. While we tend to think of energy as a unified asset, in my experience we have at least five types of energy available: physical, cognitive, kinetic, relational, and creative (or spiritual). Physical energy is the bedrock upon which all other forms of energy depend. If we're not getting enough sleep, nutrition, or exercise, it's hard to fully show up for the mental, relational, and creative demands of life. This is why I often recommend that my clients start with a simple energy audit, tracking their physical self-care and noticing how their practices impact overall well-being.

Are you getting at least seven hours of sleep on most nights? Eating whole, nutrient-dense foods at a regular cadence? Moving your body in ways that feel good? Attending to these basics becomes increasingly more difficult the more ambitious and driven an individual is, or the harsher the circumstances dealt to them by chance or systemic dysfunction.

A good-enough physical state can make all the difference in setting up our capacity to engage with life's challenges, but even

---

[4]   Csikszentmihalyi, Mihaly. *Flow: The Psychology of Optimal Experience (Harper Perennial Modern Classics)*

when we are the lucky beneficiaries of a strong physical foundation, we can get stuck in friction as we wage war against our own minds. The *Embedded Story* that shapes our *Experience* is often one of lack, limitation, or "not-enoughness." We get caught up in predictions about how things should be rather than accepting them as they are, and judge ourselves harshly for falling short of self-imposed standards.

As with the other dimensions, our experience of Energy starts with the story we tell ourselves about what is happening at each moment. Think of a time in college, work, or even right now, when you might be attempting to solve a difficult problem—say, studying for an exam or building an elaborate presentation—and you feel like your eyes are closing with every page. It is like swimming through molasses: effortful, sticky, and impossible to see through. Then a friend calls to invite you to a movie. It's the latest showing by a director you love, and another (attractive) person will be there too. Suddenly, you have a burst of energy, enough to rush around your home, shower quickly, and pick the right outfit. You arrive at the movie theater in under an hour with a pep in your step and enough energy to last you all night. What changed?

I have found it helpful to think of our human organisms as metaphoric pipes through which energy can flow. Sometimes, those pipes are open, and the life force[5] rushes through us, compelling and fueling action. Other times, our pipes get clogged; what moves through them becomes constricted by metaphoric gunk, and advancing any action becomes laborious and slow. Just as a clogged pipe restricts the flow of water, experiences like self-judgment, loneliness, or misalignment can create blockages in our flow of energy, leaving us feeling drained, heavy, or stuck. Conversely, when our pipes are unclogged—through experiences of insight, connection,

---

[5]   *I use 'life force' poetically to mean the inspired and efficient use of metabolic energy, not some unknown substance.*

or creativity—our energy can move freely and thereby feel abundant, imbuing us with a sense of vitality, lightness, and expansiveness.

Our proverbial pipes can gradually become plugged over time through the accumulation of small daily stressors or unexamined patterns of thought and behavior. We may not even realize the toll these blocks are taking on us until we feel utterly depleted. By bringing awareness to these patterns and making intentional choices to unblock ourselves, we can reclaim a sense of aliveness and engagement with the world.

Our narratives about energy directly shape the reality we experience in regard to it. What we resist persists but what we welcome sets deep, abiding roots. Working through the five dimensions of CRATE each unplugs a particular type of energy flow. Here's a simple checklist to follow when our energy becomes stagnant:

- *Do I know what my objectives are and why I want to achieve them?* (Cognitive energy is activated by Clarity, which helps us define realistic goals.)
- *Are my organism's resources sufficiently balanced to take on this task?* (Physical energy can boost or downshift as Regulation finds an internal equilibrium.)
- *Do I have the drive and focus to enact the behavior I need?* (Agency will orient us toward objectives and adapt to circumstances, thereby activating Kinetic energy.)
- *Do I have the confidence and support I need to do this?* (Relational energy becomes unlocked as Trust enables us to find courage in the face of fear.)
- *What do I do when doubt and overwhelm kick in?* (Creative/ Spiritual energy is at the very core of Energy, and it is what this final framework dimension is all about.)

In the earlier examples of my trepidation when delivering a lecture, or the hypothetical work tasks that feel like molasses, the simplest way to gain energy was the relational component. Even when we believe in the work we are doing and have sufficient physical resources to do it, isolation and self-doubt can slow us down. This is why we often benefit from engaging with someone we trust who can remind us of why we should persevere and help us regain connection to the greater meaning that motivates us. Connecting to the audience during a lecture, attending a movie with friends, or even engaging with an idea through reading are all paths to relational energy, whether it be with the humans or narratives we care about. And *care*—as we're about to discover in the next chapter—is an incredibly potent fount of energy.

EMBODIED STANCE: EMERGENCE

The Embodied Stance aspects of each dimension address how we react to whatever is occurring at a given moment. Whether that is with Curiosity, Relation, Attention, or Transformation, all of these are beneficial ways we can respond to Emergence—choosing to expand rather than constrict in the face of that which arises to meet us. In complexity science, emergence refers to the phenomenon where novel and coherent structures, patterns, and properties arise from the interactions of a system's components, exhibiting features that are not present in the individual parts alone[6]. In our everyday life, the most immediate form of emergence is the somatic ping we call an emotion. Emergence, as an Embodied Stance in CRATE, encourages us to align with the natural unfolding of energy in our lives and orient toward its most beneficial expression. That can present as cognitive insight, physical burst, kinetic momentum, relational love, or creative inspiration.

Our physical or metabolic energy is the foundation upon which all other forms of energy depend. But the felt qualities of aliveness and joy seem to *emerge* from the interplay of multiple systems—

---

[6] Goldstein, J. (1999). *Emergence as a Construct: History and Issues.*

physiological, cognitive, or relational (which includes creative and spiritual energy). This is a great opportunity to note that the three aforementioned categories present a useful semantic distinction rather than an actual one. At its core, all energy is relational. Whether that is the relationship between our organism and external nutrients, ideas, other living beings, or the systems of meaning that inspire us— how we spend or derive energy depends on our engagement with the world around us.

As human beings, we are not isolated systems operating solely on the calories we consume and the sleep we get. We are deeply social creatures, wired for connection and co-regulation. The energy we exchange with others—through our words, our touch, our shared laughter, and our tears—is just as vital to our well-being as the air we breathe. The best measure of this interplay is, once again, emotion: the complex, dynamic process that mobilizes our bodies, minds, and relationships in the face of challenges and opportunities. From a scientific perspective, the link between emotion and energy is more than just a poetic metaphor. Emotions are psychophysiological states that involve changes in the autonomic nervous system regulation, neuroendocrine activation, and motor responses[7]. Emotions redirect blood flow, modulate arousal, and prime us to approach or avoid stimuli. In this sense, they truly are "energy in motion"—they animate our experience and give it direction and momentum.

———

The past two decades of evolutionary neuroscience suggest that core consciousness—the basic awareness of being a distinct entity— arose as early as half a billion years ago in vertebrates. It emerged as a solution to the problem of triaging overwhelming amounts of data, allowing creatures to quickly assess threats and opportunities and respond accordingly. But it wasn't until much later, with the

---

[7]   Levenson, R. W. (2014). *The Autonomic Nervous System and Emotion. Emotion Review, 6(2),* 100–112. *https://doi.org/10.1177/1754073913512003*

evolution of social consciousness and theory of mind, that we began to understand ourselves as *selves* in relation to others.

The final piece of the puzzle was the emergence of the autobiographical self, which Antonio Damasio posits occurred when we began layering patterns and symbols—the complex chains that we call "stories"—onto our core and social consciousness. With language, knowledge, and reason, we gained the ability to consciously explain and predict our experience of change over time. We became the narrators of our own lives. Here's the key point: this autobiographical self, which feels so central to our experience, is actually the last to arrive on the scene. By the time we get to our conscious explanations and decisions, countless unconscious inferences and heuristics have already occurred below the surface. Our story of reality has been revised and edited by forces beyond our awareness.

Now, what does all this have to do with energy and its emergence? The more we understand the constructed nature of our experience—the ways in which our predictions and narratives shape our reality—the more space we open up for something new to arise. When we recognize that our autobiographical self is just one more layer of prediction, one more story we tell to make sense of entropy, we begin to loosen its grip. We become less identified with our habitual patterns of thought and more available to the wisdom of the present moment. We tap into the raw, creative energy of life, which becomes available to fuel its expression through us.

The energetic dimension of emotion also goes beyond our internal experience. As you might remember from the discussion of mirror neurons in Chapter 5, we social creatures are deeply attuned to the emotional states of others. In moments of co-regulation, something remarkable happens. We tap into socially-emergent energy greater than the sum of each participant's energetic capacity. This is the magic of true collaboration and emotional intimacy— by becoming as present as possible in an encounter with another, we create space for something new and unexpected to arise. In the context of human experience, emergence manifests in many forms, including phenomena such as insight, collective effervescence, and creativity.

Insight is a prime example of emergent energy. It happens when we let go of our preconceptions and open a new frame into what cognitive scientist John Vervaeke defines as the process of Relevance Realization. Here, insight denotes a kind of cognitive leap, a sudden reorganization of mental models that allows a more comprehensive perspective to emerge. While this can occur in solitude, it is often catalyzed by the generative power of relationships. When we feel safe and supported enough to share our half-formed ideas and venture into the unknown, we create fertile ground for breakthroughs to occur. Insight is thereby deeply linked to social and emotional connection.

This is why environments that foster psychological safety—where people feel free to take risks, make mistakes, and challenge the status quo—are so conducive to innovation. As we build Trust in the generative power of relationships, we open the door to emergent possibilities.

Collective effervescence is another powerful example, initially formulated by the sociologist Émile Durkheim. It refers to the heightened sense of energy, passion, and connection that arises when people come together in shared experiences, such as religious rituals, music festivals, or social movements. In these moments, individual boundaries dissolve, and we feel part of something larger than ourselves.

The emotional energy we exchange with others is, therefore, a key ingredient in the alchemy of emergence. Whether we're co-regulating with a trusted friend, collaborating on a creative project, or participating in a social movement, we are tapping into a type of collective energy[8] that has the power to inspire and uplift us.

---

[8]   *The correct term here might be "synergy," but it has sadly been co-opted beyond recognition.*

Such transformative potential isn't limited to our most intimate relationships. It's available continuously, in every encounter with another being, idea, or facet of ourselves. Many wisdom traditions speak of an all-encompassing life force (*agape, qi, prana*) that connects us not just to our immediate circles but to the greater tapestry of life itself. While these concepts may not map neatly onto modern physics, they open interesting questions about the energetic nature of our engagement with reality.

I hypothesize that during flow or expansive states, we're not spending energy fighting against reality, but instead harnessing energy to propel us forward. We become conduits for inspiration, creativity, and purposeful action. (In case you're wondering, this is why I tend to group creative and spiritual energy together. I see both as meaning-making narratives through which we converse with the reality we experience.) Optimizing our energy isn't about doing more or trying harder; it is about aligning with the natural rhythms and intelligence of life so we can notice what *is* and trust we have the resources to meet it.

This is an opportune moment to recount the work of Transformation, which we discussed in Chapter 8 while witnessing Ben and Ella struggle with their attempts at embodied trust. It is one thing to read of others engaging in such work and wholly another to move through it ourselves. There is an important distinction between solving our problems and managing our anxiety. Often, individuals who identify as efficient problem-solvers are actually people who cannot tolerate situational discomfort and, therefore, become exceedingly proficient at eliminating that discomfort as quickly as possible. To avoid falling prey to our defense mechanisms, we must become more adept at identifying the sources of our energetic blocks and experiment with strategies for clearing them. These might involve:

- Journaling or conversing to process difficult emotions and gain clarity on decisions
- Setting clear boundaries around draining activities or relationships
- Prioritizing experiences that inspire us, even if they feel unfamiliar or challenging at first

Through such conscious experimentation, we build memories of what it feels like to trust our own wisdom and develop a more fluid, responsive relationship with the energy within us. Rather than feeling at the mercy of external circumstances or habitual patterns, we begin to see ourselves as empowered co-creators of our energetic reality.

The space of emergence is where insights are born and transformations take root. It's a space where we let go of our fixed notions of who we are and what is possible so we may allow ourselves to be surprised by the unfolding of reality. It is an open sea inviting us to remember that before the story of "me" and "you," before the divisions of self and other, there is simply the gift of conscious presence and the astounding happenstance of being alive.

I have become fond of a perspective offered by the twentieth-century French philosopher, paleontologist, and Jesuit priest Pierre Teilhard de Chardin, who wrote that evolution is an intensification of consciousness whereby we become more alive and reflective[9]. Poetically, he saw this as the universe's energy becoming physical, then turning in to observe itself.

The more we attune to this observation, which consciousness affords us—through practices of presence, connection, and appreciation—the more we align ourselves with the evolutionary impulse of life itself. We become conduits for the energy of

---

[9]   *Teilhard de Chardin, P. (1959). The Phenomenon of Man. New York: Harper & Row.*

emergence, midwifing new possibilities for ourselves and the world we inhabit.

EXTENDED SELF: EMPTINESS

Some of my fondest childhood memories are in the physics lab at McMaster University, where my father spent the majority of his time and all his attention, and where I followed him around on weekends like an eager puppy. It was there, one Sunday afternoon, that I remember peeking inside a big metal vacuum chamber as a laser pierced the darkness. "Ooh, pretty!" I thought. Then the chamber became consumed by utter blackness. "Look!" my dad pointed at a screen where green numbers moved through their own blackness. "There are the particles in there." He then excitedly described all the electrons that were pinging around, reacting to each other and to the light that had just moved through. What's more, he said, barely containing himself, it was possible for quarks to jump from here to a space far away––say in China or in another galaxy––and then reappear, or maybe, maybe, exist in both places at once. He was grinning ear to ear, eyes shining with amazement. I learned two important truths that day: just because something seems empty, it doesn't mean there's nothing there; and wonder is a form of love, existing within us while simultaneously drawing from an inexhaustible font of energy around us. Many years later, that early memory helped me integrate a foundational component of many wisdom traditions into what feels to be both the end and the circular beginning of the CRATE framework.

I now see Emptiness as that space of pregnant possibility—the opportunity for something new and unexpected to emerge in the open sea that is not just around but also inside us. Emptiness is the pause between stimulus and response—the moment after the breath is exhaled or the tide withdraws, pregnant with waiting for the next wave to break on the shore, or the next inhale to fill our lungs.

As physics has taught us, energy is the most fundamental and irreducible force in the universe. It cannot be created or destroyed, only transformed. That energy moves through mostly empty space, creating and interacting with matter, and altering the space through which it moves. As such, Emptiness is also the potentiality of future form. This is why it is the concluding aspect of both the Energy dimension and the CRATE framework. After we are finished working through the Emptiness aspect of Energy, we will find ourselves ready to begin with a new kind of Clarity once again.

You may remember that the *Extended Self* aspects of the other four dimensions are Convergence and Adaptation (two ways of looking at the creativity required to move beyond ourselves via Clarity and Agency) and Release and Translucency (two ways of letting go of assumptions or seeing through them via Regulation and Trust). It will hopefully come as no surprise that each of these are invitations to let go.

Emptiness is the point where form ends. We find it when our story stops. Not just in the very literal sense of death but also in the transient, momentary experience of no thought, no narrative, no-thing-ness. It is a pure way of being without struggle, without fear, without an agenda. I suspect it is what many religions call faith, but I experience it as a trusting surrender to love. "Trusting" because I have no proof that love is there to catch me when I let go of trying, except that, objectively, it always has. "Surrender" because there is a curious loosening of agendas that happens when I near it. It's not about losing agency but also not about charging head-first towards a goal. The closest I can liken it to is a shrugging acceptance: "Whatever will be, will be."

If you are like most driven people I know, the above statement might drive you nearly out of your skin. "What do you *mean* just 'let it be'?!" you might rail. "I didn't work so hard just to give up!"

I hear you. I've been you. And you'll have to trust me (there's that word again) that what I'm suggesting here is a graduation rather than an abdication.

The core of our being—the pure awareness that underlies our experiences—is unchanging and ever-present. It is the ground from which our thoughts, emotions, and sensations arise and return. Energy arises from within us, and our "job" is to clear the paths to its free, unconstricted expression. In other words, to get out of our own way. If *Experience* is about orienting, then *Emergence* is about noticing how energy arises, and *Emptiness* is knowing that it has always been there. As the Extended Self aspect of Energy, Emptiness invites us to expand our sense of self beyond individual limitations, tapping into a broader field of potential.

When we talk about "drawing energy" what we're really pointing to is the process of aligning ourselves with this fundamental nature of flow. It's not about accumulating or generating something from nothing, but about clearing away the blocks and distractions that obscure our inherent vitality.

If we go back to the metaphor of open pipes allowing energy to move quickly and abundantly, the key is to keep our pipes free of the constrictions that form when we become overly rigid in our narratives or agendas. Hence, the key to restoring our flow lies in the practice of emptiness. Emptiness, in this context, does not mean a void or absence, but rather a radical openness to potentiality. It is the still point at the center of the turning world, the space in which all forms arise and dissolve. When we touch this emptiness, we come into direct contact with the source of our being.

Accessing this state requires a kind of surrender—a willingness to let go of our habitual patterns and identities and rest in the spaciousness of pure awareness. It means disidentifying with the contents of our consciousness —our thoughts, beliefs, and narratives[1]—and instead identifying with consciousness itself. As Thich Nhat Hanh reminds us, "Emptiness is the ground of everything.... Beyond the idea of emptiness, is the idea that emptiness is also full of everything."[2]

This is not a passive or fatalistic surrender, but an active and courageous one. It is the surrender of the wave to the ocean, the recognition that our individual self is not separate from the greater whole. In letting go of our resistance and control, we open ourselves to the wisdom and flow of life itself. We begin to see that the "I" at the center of our experience is actually a kind of mirage, a mental construct that arises in response to ever-changing conditions.

ENERGY: FLOWING THROUGH SPACIOUSNESS

Our relationship with Energy is fraught with contradictions. We chase it relentlessly, convinced that if we could harness enough of it, we'd finally feel alive, successful, and whole. Yet, in our pursuit of this elusive force, we often deplete the very reserves we seek to replenish. It's a paradox that has haunted much of my life and which I see snapping at the heels of friends, loved ones, and clients. We have been taught to equate worth with productivity, so we spend countless hours pushing ourselves to the brink of exhaustion, believing that if we just work harder, longer, and smarter, we'll eventually crack the code of contentment. The truth is, the more we chase after energy, the more it slips through our fingers.

The path to authentic energy is not one of control and conquest but of surrender and flow. It's about learning to attune to our bodies' wisdom, listen to the subtle signals that tell us when we're veering off course, and course-correct with compassion and care.

---

[1]   *Yes, those are three terms that point at the same thing.*

[2]   *Thich Nhat Hanh, The Heart Sutra: the Fullness of Emptiness, www.lionsroar.com/the-fullness-of-emptiness*

Experience is the gateway to this inner wisdom. It's the raw data of our lives, the unfiltered feedback that our nervous system is constantly broadcasting, whether we're tuned in or not. When we're disconnected from our experience—when we're numbing out with food, scrolling mindlessly through social media, or chasing the next dopamine hit—we're essentially putting our fingers in our ears and humming loudly to drown out the truth of our own discomfort.

If, instead, we become curious about our experience—willing to feel the full range of our emotions, sensations, and impulses without judgment or resistance—we open ourselves to a wellspring of insight and energy that is always available to us. We begin to discern the difference between the false promises of quick fixes and the deep nourishment of true connection.

Emergence is what happens when we trust the intelligence of our experience. It points to the natural unfolding of our potential, the welcoming of creativity that occurs when we stop trying to force the flow and instead allow ourselves to be carried by it. In moments of emergence, we tap into a source of energy that is beyond our individual selves—a collective effervescence that arises from our interconnectedness with life. This is the energy of inspiration, of "being breathed" by evolutionary systems greater than ourselves.

When we're in a state of emergence, we feel alive, engaged, and energized, not because we're pushing ourselves harder but because we're aligning to the natural rhythms of existence.

Emptiness is the space in which emergence occurs and to which it leads us. This vast, open dimension lies beneath the surface of our thoughts, emotions, and identities. When we're in touch with emptiness, we can hold our experience lightly and relate to it with curiosity and compassion rather than attachment or aversion. Such is the paradox of emptiness: it is only by embracing the uncertainty of our existence that we begin to find stability and ease. As we relinquish our grip on who we think we are, we discover the joyful flow of who we might become.

Cultivating energy requires a willingness to sit with discomfort, befriend uncertainty, and let go of the illusion of control. It demands that we confront the reality of our own impermanence and the fact that, no matter how hard we cling, everything we love will eventually slip through our fingers.

To me, this is the essence of continuous creative flow. It's a surrender to the magnitude of existence, trusting that even amid chaos and uncertainty, there is underlying beauty and wonder to be found. The energy we seek is not something we need to chase but something that is always here, waiting for us to slow down and listen. To quote Rumi once again, "What you seek is seeking you."

PART III

PAY IT FORWARD

10

THE COURAGE TO CARE

Becoming Relational

"There is nothing in the world as strong as tenderness."
— Saint Francis de Sales

Once upon a few months ago, on a window frame overlooking the Catskill Mountains, a bee became stuck in a spiderweb. The bee fought valiantly to free itself, but the more it tore at the web with its movements, the more the silky strands stuck to the bee's body, wrapping it in layers that restricted its struggle. The threads clung to the insect like a cocoon of foreboding, increasing panic while reducing its agency. As the bee began to tire, the spider moved in. It didn't have to do much. Just poke at the bee with its two front legs—enough to feed the bee's panic and keep it fighting so it would eventually exhaust itself. The spider was patient and methodical. It seemed to know just how this whole dance would go. The bee struggled, trying mightily to bring its stinger to bear, but the webby cocoon restricted even that movement. It rocked back and forth in desperation, fighting against inevitability, seemingly persevering and capitulating at once. Then, suddenly, the last strand of web tore off the window pane, and both bee and spider plummeted to the ground below.

I can't tell you what happened next. My heart hopes that the bee miraculously survived, that it managed to free itself and fly off to its hive, that its courage proved worthwhile. My mind knows that the spider likely finished it off on the ground, that nature is often red (or black) in tooth and claw; that when we fight entropy, entropy tends to fight back.

I *can* tell you that I was both riveted and conflicted. On the one hand, this scene registers as such a minor occurrence: nature naturing on a spring afternoon during an otherwise peaceful getaway at a time when the globe is pocked with much greater, *human* suffering. On the other hand, this was a real life-and-death struggle that I had just witnessed. It did not need to compare to all the bigger pain out there in the world. I like bees. I also like spiders. I try to appreciate all living things, even wasps and centipedes and New York City cockroaches that jump or fly or whatever it is they do with their freaky antennae.

We won't always win. We won't always know what to do, what to say, or even what stance to take as we step, bloodied and torn, into life's arena. I'd like to believe that we can make our peace with that. That like the bee or the spider, like the clients I see persevering in my sessions, or the fictional heroes I admire in books and on screens, each of us will be willing to stand not against, but *with* life's arrows.

Still, having witnessed the panic and struggle, having inferred suffering without truly knowing whether an insect has the capacity to feel terror, my heart aches for that bee and for all the other beings feeling pain at this moment. And so, I push rationality aside, or rather, I move past and beyond it, allowing my eyes to blur with emotion. Saint-Exupéry was right, "It is such a secret place, the land of tears."

A HOOK OR A TETHER

The Greek poet Hesiod was first to recount the story of Pandora, to whom Zeus gifted a magical urn. Curious, Pandora opened its lid, releasing countless trials into the world, including sickness, heartbreak, and death. She hurriedly shut the lid, managing only to trap one last entity, *Elpis*, the embodiment of hope or expectation.

More than two millennia later, philosophers continue to debate whether Elpis was intended as the last and worst of the trials or whether hope is the saving grace that enables us to endure. I have come to believe it is both.

Hope, like *love*, *fear*, or *hate*, is a four-letter word most of us use all too lightly, assuming that we know exactly what each other means.

"I hope it won't rain tomorrow."
"I hope I get that promotion."
"I hope I find someone to love."
"I hope I won't die of cancer."

Simple statements, each describing a reality over which we hold varying degrees of control. We use *hope* as a verb but treat it as a noun, forgetting that it is an act of the imagination, requiring us to engage in emotional projection, thereby risking disappointment.

The ancient Greeks perceived Elpis to be both a comfort to and an extension of suffering. Most Buddhists believe that attachment to expectations is at the very root of suffering. And yet, our modern achievement-driven culture is obsessed with satisfaction and happiness, while also presuming that aspiration, ambition, and expectation are all predicates to such positive states. So, who is right, and what are we to do? If we stop expecting or hoping altogether, how do we get that promotion, or fall in love, or reach Mars? Conversely, if we throw caution to the wind and hope that excelling will ward off disappointment, how do we cope when the inevitable existential crisis comes knocking? No one has yet disproven the ancients' certainty that hope and suffering, expectation and disappointment are all intertwined. Our only choice, then, is yet another attempt at making space for both, allowing each to contain its opposite.

We bring home a new kitten and know that even if we're lucky, years from now, we will mourn its passing. We fall in love and (whether we like to consider it or not) accept that one of us will outlive the other, even in the happiest of endings. We build a company or raise a child, knowing that success means our creation will eventually stand on its own, no longer relying on our presence.

Hope and expectation are best wielded with a committed heart and a loose grip. We must paradoxically merge aspiration with equanimity. To progress, we must move toward whatever peak we aim to scale with full commitment and with the willingness to turn back when necessary, so we may live to climb another day. From our very first step on a new path, we must learn to treasure success and defeat as if they are the same outcome, because they are.

I allowed myself to hope that the bee lived. Yet, each time I think of it—each time I extend my heart to the possibility of its survival—reason rushes in, pragmatically reminding me of the less-than-favorable odds. "Hope for the best, but prepare for the worst," my father taught me. I tried to listen but struggled, unable to master the move wherein I could simultaneously open my heart and also barricade it. To this day, his guidance feels like more of a contradiction than a paradox, though perhaps I'm still young, not yet having learned how to merge the pragmatism of a scientist with the courage of a poet.

Feeling hope can be a daunting prospect because it requires us to confront the uncomfortable truth that we care about an outcome over which we have little agency. Unlike science, social mores teach us to prize positivity, encouraging us to "look on the bright side" or "keep our chin up" in the face of adversity. While this optimism can be helpful, it can also lead us to suppress or even deny the more difficult emotions that form a natural response to disappointment. And (as I've noted previously), when we deny our feelings, we cut ourselves off from valuable information about our needs, boundaries, and desires. We find ourselves engaging in numbing behaviors—whether they be overworking, overeating, overdrinking, or overshopping—all in an attempt to avoid discomfort. In an about-face, we insist blindly, irrationally, that "everything will be just fine." Over time, this disconnection from reality—the swing in either direction—leads us to a sense of isolation, confusion, even despair.

True courage, then, starts with the willingness to turn toward our emotional truth even when it feels scary or overwhelming; to extend our heart and care, or even hope. It means creating a safe space within ourselves to welcome the full range of emotional investment and its accompanying potential for heartbreak without judgment or resistance. This is not an easy practice, but it is a necessary one if we want to move bravely through the world and cultivate genuine connections with other humans and our environment.

How we attend to reality at this very moment defines who we are in the next one. A client asked me recently if my stance toward hope means that I have none. To the contrary! Knowing that Elpis was both the last curse and the only possible salvation prompts me to love her even more. To me, hope and care are intimately intertwined. Why would I hope for something that does not matter to me? The things that are most dear also present the highest stakes. Engaging with them fully—loving my family, being completely present for my clients, writing these words—they all require a level of vulnerability that not only feels like standing naked in the middle of Times Square, it's akin to shedding the top layer of skin, exposing raw flesh to the elements.

THE COURAGE TO NOTICE

As we begin the last part of this book, we must slow down to ask one of my favorite questions: *For the sake of what?* Why do we bother to push ourselves far beyond what is comfortable? Even if we're to master the CRATE framework and get all flowy and serene, what's the point of it all anyway? In the introduction, I promised you that gaining Clarity, Regulation, Agency, Trust, and Energy would yield Courage, Meaning, and Resilience. Those things sound useful and most of us believe that we want them, but what are they? And what are they good for?

Throughout the beginning of this chapter, I've used *hope, care*, and *love* almost interchangeably. You might think this points to a confusion or a conflation of terms. I beg to differ. I have found that many words in our language point to something bigger and more amorphous than the words themselves. It's as if each word is a porthole around a sphere containing the ocean, and depending on which one you look through, you might see a fish, a coral, or only see the blackness of depth. Each person might insist that what they see is all that there is—after all, the fish is real, and so is the coral—but if we focus only on what is most obvious, we're likely to miss something bigger, less concrete and nameable, but just as real if not more so.

As far as I've discerned, becoming courageous requires three parts: the willingness to notice, the willingness to engage, and the willingness to accept. (Yes, these are the three aspects of the CRATE framework all over again.) We begin with an orientation toward noticing, which is the process of becoming open, permeable, seeing not only with the eyes but the ears and nose, with our skin, with our insides—including our rational prefrontal cortex (what we usually refer to as 'the mind') and our somatic nervous system (what we usually name 'the gut' or 'the heart').

We notice by slowing down and becoming present to what is happening in the current moment, rather than allowing ourselves to get carried off by thoughts into the future or become mired in the past by memories (which are also thoughts). All of that thinking, all the narrativizing and time-traveling are acts of small cowardice. Staying in the present is scary because it is vulnerable, raw. If I stay here with these words right now, I have to admit that I'm afraid you will laugh at them—that they might come out cheesy or trite or that I might fail to reach you. The beautiful thing is that the very act of noticing not only asks courage of us, it *gives* us courage. Having braved the moment and having survived it, we become a little more certain of ourselves. Speaking our truth gives us energy. And once we get that burst of internal confidence, we can't help ourselves but shift forth into engagement.

THE COURAGE TO ENGAGE

I said that we can't help it, because we seem to be genuinely wired to engage with each other and the world around us. You might remember from Chapter 2 how our behavioral traits evolved to balance stability and plasticity, encouraging us to play it safe and survive but also to venture out and interact in search of opportunity. You may also remember Jaak Panksepp—the rat-loving (and -tickling) neuroscientist whose work on the core affective dynamics of mammalian emotion defined Care as a distinct system unto its own. According to Panksepp, the emotional system of Care allows us to attend to our young and bond with our peers, and may well be a motivational factor in the forming of tribes and civilizations. Care is the drive at the root of our relational self. Panksepp discovered that this system is activated when another member within the same in-group appears vulnerable, especially young organisms evidencing distress[1]. In humans, the cry of a baby triggers our Care response

---

1   Davis, Kenneth L.; Panksepp, Jaak. *The Emotional Foundations of Personality: A Neurobiological and Evolutionary Approach. W. W. Norton & Company.*

and activates gestures of nurturance or concern. This is not learned but innate, programmed into our brains over evolutionary millennia.

Panksepp proposed that the Care system emerged as a countermeasure to the Panic/Grief system. In the wild, a young mammal's separation from its mother, with the associated sense of fear and abandonment, leads to a state of panic, often accompanied by clear vocal protests. These cries activate the Care system in nearby adults, especially motivating the mother to prioritize a speedy return. The constant interplay between Panic and Care serves to promote the survival of the species by convincing parents to move toward their offspring even in perilous circumstances.

There is also a compelling neurochemistry when it comes to Care. That system is motivated by oxytocin, a feel-good brain chemical often labeled the 'love hormone' because it is released during intimate behaviors such as breastfeeding, cuddling, and mating. Oxytocin is *also* released when we engage in acts of generosity and nurturance, providing positive reinforcement for prosocial behaviors. When we care for another person or when someone cares for us, we activate this ancient circuitry. Our capacity for compassion isn't just based on nurture but is embedded in our genetic blueprint. We're *programmed* to expend energy so as to proactively attend to another's distress.

Isn't it odd, then, that societal narratives of autonomy, independence, competitiveness, and meritocracy work to actively disconnect us from such programming? As usual, the answer is not simple. We've evolved through competition *and* we're hardwired for connection. Yet as our world becomes ever more complex, our inherent capacity for openness and connection becomes subsumed by the pull of competition. We shield ourselves against our desire to nurture others, conflating vulnerability with weakness, courage with control, and care with micromanagement. We confuse caring with controlling or fixing—be it a situation or other people's emotions—thereby hooking ourselves to a particular expected outcome and becoming entangled in whether or not it resolves exactly as predicted.

THE COURAGE TO ACCEPT

So, how do we reclaim the Care system? What would it take to offer nurturance and empathy not just to others but to ourselves? How do we become brave enough to show up completely, risking heartbreak and disappointment, and accepting the world as it is, rather than guarding ourselves in self-protection?

Deep care teaches us to courageously attend to our thoughts, experiences, and feelings with curiosity and kindness, not guilt or denial. It enables us to ask for help as a form of connection and become confident that our vulnerability is a sign of bravery rather than cowardice. Doing so helps us down-regulate and *release* tension (the final aspect of Regulation), then see through the masks of defensiveness and certainty (the *translucency* that is the final step of Trust). Once there, we are ready to set the stage for others.

As civilization evolved, much of what Panksepp defined as the biological system of Care became translated into the societal system of Conscientiousness. To the ancient Greeks, the concept of *Charis*—a form of care expressed as loving-kindness—was a fundamental principle that guided interactions and shaped their social fabric. Charis was not just a philosophical idea but a tangible presence in the lives of the Greeks, embodied as a goddess revered for her grace, beauty, and generosity. Homer first introduces us to Charis in the *Iliad* as the wife of Hephaestus, the god of crafts and metalworking who forges Achilles' shield. This divine pairing is significant, suggesting that grace and reciprocity (embodied by Charis) are intimately linked with the transformative power of creativity and craftsmanship (embodied by Hephaestus).

We will delve much deeper into the interplay between reciprocity and creativity in Chapter 12. Still, for now, it is relevant to note that Charis represented a complex web of customary obligations, embedding participants within a network of mutual care and acceptance. All deeds of generosity could be answered by an equivalent or greater gift of gratitude, not only among humans but also between mortals and gods. In practice, this translated into emphasizing hospitality, exchanging gifts, and forging enduring friendships. To favor a stranger, to provide food and bed for them and their companions, was not just a social expectation but a duty that elicited divine beneficence. Such exchange was not seen as a simple matter of *quid pro quo*. Instead, it was the deepening of social bonds—conveying respect and acknowledgment of the other.

In a profound way, the enactment of *charis* presented a recognition of human interdependence: the understanding that nobody can survive completely on their own, that we're all worthy of the goodwill of other humans, and that giving and receiving such care would enable us to overcome the vicissitudes of life. *Charis* encouraged a culture of reciprocity and mutual concern that made everyone a stakeholder in their community's welfare. In this light, acceptance can be seen as an act of great generosity—the willingness to open our hearts and accommodate the idiosyncrasies of individuals and circumstances, creating as much social harmony as is realistically possible.

Of course, the ancient Greeks were not perfect. Similar to our current predicament, their society was also marked by inequality and violence. Care—and especially *charis*—was not afforded to every human[2], let alone every living being. Yet, the idea of *charis*— the generously accepting disposition toward another—remains a powerful reminder of what is possible when we prioritize generosity, compassion, and mutual aid.

Having a generously accepting disposition may sound like a tall order. Many of my friends and clients—the majority of whom are outliers when it comes to both agency and ambition—find themselves allergic to the idea of acceptance. Five years ago, I would

---

[2]   *Enlightened as they thought themselves to be, the ancient Greeks did not allow women to participate in governance nor own property; and they thought nothing of having slaves and conquering other cultures for the purposes of exploiting their humans and resources.*

have counted myself among them. We are taught that in order to succeed, we need to compete, and in order to compete, we need to compare. Yet, in contrast to care, which promotes belonging through acts of validation and inclusion, competition and comparison are acts of distancing and separation. *I am different from you*, comparison whispers, *and one of us is better or worse than the other.* Comparison teaches us to place ourselves above or below the people around us and create a hierarchy of value. Egged on by competition for status, we experience superiority, inferiority, envy, resentment—all the divisive emotions that undermine our sense of belonging. But what would it be like to walk into our next meeting or networking event without that invisible measuring stick in hand? What if, the next time we engage in conversation with someone new, our objective is not to impress or defend, but to connect and show care? My personal hack (one I often offer up to clients to make their own) is shifting the conversation from achievements to passions—rather than telling you what I do for a living, let me share how I feel as a matter of loving. Sharing passions is, but its very essence, vulnerable and open. You might be surprised how much more effective it proves in forming deeper, more lasting connections.

The paradigm of care encourages us to know we are accepted, as long as we respect one another and act based on agreed-upon values. Our actions still matter, but there's a sense of abundance, welcoming us to arrive as we are and to continuously strive to improve within a space of psychological *and* physical safety. The paradigm of comparison, on the other hand, is one where we expect scarcity; the spoils go to the winner, and those who are not at the top automatically lose. One offers a win-win, infinite game of cooperation, while the other is a finite, zero-sum struggle of competition.

I would still argue that the choice between these two options comes down to courage. It is a much braver stance to declare that there can be enough resources, time, and affection for all of us to share, that even when there isn't enough (which absolutely *does* happen), we will engage with reality and work to distribute what is available or to create ways to generate more, and that we will do so together, openly and without obfuscation.

Ultimately, that stance is a choice: a decision to orient toward, not away from each other. I don't know whether this choice is equally available to every human or genetically predisposed in some of us, but I do know firsthand that it *is* available. I also know that those of us who have the means to choose care and connection stand to benefit—both for ourselves and the world—as we do so. That way lies meaning.

11

THE MEANING TO ACT

Aligning Your Why

"From the center of my life came
a great fountain, deep blue
shadows on azure seawater."
— Louise Glück

What exactly *is* meaning? That's the perennial question, and the teenage late-night question, and simply the human question. Meaning, in the way I have come to understand it, is not theoretical. Because of this, it refuses to fit neatly into the analytical, long-term, rule-of-thumb framing into which we keep trying to shoehorn it. Meaning is contained in the literal *and* the figurative senses. It is breathed into, felt, lived, imbued, and interpreted. Most of all, it is loved. It is the things we love, the living beings and ideas that are most dear to us, the tangible and intangible symbols that are most salient, that shape our meaning.

And since the largest concepts most worthy of our love are best understood non-linearly, allow me to tell you about a gentle yet fierce Frenchman who loved flying planes almost as much (and sometimes more) than he loved writing words.

It was June of 1940, and France had just fallen to Nazi Germany. As the Axis advanced, the French government signed the Armistice of June 22nd, dividing the country into occupied and unoccupied zones. The writer, who had been serving as a reconnaissance pilot in the French Air Force, found himself facing a devastating choice. He couldn't bear remaining under occupation or, worse, being forced to collaborate with a regime he abhorred. Moreover, as a famous author who had been vociferously critical of Nazi ideology, he faced persecution and even death. Worst of all, the Armistice meant the demobilization of the French military, robbing him of access to his beloved plane. Heartbroken and disillusioned, the writer chose exile over submission. He left France not just to escape danger but as an act of resistance. In December of 1940, he stood aboard a ship watching Lisbon recede on the horizon, hopeful that in New York he could find a new hope.

But the bustling sidewalks of New York City, far more harried and noisy than his beloved French countryside, just made him feel more adrift. He traversed the streets and the continent, finding himself ill at ease in both New York and Los Angeles, submitting to fever, then depression, as he became overwhelmed by the darkness in the world and in his heart. Who was he if he couldn't fly, couldn't defend his country, couldn't protect the world from a wave of blood that was swallowing it whole? How was he to write when everything that he had held dear proved weak—even cowardly—in the face of aggression?

To salve his heart and pass the time, a French actress and friend sat by his hospital bed and read him the fairy tales of Hans Christian Andersen. They spoke of the darkness that permeated children's stories, how each was a journey away from, and back to, whatever home meant. They spoke of the truths that children know and then forget, and whether it was possible to remember them again. The writer talked about a young boy with the purest laugh, of how he could almost glimpse him out of the corner of his eye and how much he wished he could hear what that boy had to say.

Time passed. One day, in a restaurant in what is now the West Village, the writer found himself in conversation with his publisher and the publisher's wife. Absent-mindedly sketching on the tablecloth, he gasped as a small, golden-haired boy appeared under his pen. Prodded by his companions' questions, he began talking wistfully about the boy, how he kept showing up in his thoughts, and how he always looked as if he were about to ask for something.

"Maybe you should write his story?" the publisher's wife playfully suggested. "That way, he'll say his piece, and then he might stop bothering you."

The writer listened. He retired to a friend's home in Northport, Long Island, where he wrote and sketched and then wrote some more. On his pages appeared a young boy who looked small but stately. He had a lightness, a spaciousness about him, a young face with the deepest, most inquisitive eyes. He looked up and said, in that way that the realest of characters speak to a writer, "Please... draw me a sheep...."

As I tell you this, recounting the story as closely as I have researched and then imagined it, I find myself overcome with emotion. I am, of course, writing here about Antoine de Saint-Exupéry and how he first came to meet The Little Prince.

Over the following days and weeks, as the Little Prince shared his interplanetary journey, Saint-Exupéry excavated the deepest truths he had learned as an aviator, explorer, and human. Through the eyes of that golden-haired boy and the book's narrator (a pilot having suffered a perilous crash into the Sahara desert, much as the author had years earlier), he remembered the essence of what gives life meaning: having someone you tend to, someone you trust, someone you love so deeply that you cannot help but return to them, no matter the cost.

"It is only with the heart that one can see rightly," the fox tells the Little Prince, "What is essential is invisible to the eye." In uncovering this story, Saint-Exupéry wasn't writing a children's book; he was articulating a philosophy of meaning that would guide his actions during humanity's darkest hour.

As "The Little Prince" took shape, so did Saint-Exupéry's resolve. Having birthed a tale of cosmic significance amidst earthly turmoil, it became a declaration of what he himself held to be most meaningful. Saint-Exupéry knew that he, too, had to return home. In 1943, with "The Little Prince" published and slowly making its way around the globe, the author made a choice that likely felt inevitable. Despite being older than the age limit and in poor health, he petitioned relentlessly to be allowed to fly reconnaissance missions for the Free French Air Force. His country, his people, the values of care and human dignity—these were not abstract concepts to him but living truths he had remembered while writing.

Saint-Exupéry's choice to return to active duty was not born of a desire for glory or simple patriotism. Instead, his actions were the natural culmination of a life spent seeking meaning and then acting upon it. In his 1935 memoir about the Saharan plane crash, he had written, "Each man must look to himself to teach him the meaning of life. It is not something discovered: it is something molded."[3] As he chose to fly dangerous missions over occupied France, Saint-Exupéry crafted his life into a final, profound statement about what he believed to matter most.

On July 31, 1944, just a year after the publication of *The Little Prince*, the writer took off on a reconnaissance mission from which

---

[3]   *Antoine de Saint-Exupéry, Wind, Sand and Stars.*

he did not return. Four years earlier, in a letter to his friend Léon Werth, he had written presciently, "I have a feeling it will be a long flight. Into the night.... In which case, I shall enjoy it. Night flying is wonderful!"[4]

The Little Prince, born from longing and hope, spoke not only to his author but left a mark on hundreds of millions of readers across more than one hundred and fifty languages—among them Bulgarian. There, he found me, too, at the age of six and has not since left my side.

MOLDING MEANING

If Saint-Exupéry was right, and meaning is indeed molded, where on earth do we find the clay? What happens when most of us do not get a character—or even an idea—to appear under our pen or whisper in our ear?

My next statement is likely the most "out there" assertion in this entire book: I have a hunch that care and creativity are actually the same impulse: the desire to birth and tend to something we hold dear. *This* moves us to action, thereby producing momentum coupled with salience, and it is *that* that we call "meaning."

I have racked my brain and failed to find an example—real or imaginary—of true creativity without care. This is why building up the courage to care enables us to discover—even unlock— the meaning to act and the resilience to create. It *moves* us—as in, sends us in motion—on a journey through which we gain clarity, agency, trust, and energy. Regulation, on the other hand, does not automatically arrive with care or meaning. If anything, the passion inherent in such strong convictions can be dysregulating. We can become so flooded by what appears important that we lose sight of actual reality, a pattern most of us have all glimpsed when becoming

---

[4]   *Antoine de Saint-Exupéry, Letters to a Friend.*

caught up in romantic obsession, a competitive goal, or even a shiny new purchase.

Conversely, I suspect some of you might be reading this and thinking, "Passion, what passion? I haven't got the first clue where to find such passion." Becoming overly attached or being unable to find what we care about with a magnifying glass are two sides of the same dysregulated relationship to meaning. They are both ways we unconsciously try to protect ourselves from pain by closing off and prioritizing control. In doing so, we often become performative, adopting existing narratives—especially those fed to us by social media and advertising—leaving us little room for the surprise inherent in truly falling in love with someone or something. As a result, much of the meaning we encounter is pre-rehearsed, delivered to us on a platter of platitudes or ideology. It is synthetic meaning, lacking the immediacy and surprise of meaning-*full* engagement and discovery.

To summarize, meaning does not happen just in your head. It happens when you allow yourself to be interrupted by living beings and ideas larger than yourself—and then you allow yourself to *care* about them full-heartedly and with every fiber of your being.

MEANING AND FLUIDITY

Meaning needs coherence, significance, and mattering; it needs to make sense, to feel real, and to have relevance outside of us. This is the lesson taught by Dr. John Vervaeke—cognitive science professor and author of *Awakening from the Meaning Crisis*, whose Relevance Realization theory I mentioned in Chapter 9, and who is one of my most influential teachers. Vervaeke emphasizes that *meaning*, when it's fully coherent, is 4E-accordant: it is embedded, embodied, enacted, and extended. Discovering meaning is a continuous journey from salience to significance to synthesis. It's a process of revealing what we sense, know, learn, and co-create to be true. Noticing and recognizing meaning are both forms of remembering: re-encountering what we feel to be deeply real, important, and precious to us.

Vervaeke's work offers a comprehensive framework for understanding and navigating the challenges of meaning-making. He argues that we are currently facing a profound crisis characterized by a breakdown of traditional sources of significance, coupled with a growing sense of alienation and fragmentation. In response, he urges us to develop a new "ecology of practices" for cultivating meaning and wisdom.

Central to Vervaeke's approach is the idea of participatory knowing—the recognition that meaning emerges from a reciprocal dialogue between self and world, subject and object. This aligns with the notion that our relationship to meaning is first experienced by the senses (what some may term intuition) and only secondarily interpreted by the mind.

Think of it like this: meaning isn't a static thing you can pin down and dissect. It's more like a dance between you and the world. Things catch your attention (that's salience), then some of those things start to feel important (that's significance), and finally, you weave them into your understanding of life (that's synthesis). Tying this to the CRATE aspects once again, salience orients us toward our story. Significance decides our stance. And synthesis becomes integrated into our sense of self. All of this is pretty similar to falling in love: you notice someone, they become important to you, and then they become part of your story.

And here's what's crucial: the process of meaning-making isn't just happening in your head. It occurs in your gut, in your hands, in the way you move through the world. That's what Vervaeke means by embedded, embodied, enacted, and extended. You're not just thinking about meaning—you're living it, breathing it, creating it in every interaction.

Most prosaically, we can summarize our meaning by answering the question, "Why bother?" Why do we get up in the morning? Why do we exert effort? What is our objective, goal, or purpose, and how important is it to us? I can wake up today and decide that I would like to climb Mount Everest because it sounds like a cool and significant thing to do. Still, if that goal does not hold a profound importance to me, I will likely give up on the plan as soon as I discover the complicated logistics of planning a trip to Nepal, the cost of curated adventure packages, or the baseline physical fitness necessary. However, if climbing Everest had been my father's life-long dream and I was yearning for parental approval, or if the recognition of my peers was of primary importance to me, or if being in the mountains felt like a transcendent spiritual practice, I would be less likely to capitulate. The amount of effort we are prepared to expend—the price we are willing to pay—is proportional to how meaningful a given goal is to us. But how do we know that our emphasis on something is worth it?

How do I know if the meaning I've found is real? What if I'm just fooling myself? These are fair questions to ask, which have haunted philosophers and non-philosophers alike for centuries. The Roman Inquisition was so troubled by such questions that they burned Giordano Bruno alive at the stake for daring to suggest a system of meaning that directly contradicted theirs[1]. We assume that the realness of meaning is about some objective, universal truth. This is valid when it comes to whether we consider the Sun to be a star at the center of our solar system, and less applicable when it comes to whether I consider the Rocky Mountains to be more *real* as mountains than the Catskills. Realness can be measured, debated, and ascertained based on agreed-upon definitions. Yet, the moment

---

[1] *Bruno proposed an infinite universe with countless stars and possibly other inhabited worlds, challenging the geocentric model of the universe and the uniqueness of Earth as suggested by the Roman Church.*

we start desperately grasping at meaning, insisting that our version of reality is the only right one, we lose the plot. We've traded the fluid, living thing that is meaning-*full* for a rigid, dead thing that's more like an ideology.

Instead, what if we held our sense of meaning and even realness more lightly? What if we allowed it to be fluid, to shift and change as we encounter new experiences, new ideas, and new ways of being? The author David Chapman calls this the "fluid mode of meaningness." It's an approach that acknowledges the inherent uncertainty and ambiguity of existence without falling into nihilism or relativism.

As with most of life's most captivating instances, this is an engagement between pattern and nebulosity, between the structures that give our lives coherence and the openness that allows for creativity and change. Taking us all the way back to the primary meta-traits we encountered in Chapter 2, it is in the tension between Stability and Plasticity that fluid meaning (or "meaningness"[2]) emerges. When we find a balance between the solidity of our individual narrative and the fluidity of the larger story in which we continuously find ourselves embedded, we realize that we are both sailing the sea and becoming the water within it.

MEASURING WHAT MATTERS

The above ideas might sound abstract, but they play out concretely in how we approach our relationships, work, and sense of purpose. Do we insist on rigid roles and expectations or allow for growth and change? Do we cling to a fixed idea of success or remain open to new possibilities? Do we demand certainty in our beliefs, or do we cultivate a sense of wonder and curiosity about the mysteries of existence?

---

[2]   *For a thorough and thought-provoking discussion on the nebulosity of meaning, visit David Chapman's writings at Meaningness.com*

The fluid approach to meaning-making isn't about having it all figured out. It is being willing not to know, to sit with uncertainty, to allow ourselves to be surprised. It's also about recognizing that we don't achieve meaning once but continually discover, create, and reshape it through our engagement with the world.

Our sense of meaning evolves together with our sense of reality and what matters in it. We mold meaning by discovering, growing, and leveraging it. We discover it by encountering what is beautiful (awe-inspiring), good (beneficial), and true (real and realizable). We grow it by coming into a trusting relationship with what we feel to be meaningful and then seeing into it (insight), thereby allowing it to change us. We leverage it by drawing upon its energy to source courage and overcome friction, to preserve what is good, true, and beautiful so we may share it with others.

This process of discovering, growing, and leveraging meaning aligns with Aristotle's concept of *eudaimonia*, or human flourishing. For Aristotle, *eudaimonia* was not a fleeting emotional state but a way of living that enables us to fulfill our potential and live in accordance with reason and virtue. It is achieved through the cultivation of practical wisdom, the development of moral and intellectual virtues, and the pursuit of a life of contemplation and service.

So, how do you go about foregrounding meaning? And how do you know that the meaning you find is real, and not subliminally suggested to you by external manipulative forces? Luckily, there is a way to track what is most salient to you, and it is not through what you think or say but rather through how you act. Time and money are the currencies we spend on whatever we find to be important. They are also wonderfully convenient behavioral proxies.

You can examine your own by gathering your monthly and yearly expenses and sorting them so you can easily see the top five categories where your money goes. While the default assumption is that many of our most significant expenses are inevitable, I encourage you to challenge this. If your largest expense is rent or mortgage (as in the case of most of my clients and friends living in major metropolitan areas), something in your belief system led you to think that this is where the best jobs are, or this is where the zeitgeist is accordant with yours, or even that this is where you happened to be born and where your friends and family reside. Consciously or unconsciously, you bear the cost for what you deem to be most crucial. Similarly, with expenses for food, travel, education, and clothing: whatever you buy for yourself or loved ones is what you believe is essential for surviving and thriving—including where you aim to be in your social status.

Now, use this same form of accounting for your time. Over the next two days, track your time by the half hour and see what the top five categories are that cost you the most hours and attention. If you are lucky, sleep and relationships are high in the top five, and you have listened to your body and what it needs to flourish from an evolutionary perspective. But I have worked with many executives (especially startup entrepreneurs) where sleep came sixth, even seventh, and personal relationships only made the list if you included team.

Ask yourself, is your spending of money and time aligned with what you hold most dear? If the answer is 'yes,' congratulations! Keep going! Check in with yourself regularly to ensure you remain aligned and nudge the order of priorities (wherever you can) to reflect what you most care about. If it is a 'no,' there is no need to despair. You're in good company. Most of us become misaligned at different times, usually due to overwhelm.

To keep myself and my clients accountable, I've created a set of coaching tools, designed to help us discover or return to alignment—

among them is a version of KPIs[3] and OKRs[4], which I call *Key Meaning Indicators* and *Objectives and Meaningful Results*. To give you a taste, here is a very brief overview.

Key Meaning Indicators (KMIs) and Objectives and Meaningful Results (OMRs) are complementary tools that work together to align your actions with your deepest values and sense of purpose.

KMIs serve as your compass, providing ongoing measurements of what brings meaning to your life. They help you stay aware of the areas that contribute most to your sense of fulfillment. OMRs, on the other hand, are your roadmap. They translate the insights from your KMIs into concrete objectives and results that move you toward greater meaning and purposeful action.

Think of Key Meaning Indicators as the constant backdrop against which you set and evaluate your Objectives and Meaningful Results. To make this even more concrete:

Start with KMIs:
- Reflect deeply on what brings meaning to your life.
- Identify 3-5 key areas or experiences that consistently contribute to your sense of fulfillment and flow. *(For me, that happens to be loving, learning, and looking at the world.)*
- Develop ways to regularly assess these areas, such as journaling, self-reflection, and monthly check-ins. *(In my example, I check weekly whether I have spent sufficient time with family [loving], whether I have read at least 4 out of 7 days [my*

---

[3]   KPIs: Key Performance Indicators. *Quantifiable measurements used by organizations to gauge or compare performance in meeting strategic and operational goals. These metrics are typically used in business contexts to evaluate the success of an organization, employee, or particular activity. Examples of KPIs include revenue growth, market share, customer satisfaction scores, and employee turnover rates.*

[4]   OKRs: Objectives and Key Results. *Goal-setting framework, originally created by Google and used to define objectives and track their outcomes. Here, Objectives are viewed as clearly defined goals, while the Key Results are specific, measurable actions taken to achieve that Objective. OKRs are typically set at the company, team, and personal levels to create alignment and engagement around measurable goals.*

proxy for learning], and whether I have at least one easy-to-cite occasion of encountering art, deeply relating to another person, or being in nature [this is what I think of as truly looking].)

Next, develop OMRs based on your KMIs:
- Look at each Key Meaning Indicator and ask, "What objectives could I set that would positively impact this area of meaning in my life?"
- Ensure each objective has both quantifiable results and qualitative meaningful outcomes. *(e.g. If you decide that being a good leader is an important source of meaning in your life, you might set objectives such as mentoring others as they attempt to solve problems, identifying relational blind spots, and potentially growing your team in a way that expands the depth and breadth of your leadership. You can then set ways to check the quality of your engagement with others and also track the time you spend on each of these tasks, so as to gauge whether you are being successful.)*

Lastly, align and iterate:
- Regularly review your OMRs against your KMIs. Are your objectives truly serving the areas most meaningful to you?
- Be willing to adjust. Encourage your sense of meaning to remain fluid and continue evolving, then allow your objectives to follow it.

Most of all, make sure not to get lost in three-letter acronyms or rigid mechanisms of any kind. While structure can be useful (this book details a framework after all), they are a map, not the actual world that awaits our attention. You can find links to all CRATE assessment tools in the Appendix, as well as links to other authors and a *Measure What Matters* lesson inside the app. Balancing short- and long-term objectives is not easy, and neither is setting a regular review cadence. Faltering is human and happens to all of us, so beating ourselves up is truly a waste of time.

Instead, it serves us to remember that the search for meaning isn't about finding the right answer but about developing the courage to care about the most difficult, vulnerability-inducing questions, finding the resilience to keep exploring them even when the path is unclear, and having the openness that allows our sense of meaning (and narrative of self) to be continuously transformed by what we encounter. It's the *practice* of being human—with all its iteration, uncertainty, and potential for wonder.

The clay is always wet. The sculpture is never finished. That's not a bug—it's a feature. The fluid nebulosity of meaning is what keeps us growing and attuned to the possibilities of each moment. Just as it did for the Little Prince, this compels us to notice the beauty of our particular rose.

12

THE RESILIENCE TO CREATE

Welcoming Uncertainty

"There is a crack, a crack in everything.
That's how the light gets in."
— Leonard Cohen

hings being what they are, now what? The familiar phrase pops into my mind, seemingly unbidden, snapping me out of panic and stilling the nausea that threatens to overwhelm me. Heat spreads along my chest and neck, up to my cheeks. My stomach feels like I'm on a rollercoaster. Still, the words work their magic. I've used them with clients and loved ones, especially in moments that seem dire. The phrase is meant as a reminder: "Things might be horrible, but you're still standing." Now, it calms me. My hands shake slightly less as I attempt to call the unknown number from which my mother left a sobbing voicemail, saying she was in a car accident. I've missed four calls and two voicemails while coaching, and now a bone-chilling terror races through my nervous system. A string of unsuccessful attempts force me to let several more minutes pass. Time stretches and becomes very still. I stand, holding onto my desk, trying to slow my breath. In the space between moments, I notice the individual emotions: guilt about being five hundred miles away, fear that she might be terribly hurt, panic that my dad might be dead. I examine the possibilities and try to make space for each one. I know how to navigate this, yet I feel as if I'm a pebble skipping along the water's surface, touching reality for only a second, doing my best not to sink or drown.

Eventually, my mother calls back. Things are bad (the car is totaled), but she is alive; traumatized and shaken, yet, thankfully, able to go on without hospitalization. I help with logistics and comfort. I do my best to offer all that an adult child can do when her elderly parents are far away and in need. In the days that follow, I assist with insurance and do my best to soothe my mom when the nightmares roll in.

When the dust settles, I'm left wondering: what is it that can prepare us for such cataclysmic moments? How do we ensure that when the volume of emotion gets turned all the way up, we can still tread water and see the horizon? The truth is that we can't prevent uncertainty from happening. The more we try, the more we fall prey, like the bee trapped in the spider's web. Constriction wraps us in its tendrils, exhausting us with struggle until we lose the will to fight back.

My mother is one of the most incredible survivors I've ever encountered. When there is no path visible, she forges a new way forward, whacking through the bushes and bramble of life. Yet the same force of nature that propels her often threatens to send her careening off-course. The irony is not lost on me: her accident was an instance of unintended acceleration. The software in their hybrid car malfunctioned, causing a crash she had no way to control or prevent. Miraculously, no one else was hurt, and the occasion is now a glitch—rather than a rupture—on the graph of our entwined lives. When I tell my friends what happened in the days following, everyone is horrified, both out of concern for our family but also out of alarm for their own existence. They want to know the exact make and model of the car, the precise conditions that caused the malfunction, the minutiae of weather and circumstance.

I oblige with details and then try to change the topic. The reality is that there is no amount of information or preparation that can prevent uncertainty. There's no knowledge or practice that can keep us safe from living. Still, we keep looking for a talisman, a magic spell to ward off the terror of reality.

THE THREE FACES OF RESILIENCE

CRATE is not a talisman. By now, you've hopefully begun to internalize it as a set of tools that can ground us at moments when overwhelm becomes most threatening. When it works best, the framework functions as a lighthouse; when it falls short, it's at least a reminder of the night sky. While we can't ward off uncertainty, we can develop systems that not only withstand volatility but potentially benefit from it.

This concept, defined by the statistical scientist and risk analyst Nassim Nicholas Taleb as *antifragility*[5], describes systems that gain from disorder or stress. In the context of living systems, we can view our responses across a spectrum from fragility to antifragility, with resilience describing the process of surviving, persisting, and propagating. Such extended resilience enables us to build our capacity to respond to life's challenges, aiming not just for stability but for states where perturbations can lead to growth and creativity. Adapting Nietzsche's famous quote,[6] we could say that what doesn't

---

[5]   *Taleb, N. N. (2012). Antifragile: Things That Gain from Disorder. Random House.*

[6]   *Nietzsche, F. (1888). Twilight of the Idols, or, How to Philosophize with a Hammer. (W. Kaufmann, Trans., 1954). Penguin Books.*

kill you might not always make you stronger—but when it does, that's antifragility at work.

As we navigate uncertainty, we benefit from one of three types of resilience[7].

First, there is the *Resilience to Get Up*. Often associated with *survival*, this is the most fundamental form of resilience: the ability to rise when we've been knocked down. This is the type of resilience that my mother embodies. It is about facing the immediate crisis, dealing with shock, and taking the first crucial steps forward in the aftermath of unpredictable change. It's the resilience that helps us breathe through panic, make that difficult phone call, or simply get out of bed on the hardest of days. In CRATE terms, survival resilience draws heavily on Regulation and Agency. We regulate our immediate emotional response and then take decisive action to address the situation at hand.

Second, there's the *Resilience to Keep Going*. Once we're back on our feet, we face a different challenge: *persistence* over the long haul. This type of resilience sustains us through prolonged periods of difficulty or uncertainty. It's what keeps us moving forward when the adrenaline of crisis has faded, yet the path ahead continues to daunt us. In the aftermath of my mother's accident, this persistence-type of resilience is what I most needed to access. Helping with logistics, soothing nightmares, and listening as the stress continued, required a steadier, more enduring kind of strength. Persistence resilience is closely tied to the Trust and Energy dimensions of CRATE. We must trust in our capacity to endure, to find meaning in our struggles, and to maintain the energy needed for sustained effort.

Finally, there is the *Resilience to Create*. This *generative* form of resilience is not just about surviving or enduring—it's about creating something meaningful from our experiences. This is the resilience that transforms adversity into art, pain into purpose, and challenges

---

[7] *There might be more or differently-framed types of resilience. Still, I find that grouping and remembering things in threes is a useful way to find the broad outlines of a concept.*

into opportunities for growth. Generative resilience allows us to take the raw material of our experiences—even the most difficult ones— and fashion them into something that adds value to our lives and the lives of others. Surviving for our own sake can be difficult, especially when we feel most depleted. Following my mother's accident, it prodded me to turn away from countless work tasks and prioritize a family trip with my parents, where we could spend time connecting in nature over vistas that had life-long meaning for us and passing those memories to the next generation.

In the context of CRATE, generative resilience draws on all dimensions while emphasizing the framework's alpha and omega: Clarity and Energy. We need clarity to see beyond our immediate circumstances and envision new possibilities. We need energy—not just physical, but creative or spiritual energy—to bring those visions into reality. Being generative requires us not just to withstand but to welcome and integrate uncertainty, much like how we might design technical systems to have antifragile properties.

On teams, having such a mindset encourages us to foster conditions where we can safely experiment, fail, learn, and iterate, gradually building our capacity to thrive in the most unpredictable and volatile environments. The CRATE framework itself is a product of this type of resilience. It emerged from my own struggles with overwhelm, my search for meaning, and my desire to create something that could help others navigate the challenges they faced amidst the pandemic.

A CONTAINER TO HOLD REALITY

The process of breaking and remaking our cognitive frames is where resilience and creativity intersect most powerfully. It's a continuous shift, which converts difficulties into insights, deeper connections, and meaningful output.

When we're resilient enough to live with our discomfort, curious enough to explore it, and creative enough to reshape it, we open ourselves to tangible growth. I am not advocating blind positivity or denying the reality of human pain. Rather, I am hopeful we can develop the capacity to view our experiences—even the most challenging ones—with a spacious awareness that allows new possibilities to emerge and offers us an ever-unfolding understanding of the reality we inhabit. I've come to believe that our patterns of behavior are neither inalterable nor completely mutable; instead, they are perpetually in a state of movement and confluence, subject to change and modification as life shifts around us and we around it. For the most part, the dynamic of our inner life tends to unfurl at a slower tempo than the ceaseless, sometimes panicked, oscillations of our external environment. As a result, we cling to ways of being, beliefs, and habits long after they are no longer feasible, productive, or even reflective of our current lived experience.

To continue growing, our capacity for improvisation becomes the very core of our resilience. As we learn to interact with the world without relying on pre-existing patterns, we tap into a deeper source of convergence, adaptation, and the much larger concept that contains them both: creativity. The more creative we become, the more we trust in our resourcefulness, meet each moment with openness and curiosity, and no longer fear drowning in overwhelm.

———

I'd like to make all this as tangible as possible because even the most poetic concepts are of little use to us if we cannot turn them into embodied actions. Given that this is our last chapter together, I'd like to briefly cover some questions I've encountered from clients and friends, so as to provide the most concrete pointers on how to engage with CRATE and harness your own courage, meaning, and resilience:

- *Why should I bother with any of this? Things are okay enough, and all this navel-gazing seems like a lot of work.* Building resilience in times of peace is useful for when you're under siege. What that means pragmatically is that the more comfortable we become with tolerating and addressing small discomforts, the better we'll be when we experience a big and uncomfortable one. Within our professional lives, it means building the capacity to engage with and solve low-stakes disagreements, so that by the time we face serious internal or external adversity, we have gathered enough relational trust to ensure that our team or organization doesn't break. The relationship psychologist and author Esther Perel writes about "the distinction between the 'flaccid safety of permanent coziness' and the 'dynamic safety' of couples who fight and make up and whose relationship is a succession of breaches and repairs." Our relationships with others get stronger when we learn how to address challenging topics and even have passionate disagreements while still caring for one another. This is also true for our relationship with ourselves.

- *Okay, so is the whole point of CRATE that after I move through the different framework dimensions, I won't feel upset or overwhelmed?*
  That was my hope when I started building the framework: that I would figure out how to navigate all the uncomfortable emotions, and then they would be gone. But what emerged was far more interesting. As I worked with clients and with my own emotions, it became apparent that the way to navigate difficult feelings was not just to go 'through' them but instead to move 'with' or even 'as' them. That means that we don't just hold our breath till the painful moment passes; we learn to sit with the feelings, integrate them both from the top down (cognitively) and

from the bottom up (somatically); we can then accept and embody them as the important messengers that they are.

- *Aren't there easier ways? Why can't I just distract myself or watch something when I'm having a bad day?*
  You can't permanently ignore an emotion. You can try to sublimate it, project it, or deny it, but it always comes out sideways. As Jung wrote, "Your vision will become clear only when you can look into your own heart. Who looks outside, dreams; who looks inside, awakes."[8] While it is strategic to sometimes park intense emotions until we can engage with them in a safe setting, such delay is ideally kept to a matter of hours or, at most, of several days. Much as folk wisdom tells us to avoid going to bed angry at our spouse, we are best served if we avoid going to bed still carrying unfelt anger, sadness, guilt, longing, or any other emotion we find uncomfortable—even if it's happiness.

- *So what do I actually have to learn? You said the main parts of the framework are Clarity, Agency, and Trust, right?*
  CRATE does not have primary versus secondary dimensions. It does make a distinction between primarily-cognitive dimensions (Clarity and Agency) and primarily-somatic ones (Regulation, Trust, and Energy). It may be useful to focus on these in order, as their sequencing is deliberate. Clarity helps you figure out what's important to you, what thing gives you courage. This thing, in turn, gives you meaning, which empowers you to act, which then gives you a sense of Agency. Then, Trust and Energy give you resilience, and an impetus for creativity or generativity. Regulation helps you turn the intensity down or up as

---

[8] Jung, C. G. (1960). *The Structure and Dynamics of the Psyche. Collected Works, Vol. 8.* Princeton University Press.

needed. All of them together create a sense of being able to flow with life, able to include even the most difficult emotions.

- *After all that thinking and practice, what happens? Will something be different?*
  Your mileage may vary, but I can tell you that life doesn't have as many hooks for me these days. Put another way, my mental models are not as rigid. It feels as if reality flows like water, and I flow along with it, and my sense of an *I* is also part of that flow; and when a loved one is upset, or I get tired, it's just like there's this bit of frothy foam on top of the waves, and I know it will dissipate soon enough and that it's just another appearance of the same water.

- *Does that mean that everything is mostly fine all the time?*
  It does—most of the time. Some things are exciting, other things are heartbreaking, and others are peaceful and beautiful. Of course, we can still have a preference, but my experience is that I am (usually) willing to welcome whatever happens and see what I can do about it.

- *How does this apply at work? Will it help me get a promotion?*
  Quite likely. At the very least, it will help you become significantly more present during any conversation and respond (rather than react) to whatever is happening. It will then help you make decisions aligned with your whole organism, resulting in curiosity, attention, adaptability, and the energy to follow through with your very best effort.

- *Aha! So it's not just equanimity or whatever?*
  It's a different kind of calm. My friend and teacher Charlie Awbery calls it a "spacious clarity" and says

that it encompasses and accepts everything "without
ignoring, rejecting, or cutting it off."[9] My version of that is
courageous caring. It prompts us to engage even more full-
heartedly, giving us the *meaning to act*, to know how to parse
information based on what is most salient or relevant, and
then orient accordingly. In Vervaeke's terms, that's the
point when care adds fuel to Relevance Realization and
makes things meaningful.

- *What about when your team doesn't perform or your boss
  gets stressed and takes it out on you? In other words, how
  does this help when things are out of your control?*
  That happens. Within teams, there are many possible levels
  of anxiety, across the entire spectrum of acceptance (or
  lack thereof). When I work with individual leaders, I do
  my best to get each one to a place where their work and
  life can feel aligned; but often, the organization itself can
  become a path of growth, a means of forcing them to figure
  out whatever they're conveniently ignoring. Organizations,
  teams, families: they're basically all group organisms that
  reflect the health of their individual members, just as our
  body sooner or later surfaces anything amiss with an organ.
  Work can force us to face some of our most sublimated and
  inconvenient emotions, especially as we rise through the
  ranks and become responsible for others.

- *How does CRATE work when applied to entire teams? Is
  it like a 'Kumbaya' group session where everyone shares
  their feelings?*
  You can pretty much bet I won't be asking anyone to do
  trust falls. Still, Trust is the most important dimension to
  foster within teams. Without it, it is impossible to deeply

---

[9]   *Awbery, Charlie (2023). Opening Awareness: A guide to finding vividness in spacious clarity.
Evolving Ground Limited.*

care about work, each other, or even ourselves. Clarity and Agency are where I start when I go into organizational coaching because, objectively, that maps right onto strategy and tactics. It's a great way to begin with surfacing constraints and affordances, but Trust is where we inevitably need to end up.

- *Will CRATE help me be less stressed?*
  Especially in a professional context, one of the first places to see results with CRATE is clearer decision-making, which directly reduces stress. The big secret—which is not really a secret—is that overwhelm and flow are two facets of the same intensity. We experience overwhelm when we attempt to exert full control over our environment, and the reason we want control is that we are driven to minimize surprise while maximizing inference. When the framework can help people reframe their relationship to control, their teams, their families, and their whole lives begin to shift.

- *A lot of what you've described in this book sounds related to things I've heard about meditation practice. Is there a relationship between CRATE and seated meditation? Should I be meditating (and if so, how)? Or is this more of a dialogue-based system?*
  Meditation is an excellent practice to utilize within the Regulation, Trust, and Energy dimensions. It is a path inward that enables you to listen to your body and recognize your internal narratives. Focusing (which is a style of meditation) can help you note the pings of your nervous system with greater nuance, which will help especially in the Recognition aspect. Both meditation and contemplation are toolkits that will allow you to go deeper within the framework, but it is not a showstopper if you don't have a seated practice (or if you don't want to

interfere with what you are already doing). Simply put, CRATE can function as another path in or a widening of your existing path toward greater self-awareness.

- *This sounds too good to be true. What can't CRATE do?*
  First of all, it doesn't *do* anything; you are the one doing (or not doing) any of it. The framework is just a map—it's up to you to navigate it. Second of all, while CRATE increases your engagement with the world, it cannot tell you what to care about or how to integrate that care into a worldview that feels true to you. So if you're looking for answers on how to live, this framework (and book) might help quiet the internal chatter and let you begin truly engaging with the world. But the rest is up to you.

- *You've convinced me, but what can I do right now?*
  Pick any one of the Embedded Prediction (or *Story*) aspects: constraint, recognition, affordance, temporality, or experience. Each of them is a way of becoming more aware of what is going on right at this moment. Spend your day finding as many instances of, say, temporality, as you can. Every time you think about the past or the future (even for something as simple as the next email you have to write), notice the time travel. See which reality you are inhabiting and how that is helping you, even if the "help" is just a distraction from something unpleasant. However you choose to dive in, *do* dive in and test for yourself what works best and which approach keeps you continuously engaging with it. Most importantly, as I often say in the CRATE app: be brave, be kind, and go do what scares you!

CREATIVITY AS LOVE

Creativity deserves (and has prompted) entire books attempting to decipher its magic. For me, creativity is close to what others term a spiritual practice. This is because actual creativity—the birth of new ideas that can move and expand us—necessitates exactly the kind of egoic abdication I have been urging throughout this book. Writing, art, design, building a new business, starting a family—it all requires vulnerability, a letting go of the illusion of absolute control, and the embrace of forces that feel larger than us. All creative output is born in a relationship, whether that is to an idea, a natural phenomenon, or another person. Both insight, and the creative results born of it, require a participatory stance closer to channeling than to autonomous invention.

The phenomenal writer, producer, and director David Milch is my best example of such channeling and the exemplification of creativity as an act of resilience. I believe that his television shows *Deadwood* and *John from Cincinnati* are some of the most noteworthy twenty-first-century literature to date. While working on this chapter, I found myself unable to clearly express why resilience was instrumental in creativity until I rewatched a particular episode from *Deadwood*. The show is set in the settlement of Deadwood, South Dakota, during the Black Hills gold rush of the 1870s, before the territory was annexed by the United States. The drama revolves around a morally-complex cast of characters, most of them on the wrong side of the law or at least keeping it at arm's length, who converge on this outpost in an attempt to be subject to no government and heed no order. Yet despite themselves, they begin orienting toward one another, and in the process form a community organized by invisible rules of care.

I encountered *Deadwood* shortly after it was first released on HBO in 2004 and became fascinated with its creator. In the two decades since, Milch's lectures and approach to life have made an even more formative impression on me than his incredible writing. A victim of childhood physical and sexual abuse and a "degenerate gambler and junkie" by his own estimation, Milch is a true Milchian character—full of foibles, disagreeable, on occasion explosive, yet also tremendously generous, humorous, easily moved, and imbued with care for others, including (according to numerous accounts) complete strangers. During the height of his television career, he was so ensnared by a combination of obsessive compulsion, attention deficit, and terrible back pain that the only way he could write was to lie on the floor of his office, watching a giant monitor as an assistant typed the words he spoke. In that way, he would channel entire scenes, speak them out as if in a trance, then bark edits, retracing his steps and reciting lines over and over again until their melodies resonated. With this combination of debilitating neurosis and awe-inspiring creative genius, I'm certain that were it not for the characters and real-life humans he loved so unconditionally, Milch would have long since died. Instead, his torment enabled him to exist in that space Saint-Exupery intuited: the realm where the heart sees clearly what is invisible, then finds means to share it with the rest of us.

Milch's work teaches—not through telling but through showing—that the illusion of separateness is often just that: an illusion. His own saving grace, which carried him through trauma, addiction, and the demands of an all-too-potent mind, is that he loves the haunted world he observes with every ounce of his being. His writing exemplifies compassion for the most broken degenerates of humanity because he counts himself amongst them, and can therefore see, reflect, and amplify the beauty in each one. Rewatching "Deep Water" (the second episode of *Deadwood*'s first season), I was struck not just by the plot, acting, or cinematography, all of which are masterful, but by the tender yet tumultuous energy of the show. In the episode, multiple characters tend to an orphaned and injured Mennonite girl, Sofia, who, without speaking or opening her eyes, begins to create meaning between them. In Greek, Sofia means wisdom. Here, too, the girl symbolizes the wisdom of care as a unifying factor, not only for this group of humans but also for each of them individually, as they overcome internal barriers and open their hearts. Milch writes about this in his memoir, *A Life's Work*: "The camp's care for Sofia, over time, is as much in who stays away as in who steps in to care."[10]

The most notable part of "Deep Water" is how alive the characters become as they interact in the tensest moments, not through significant dialogue but through the internal conflict conveyed by eye contact, body language, and facial expression. Milch describes in his memoir how he struggled with finding the ending to the most emotionally fraught scene in the episode, in the end instructing the actors playing Al Swearengen and Doc Cochran to walk toward one another, each focusing on their character's darkest worries. As Milch puts it, the scene wrote itself in two lines.

Reflecting on the process, he notes, "If you're sticking with your work, you discover truths about it that aren't present when you begin, and that's the real fun. Symbols, signifiers, they generate their meaning out of the submission of energy from the believer. They're fluid rather than stable. They mean different things at different times. The same nugget of gold can be a source of wealth or it can be a source of destruction. The symbolism as it strengthens and stabilizes generates more and more complicated social institutions."[11]

We, too, are "fluid rather than stable... [meaning] different things at different times." That humble "submission of energy from the believer" is the participatory stance that CRATE encourages and attempts to enable at every step of the way. I do not think I would have found my way to it so clearly, were it not for the incredible wealth of wisdom, and especially care, that Milch revealed to me.

At the time of this writing, David Milch resides in a long-term memory-care facility, having been diagnosed with Alzheimer's. His beautiful brain is covered with plaque, and it appears that on

---

[10] Milch, David. *Life's Work: A Memoir* (p. 173). Random House Publishing Group.

[11] *Ibid.* (p. 172)

most days he does not have access to the full breadth of its faculties. Nonetheless, in the past year, together with long-term collaborators, he has completed another TV script and continues work on a multi-decade project about William, Henry, and the entire James family.

Creativity is a form of generative care. We need serious effort and vulnerability to fully invest ourselves in creating something we care deeply about. The more we care, the more vulnerable we feel, and the scarier it becomes. Like hope, creativity is an act of the imagination, of loving the question—the person, the problem, the world—enough to engage with it fully. It is a birthing process, messy and full of hope. As with birth, it is incredibly painful and feels like it will rend us in two. It requires us to tear ourselves open and survive it, and the more we do, the more trust (i.e., resilience) we build that we can do it again.

The title of this chapter is 'The Resilience to Create,' but the process is cyclical. The more courage we can find, the greater our capacity to care. The greater our capacity to care, the more meaningful our interactions with that which we care about. The more meaningful our interactions, the more courage we now have to defend it. As we go through this, we become more resilient, more courageous, more willing to withstand effort and risk heartbreak. Out of all this emerges further meaning, not just for ourselves but for those around us.

I suspect this is how *Deadwood* and *The Little Prince* happened. And, on a much smaller scale, how this book came to be. This virtuous feedback loop is the secret to writing, marriage, parenting, innovation, and building startups. Every endeavor in which you set out into the unknown without any guarantee of success helps you arrive at new, stronger versions of your self, and then pay it forward.

———

As I complete these final pages, the world feels to be tilting off its axis. My stomach sinks at every news alert, in every conversation with friends and clients. Each of us is trying to build something meaningful while reality feels to be unraveling. The temptation to shut down or look away has never been stronger.

Still, I keep thinking of Carl Jung and his *Red Book*[12]; not only for its revelations but for the raw courage of its timing. On most evenings, as Europe teetered on the edge of what would become World War I, Jung sat in his study, and allowed his psyche to expand into the coming terror rather than contract away from it. He called this practice of diving straight into the images and emotions that terrified him—letting them speak openly rather than defending against them—'active imagination.' He didn't do this to bypass reality, but to meet whatever emerged from it with full awareness. The result was a beautiful piece of art—part psychological treatise on becoming human, part mystical poem—interwoven with mesmerizing illustrations that entwine mandala patterns with Blakean visions. *The Red Book* offers more than insight; it is a record of transformation, a path to metabolizing collective fear into individual meaning.

This process of becoming our full selves and engaging with everything the world delivers is the opposite of pretending that everything is fine. It asks that we remain porous enough to let pain move through us without drowning—finding the sweet spot between numbness and overwhelm where generativity becomes possible. Like Jung in his study, we can access enough Trust to keep our hearts open, even as the ground shifts beneath our feet. I suspect this is what the resilience to create gives us on a tangible level: not an impenetrable shield but a continuous willingness to engage—letting ourselves be changed by what we encounter, then shaping something new from whatever remains.

The work I've explored in this book—the whole point of learning to navigate overwhelm and access flow—becomes even more vital when our collective anxiety threatens to swallow us

---

[12]   *The Red Book, or Liber Novus, is Carl Jung's most personal work, created between 1914 and 1930, but kept private until its publication in 2009. Written and illustrated by hand in the style of a medieval illuminated manuscript, it documents Jung's journey of 'active imagination' during a period of intense personal and collective crisis.*

whole. It's precisely when everything feels most uncertain that we must remember how to let intensity move through us rather than obliterate us. We cannot predict or control what happens next in our tumultuous world, yet we can choose how to meet it. We can contract in fear or expand with care. We can let our overwhelm isolate us, or allow it to connect us more deeply to what matters most. The tools I've shared here work not only for individual growth, but also for remaining connected, even when engagement feels nearly unthinkable. Leveraging them, you will find flow despite the chaos, and with a newfound courage to sail directly into it.

If all of this sounds big and overwhelming, that's because it is. Love, when felt all the way through, is overwhelming, intimidating, and terrifyingly beautiful; and the Story, Stance, and Self—meaning our dissolution, extension, and evolution—is to let it be that way. Welcome it. Rest your head in the mouth of the dragon of overwhelm and say: eat me if you wish. That moment—from different angles—is precisely what I mean by all the final aspects of the CRATE framework: Convergence, Release, Adaptation, Translucence, and Emptiness. Each of them is a way we step into the emergence of form that we call 'creativity.' You, me, we are not alone in this engagement with uncertainty. We are each, in our own way, working to get up, to keep going, to keep creating while continuously standing against entropy.

It's a leap and a dive, an act of welcoming emotion much larger than our individual selves, and allowing it to begin unfolding within us. There is an exhale. An expansion. The wave of overwhelm passes right through us as we take a deep breath and anchor with each other. We turn and *return* to our most natural state—a state where we can breathe water—a state of overwhelming flow.

INDEX

ACKNOWLEDGEMENTS

It will likely come as no surprise that if one chooses to study overwhelm with all its foundational causes, nuances, and potential flipsides, it is likely because they themselves are no stranger to overwhelm. I've spent my life humaning with a lot of thought and a lot of emotion, and the reason I'm still standing and able to write about it is thanks to the incredible humans I've had the luck to encounter and love. To each of them, I owe a debt of gratitude.

Thank you, Lawrence, for being my lighthouse and my night sky. Cassandra, you inspire me each day with your brilliant mind and the spirit of a warrior poet. William, you have become a young man of thoughtfulness and strength while still retaining the courage of a gentle heart. Bebba and Kosta—Mom and Dad— you sacrificed so much and gave me all that you could, so that I could be here to tell this story and pay it forward. Marty and Nicole, thank you for loving us always.

Thanks also to my dear friends for your continued and unconditional support: Ken Hughes for daily encouragement and warm historian catholic Yoda wisdom; Michael and Blanca Freydin for always being there for us and making me laugh till my mascara runs and I get raccoon eyes; Kristin DePlatchett and Margaret Timmons—your fierce friendship is the stuff of books; Doba Parushev and Geri Kirilova, you gave me the courage to leap, way back when doing what scares me was absolutely terrifying; Wendy Suzuki, I am humbled by your friendship and tireless willingness to answer all of my science questions.

Thank you as well to Caryn Effron for your continued love and support—you are the champion every woman needs; Samantha Katz for being my accountability buddy and passionate friend, and Krista Mitchell Cornell for always checking on me and being in my corner; Charlie Awbery for so much warmth, deep care, and invaluable teachings; Martina Welkhoff, Marco DeMiroz, Blake Janelle, David Wang, Lucas Nelson, Aaron Holiday, Nnamdi Okike, Virginie Raphael, Elizabeth Abrams, Sejal Gulatti, Olga Yarmolenko, and Guerin Schwarberg—you each supported me in hard moments, believed in me, and shared my joys.

To my teachers and mentors: Rachel Rider for the years spent teaching me how to hear the wisdom of my body—my back is at peace thanks to you; David Pezenik for engaging in countless elucidating conversations; John Vervaeke for your generosity of ideas and spirit; and Terry Real and Esther Perel for your willingness to openly share your tremendous skill and insight.

To the talented humans who helped this book become a reality: Lawrence (once more) for being the most patient editor and thought-partner one could ask for; Rachel Jepsen for your warm assistance with structure, editing, and feedback; Caitlin McCoskey for your incredible intuition and for trusting in me before I fully knew how to trust myself; Omri Cohen for being a phenomenal idea midwife; Andrew Blevins for your perceptive comments and meticulous audio editing.

And, of course, to my clients: each of you has trusted me with your stories, your dreams, and your emotions. I am humbled by your courage during each session and continue to learn alongside you as we navigate together this wild ride of becoming our multitudinous selves.

Last but not least, to you, dear reader: thank you for making it through this lengthy book. I hope for you all the courage, meaning, and resilience you need to navigate your journey. And most of all, I wish you love.

ABOUT THE AUTHOR

Dessy Levinson has devoted her career to understanding how humans navigate complexity and create meaningful impact. As the creator of the CRATE Framework and founder of crate.com, she combines psychological insight with practical business experience to help leaders transform overwhelm into flow.

Her unique perspective derives from over two decades spanning three distinct careers: first as a Creative Director developing consumer campaigns for Fortune 500 brands, then as Managing Director at 645 Ventures where she specialized in early-stage consumer startups and emerging technologies, and now as a coach and founder helping high-performing individuals align their narratives and behavior to achieve lasting transformation.

Levinson's approach is grounded in extensive study of psychology, cognitive theory, and relational dynamics. She trained with leading experts including Terry Real at the Relational Life Institute, Executive Somatic Coach Rachel Rider, and psychotherapist David Pezenik, LCSW. Her work is further informed by studies with relationship expert Esther Perel and cognitive scientist John Vervaeke.

Her sought-after workshops include 'Do What Scares You,' 'Containing Overwhelm,' and 'Thinking in Story.' Through these teachings and her coaching practice, she helps founders, leaders, and teams find the courage to care, the meaning to act, and the resilience to create.

Dessy studied Critical Theory, Literature, Classics, and Psychology at the University of Alberta. She lives with her family in the New York metro area, where she continues to explore the intersection of psychology, creativity, and transformational growth.

ABOUT THE TYPE

This book celebrates three complementary typefaces. Chapter titles are set in Saol, a contemporary serif typeface designed by Schick Toikka that combines classical proportions with modern sophistication. Its distinctive character draws inspiration from both high-contrast Didone typefaces and nineteenth-century oldstyle fonts.

Chapter subtitles appear in Geograph, a geometric sans serif designed by Martin Wenzel and Fabian Deorowicz. Its clean lines and balanced proportions provide clarity while maintaining warmth, reflecting the book's integration of precision and humanity.

The body text is set in Janson, a typeface long misattributed to Dutch punch-cutter Anton Janson but actually created by Hungarian printer Nicholas Kis in the late 1600s. Known for its excellent readability and elegant character, Janson combines Renaissance harmony with baroque expressiveness, creating an inviting texture for extended reading.

ADDITIONAL MATERIALS

Thank you for reading *From Overwhelm to Flow*.
To access your complimentary resources, please visit
crate.com/extras
or scan the QR code below:

Enter code **FLOW25** to receive:
· Three months of premium access to the CRATE app
· CRATE assessment toolkit
· KMI/OMR frameworks
· Discount codes for upcoming classes
· Additional reading recommendations

The above webpage will be updated regularly with new tools,
research, and insights to support you on your journey.